Woman to Woman 2

A second selection of Christian articles or women by women

Compiled and edited by

Sylvia Penny

ISBN 978 1 78364 722 4

Printed in the UK
First published in 2023

The Open Bible Trust

www.obt.org.uk

****

Publications of The Open Bible Trust must be in accordance with its evangelical, fundamental and dispensational basis. However, beyond this minimum, writers are free to express whatever beliefs they may have as their own understanding, provided that the aim in so doing is to further the object of The Open Bible Trust. A copy of the doctrinal basis is available on **www.obt.org.uk** or from:

THE OPEN BIBLE TRUST
Fordland Mount, Upper Basildon,
Reading, RG8 8LU, UK

Preface

This book is made up of a selection of different articles, many of which first appeared in *Search,* the bi-monthly magazine sent out by the Open Bible Trust. They are written by women, for women.

These articles cover a wide variety of different topics, ranging from *Women in the Bible* to *Christian Living*: from articles on the *Lord Jesus Christ* to those on *The Person of God*. There are others on *The Bible* and a good section on an assortment of *Spiritual Subjects*. Not only are these good for personal reading and reflection, but they can also be used as a basis for leading home groups and Bible Studies.

My prayer is that you may find them interesting and helpful, and enjoy reading them as much as I have enjoyed compiling and editing them.

Sylvia Penny
Compiler and Editor

Contributors to this book are

Karen Bismark
Laura Kestly
Andrea Marple
Sylvia Penny
Hazel Stephens
Vicky Wilkinson

Contents

Women in the Bible

1. Eve 8
2. Sarah 17
3. Rebecca 22
4. Rachel 28
5. Rachel, Leah, Bilhah & Zilpah – the four mothers of Jacob's sons 33
6. Michal 39
7. Abigail 42
8. Martha's Memories (from two days before the crucifixion) 46
9. Tabitha (Dorcas) 50
10. Lydia, a dealer in purple cloth from Thyatira 53

Christian Living

11. Submission 60
12. The Will of God 63
13. Do not judge 65
14. Riches at Christmas 68
15. How do we spend our time? 70
16. Gifts and Talents 73
17. Christianity in Society 76
18. Believers and Atheists 79
19. How to be Happy! 81
20. Let us Love one Another 85
21. Motivation is important 89
22. Life is so daily! 94
23. Balance 97
24. Love 100
25. Thankfulness 103

26. Summertime 106
27. Rise above on eagle's wings..110

The Lord Jesus Christ

28. The final journey..114
29. The Ascension 116
30. The Miracle Baby – God and Man.......................................120
31. Jesus' life in danger 123
32. The Resurrection...127
33. The Son of God..131
34. A Child is born … and he will be called … Everlasting Father 136
35. Jesus, Firstborn from among the Dead (Colossians 1:18)......139

The Person of God

36. Only God is Good and Holy 144
37. Omnipresence of God 146
38. Eternality of God 149
39. Omnipotence of God...151
40. Omniscience of God..153
41. Why is the Universe just right for life? 156

The Bible

42. Reading the Bible..162
43. What does the Bible say to *me*? 167
44. Genesis – Should we take it literally? 171
45. Genesis 2 – The Two Trees 175
46. Ecclesiastes and the meaning of life 182
47. Luke 6 - Blessings and Woes 187

Spiritual Subjects

48. Three Challenging Verses (1 Thessalonians 5:16-18) 195
49. Is faith God's gift to man? 202
50. Faith and healing 206
51. Is prayer scientific? 211
52. Problems with prayer 217
53. Serendipity and prayer 221
54. The Good Wolf and the Bad Wolf 224
55. The Christian Hallmark 228
56. Water miracles and the miracle of water 234
57. Made in the image of God 238
58. The Judgment seat of Christ and the Great White Throne 243
59. Augustine and the problem of evil 247
60. Prophecy at Easter 253
61. A Valentine Letter from God 260
62. Christmas and the Promised Seed 263
63. Christmas – A True Story 267
64. Grace Reigns 269
65. Let the weak say "I am Strong" 271
66. Never too late to repent 273
About the Author 278
Also by Sylvia Penny 279

Women in the Bible

1. Eve

Sylvia Penny

In this article on Eve we will first look at the relationship between Eve and Adam. Then we will go on to look at Eve's role in the Fall and *why* Satan was so successful in his deception of Eve.

Eve's relationship with Adam

First, what does the beginning of Genesis tell us about the relationship between Eve and Adam and, more generally, what does it tell us about the relationship between husbands and wives?

Many think the early chapters of Genesis teach that God required wives to be subordinate to their husbands from the very beginning; that they should be under his authority. There are four main arguments used to show this:

1. The woman was *created after* the man, and is therefore secondary to him.
2. The woman is *taken from* the man, and is therefore secondary.
3. The woman is *named by* the man, and is therefore subordinate to him.
4. The woman is *created to be a helper* for the man, and she is therefore under his authority.

For these main reasons, and particularly the last one where she was created to be Adam's helper, it is argued that Adam was created to be the leader, and the woman was created to be the follower. However, if we look back at chapter 1, we see that no such hierarchy exists. Genesis 1:27 says: "So God created man in his own image, in the image of God he created him; male and female he created them." Then he blessed them, and told them to be fruitful and multiply.

Both male and female are created in the image of God. There is no separation or distinction. They are complementary parts of a whole –

each is necessary to the other. They are equal. In chapter 2 however, we find these two, male and female, are to have different *roles*. Adam is incomplete without the woman, and needs her to help him. Equally, the woman is incomplete without Adam. Together, they were to be *one flesh*.

If we look at the four arguments given for thinking that God required Adam to be in authority over the woman, we find that, individually, they don't stand up to closer scrutiny:

1. The fact that Adam was created first does not prove his superiority or authority over the woman, or else we could also argue that the birds, fish and animals are superior to, or in authority over, man which no-one would agree with.
2. The point of emphasising that the woman was taken from the man is not to show that he is in authority over her, but to show the complete unity of male and female, as they both came from one identical substance, not from two separate creations out of the dust. Adam had no part in the creation of the woman, and her first contact is with God, not with Adam. God then presents her to Adam as one half of a complete whole. Adam immediately sees this, as the first thing he says is: "This is now bone of my bones and flesh of my flesh". He sees an equal, not a subordinate. Even today, in English, we sometimes refer to our husband as our "other half"!
3. Adam doesn't give her the name *Eve* until after the Fall. When she is first brought to him by God he simply calls her *woman* which refers to her gender – but this is not her name. However, it is true that on many occasions in the OT naming people *does* imply that the person doing the naming has authority over the person being named. It is interesting, therefore, that Adam only names Eve after the Fall, and not before. Why is this? In Genesis 3:16 God says to the woman:

   > "I will greatly increase your pains in childbearing; with pain you will give birth to children. Your desire will be for your husband, and he will rule over you".

   This is the *condemnation* from God as a result of sin. This was the *punishment* of the woman for breaking God's command. Instead of her position of equality with Adam, sin had spoiled this relationship. For the man to rule over the woman was not God's original intention. Shortly after this we see Adam exercising this new-found authority over the woman and naming her *Eve*. His ruling over Eve was a consequence of sin, just as pain in childbirth was, and just as the ground was no longer going to produce food easily for them to eat. Originally God had created Adam and Eve equal, but as a result of sin this was no longer going to be the case. And so, from the very beginning, and throughout history, it has been true that in most societies, men have been in charge.

4. Fourth, the fact that the woman was created by God to help Adam does not indicate that Adam was her superior, or in charge of her. A person who requires help may sometimes be considered to be the weaker one. Having a helper, or being a helper, does not necessarily imply either inferiority or superiority in and of itself – it depends on the circumstances. This was so with Adam and Eve. Thus, we assume an equality between them unless we are told otherwise.

Eve's role in the Fall

Having established the equality of Adam and Eve in the beginning, *before* the Fall, we will now look at Eve's role in the Fall. It is clear from three passages in Scripture that it is Adam, rather than Eve, who is blamed for bringing sin into the world. These three passages are:

1 *Like Adam*, they (Israel) have broken the covenant – they were unfaithful to me there. (Hosea 6:7)

2 Therefore, just as sin entered the world *through one man*, and death through sin … death reigned from the time of Adam to the time of Moses, even over those who did not sin by breaking a command, as did Adam … (Romans 5:12,14)

3 For *as in Adam all die*, so in Christ all will be made alive. (1 Corinthians 15:22)

In each of these, the blame for sin (and ultimately death) entering the world is clearly placed on Adam's shoulders, not Eve's. But why is this? Different answers are suggested by different commentators and Bible students.

Some believe that Eve is *excused* from blame for her sin, because she was deceived by Satan, whereas Adam was not. It is argued that Eve sinned and ate the fruit *thinking* she was actually doing the right thing, as she believed what Satan had told her, whereas Adam sinned because he *knew* that Satan was lying, and *knew* that what they were both doing was wrong. Although this is true in itself, nowhere in Scripture is anyone ever excused from the guilt of their sin simply because they are deceived, or because they are ignorant of what is right. Even in our present-day law courts, ignorance is no defence in the eyes of the law.

Others believe that Adam committed the first sin by not taking care of Eve properly in the garden, when God had told him to do this. This is based on Genesis 2:15 which says, "The Lord God took the man and put him in the Garden of Eden to work it and *take care of it*." However, this was *before* Eve was created. The working and taking care of the Garden of Eden referred to the garden itself, not to Eve. Eve was subsequently created by God to help Adam, and join with him in taking care of the garden, not to be an added responsibility. In fact, we have seen that one of the *punishments* of Eve for her sin was that Adam would *now* rule over her. Originally this was not how things were meant to be.

And there are several other possibilities put forward by different commentators.

One final suggestion is that perhaps theirs was a joint sin, committed at the same time, but Adam was the one who was culpable because he was the one who had heard God's command first hand not to eat the fruit, whereas Eve had not. Like Christ, during His temptations in the wilderness by Satan, Adam should have quoted God's words correctly to Satan, and then he should have refused to eat the fruit. However, he chose to remain silent, and knowingly joined Eve in a rebellion against God's word, and so Satan had the victory. Because Adam had heard God's word first hand, he had the responsibility to step in and protect Eve. But he didn't. Perhaps it was because of his silence that the blame for the first sin fell *only* on his shoulders, and not on Adam and Eve jointly. However, even this explanation is not entirely satisfactory.

At the end of the day, we need to accept what Paul says in the New Testament, and see the importance of the analogy, in 1 Corinthians 15:45, between the first *man*, Adam, and the last Adam (Christ). It was the first *man*, Adam, who sinned and fell, and it was the last Adam (Christ) who did *not* sin, and so had the victory over Satan. The analogy breaks down if we say that a woman, Eve, was the first one to sin.

The deception of Eve

Having looked at Eve's role in the Fall, we will now look at why Satan was so successful at deceiving Eve.

2 Corinthians 11:3 refers to Eve's deception, and says, "But I am afraid that just as Eve was deceived by the serpent's cunning your minds may somehow be led astray from your sincere and pure devotion to Christ", and a few verses later, in verse 14, it says, "for Satan himself masquerades as an angel of light." It therefore seems most likely that Eve was deceived by a cunning yet beautiful shining being, an angel of light, rather than by a talking serpent. If this is how he presented himself to Eve, perhaps it is no wonder that she believed what he told her.

Satan was also the master of subtlety. What he suggested to Eve sounded very reasonable and plausible. Surely, he suggested, there was nothing wrong with eating the fruit? Surely God shouldn't mind about such a little thing? He implied, therefore, that God must have had an ulterior motive for not wanting them to eat the fruit. He implied God had kept something important from them, whereas he, Satan, was very willing to tell them. Satan suggested God had lied when he told them they would die, because he knew if they ate the fruit they would become like him, and he didn't want that (see Genesis 3:1-5). Satan tempted Eve with the same temptation that he himself had found irresistible. He had wanted to be like God (Isaiah 14:14).

All of this Eve found irresistible. The fruit looked good, and it was obviously good for food; here was a beautiful being telling her that she would *not* die if she ate it, added to which, if she ate it, she would also become wise, knowing good and evil, just like God. Thus, in the end, Eve believed Satan rather than God. She was completely deceived by Satan's lies and she took the fruit and ate it. And she also gave some to Adam to eat. In one fell swoop Satan undoubtedly thought he had succeeded in spoiling God's plan for the human race, right from the start.

However, as we know from other Scriptures, God foresaw all that was going to happen, and had *already* provided a way of redemption for mankind, a way back to God, despite being tainted by sin. We learn this from 1 Peter 1:18-20 which tells how we were redeemed by the blood of Christ, the Lamb of God, who was chosen for this purpose *before* the creation of the world. Therefore, we know the plan for the salvation of the human race was put in place by God long before man first sinned and fell.

Eve's mistakes

When we look closely at Satan's method of deception and temptation here it is very informative. It can help us understand, even today, how we can go from accepting and trusting and obeying God's word, to doubting, questioning and finally disobeying it. The downward steps that Eve took are quite clear, and if we look at these carefully, they can help us avoid the same mistakes Eve made.

1. Satan started by questioning her understanding of what God had said, and Eve's reply shows she got this slightly wrong. She told Satan that they could not eat, *nor even touch*, the fruit from the tree in the middle of the garden. She *added* the part about not touching the fruit. Do we today add unnecessary rules and regulations for Christians to follow that have never been required by God? If so, have such unnecessary rules put others off when we have tried to witness to them? Do we misunderstand what God wants and so go astray, and also lead others astray?

2. Eve also underplayed the penalty for disobedience that God had warned about. God had emphasised they would "surely" (i.e. definitely) die. Although she did mention to Satan that God had said they would die, she softened it by dropping the "surely", and so dropping the emphasis on this. This was something that Satan immediately picked up on. Similarly, if we're not sure what Scripture says about something, this could be something that Satan uses to his advantage with us. This is why we need the armour of God (in Ephesians 6) to help protect us from the "flaming arrows of the evil one". We need to know and understand God's word.

3. Satan picked up on Eve's slight alteration of God's word and directly contradicted what God had said, and told Eve she would *not surely* die. By this Satan cast doubt in her mind, and made her question whether God's words were true. When we do not understand the Scriptures, and do not understand the way God has spoken and acted in the past, do these things raise doubts in our minds about God and about what kind of Being he truly is? Is he always right, and is he always truthful all of the time? Do we question the truth and authority of the Scriptures - God's word? Some Christians do. If so, this can damage both our witness and our faith, and Satan has the victory.

4. Next, in this downward spiral, Eve listened to Satan's slander of God and began to doubt that God's motives were good, rather than immediately rejecting any aspersion cast on his character. If we start to entertain any thought, no matter how small and seemingly harmless, that God's actions may not always be motivated purely by love and righteousness, we could start down the same road as Eve, and end up questioning God, and our faith in him, unnecessarily. For example, sometimes the problem of pain and suffering in the world can result in a person questioning God's love and goodness. This can quite often happen when a loved one becomes extremely ill, or has a terrible accident, and goes through a lot of pain and suffering, even after a lot of prayer. This is when some Christians are most likely to start questioning God, and their faith in him. Or it can happen after

a bereavement, and people feel deserted and alone. This is a time when Satan's schemes are most likely to be most effective.

5. Next, Eve ended up wanting what God had forbidden, and she let herself be persuaded by Satan that it would be alright to disobey God. Have we ever been persuaded to do something wrong, and justified our actions in our own minds, when we have actually had clear evidence or teaching to the contrary? Or have we seen other Christians do this? For example, in Britain, living together and having sex before marriage among many Christians is seen as acceptable now, and it's justified by the expectation of getting married in the future, and also because it is now the socially acceptable norm. Do we go along with this, or do we speak up for what the Bible teaches?

6. Not only did Eve break God's command, so did Adam. Although *she* was completely deceived by Satan, Adam was not, and yet he joined Eve in going against God's will. Paul says, in 1Timothy 2:14, "And Adam was not the one deceived; it was the woman who was deceived and became a sinner." Together they ate and together they sinned, and in doing so involved the whole human race in ruin. And so Satan's victory (at this point) was complete. If we allow ourselves to stray from the Christian pathway, we may unwittingly encourage others to do so as well. And maybe worst of all, we could be in danger of detrimentally affecting those we love most in this world, just like Eve. So, our actions may not affect only ourselves, they may also damage those around us.

By reading these verses, and studying what they say, we can learn to avoid the same mistakes that Eve made. And we can also see how sin entered the world. It is made very clear that Satan was responsible for the temptation and deception of Eve, which ultimately led to the first sin.

Conclusion

There is much we can learn from the account of Adam and Eve in Genesis 2 & 3. In this article we have considered two of these. First, we looked at the nature of Adam and Eve's original intended relationship before they sinned (one of equality) and contrasted it with their relationship after the Fall (one of Adam ruling over Eve). And second, we looked at the mistakes Eve made as she listened to the very convincing lies of Satan, how she was thoroughly deceived by him, and how we might avoid doing likewise.

2. Sarah

Hazel Stephens

The first mention of Sarah in the Bible is in Genesis 11:29 where she is introduced as the wife of Abraham but, in this verse, they are referred to as Sarai and Abram. The name *Sarai* translates as "princess". In the next verse, Genesis 11:30, we are then told she was barren and had no children. In that society she must have been married for at least ten years for this to have been assumed.

At this time, Sarah was living with Abraham's family in Ur of the Chaldees (present-day Iraq). Ur was then a significant port city on the Persian Gulf, which was continuously inhabited for nearly 3,000 years up to 360 BC. It was also an important part of the trade routes of the time, stretching to India in the east, and Rome and Greece in the west, as well as to Egypt and Africa. The people in Ur were also devoted to the worship of the moon god Nanna, and Ur was one of two sites of significant worship of this deity, the other being Haran in the north.

The city of Ur was at its height of importance in around 2,000 BC, and it was around this date that Sarah was born. Terah, who was both Abraham and Sarah's father (through different wives), may well have benefitted from the trade routes passing through Ur at the time. However, in Genesis 11:31, we are told that Terah moved his entire family to Haran. But, in Acts 7:2-5, Stephen reveals that Abraham had already received the call from God to go to the land of Canaan *before* Terah took his family to go and live in Haran.

Therefore, Abraham and Sarah followed the Lord's directive in two stages, as it was after Terah's death that Sarah and Abraham finally moved on to Canaan. The family had prospered in Haran and they took all their wealth and possessions with them when they moved (Genesis 12:5).

But what of Sarah? She appears to have been a dutiful wife, following her husband wherever he led. However, whether she worshipped the moon God while they had lived in Haran, while Terah was still alive, is not clear. At this point, Sarah is no more than a name in Scripture, with no hint of her future role in the nation of Israel. It is only at the death of Terah that things began to change.

In Genesis 12:5 Sarah began a new life with Abraham. It was a nomadic life, moving from place to place for most of their lives. It is generally accepted that Sarah was 65 by this time, and Abraham was 75. When they arrived in Canaan they began to travel from place to place, with the Lord directing their footsteps. Abraham set up an altar in Bethel, calling upon the name of the Lord. If Sarah had ever worshipped the moon god Nanna in Haran, this shows that any such worship on her part had now ceased, and that the family had all placed their faith in the one true God. A famine in the land of Canaan quickly followed, which could have been Satan's attempt to get the family to return to Haran. However, instead, Abraham and Sarah went south, to Egypt, to search for food.

In Genesis 12 it is clear that Abraham did not recognise Sarah's place in God's plan, as he placed her in jeopardy because of his fear for his own life. As they neared the border of Egypt, he insisted that because of her beauty, the Egyptians might want to kill him if they knew that he was her husband. So, he told her to say that she was his sister, thereby saving his life for the future that had been promised to him by God. Once they crossed the border, Abraham's fears were realised, and Sarah was taken to Pharaoh's palace for his pleasure.

This has echoes in the book of Esther, who was also beautiful and desirable, and taken to the king's palace. Esther was placed within the king's household to thwart Haman from his murderous intentions toward the Jewish nation. She used her position as queen to allow her people to defend themselves against their enemies.

Sarah's position, however, is less obvious. She may have thought herself unable to have children with Abraham, but maybe she wondered whether another partner would end her childlessness? Was this how God's promise of a nation would come to fruition? So, when Pharaoh was told that Sarah was Abraham's sister rather than his wife (in Genesis 12:13), maybe she viewed this as an opportunity to have some children.

However, the Lord immediately plagued Pharaoh's household, stopping any possibility of this. When Pharaoh finally realised that the cause of his problems was the deceit of Abraham, he was furious with Abraham for omitting to say that Sarah was his wife, which had put him in this difficult situation. He gave Sarah back to him, and sent him on his way with gifts of restitution, even though he was innocent of intentional wrongdoing. It may be that Hagar joined Sarah's household at this time, and left Egypt with her mistress.

This incident foreshadowed Israel's subsequent bondage in Egypt. Whilst Sarah was in no immediate danger, the future of the nation certainly was. It should have shown both Abraham and Sarah that the promise of a future nation from the two of them was not just a possibility, but a solid promise. Otherwise, God would not have stepped in so decisively, preserving the purity of the marriage for His future plans. However, Sarah's importance to God's future plans were not recognised by either of them at this point.

Sarah is next mentioned in Genesis 16. Ten years after leaving Haran, she was still childless, and Abraham had once again received confirmation that he would have a son to inherit all his property (Genesis 15:4). Sarah was 75 years old, and acknowledged that her childbearing years were now behind her. However, God had promised an heir to Abraham, so to fulfil the promise, she asked Abraham to give her a child through her Egyptian handmaiden, Hagar. The resulting child could then be adopted, and raised as the heir. This was an accepted part of the Babylonian law at the time, and both would have been comfortable with the arrangement. Hagar remained under Sarah's control and was never accorded the title of second wife. Hagar produced a male child on the first try, so no further relations were necessary between the two.

However, once Hagar conceived, she treated Sarah with contempt. Sarah realised that her own plan to fulfil God's promise had gone awry. She confronted Abraham about Hagar's attitude, but Abraham turned the argument back to Sarah, telling her that Hagar was *her* servant, and therefore it was for her to deal with the situation as she saw fit. Sarah was harsh with Hagar about both her attitude and her place in the scheme of things. Hagar fled from their tent home into the desert, but after God's intervention, she returned and was accepted back by Sarah, although no mention of having the baby adopted as heir was subsequently raised. Sarah was 76 years old by the time Ishmael was born.

In Genesis 17, thirteen years later, God returned to Abraham and changed both his and Sarah's names to emphasise the changes that were to come upon them. Sarah had her name changed from *Sarai* (princess) to *Sarah* (Mother of Nations). By now Sarah was 89, but God told Abraham that the next year a son would be born to her.

Soon after this, Genesis 18 states that three angels arrived at their tent on their way towards Sodom and Gomorrah. They were made welcome, and a feast was laid out for them by Sarah. Abraham was then told that the angel would return soon, and that Sarah would bear a son. Overhearing this pronouncement, Sarah thought to herself that her body was well past any childbearing, and so she laughed to herself at this impossibility. The Angel heard her laugh, and challenged her about her disbelief, which she vehemently denied. Sarah was told that in spite of her disbelief, this would come true, and that the Angel would return at the appointed time, and that Sarah would indeed have the son of promise.

Genesis 20 says that after the angels left, Abraham and Sarah moved south, to the Negev, and once again, Abraham was in fear for his life from his new neighbours. Again, he presented Sarah as his sister, and this time he gave her to Abimelech the king of Gerar to be a part of his household, repeating the events that had taken place in Egypt some 23 years before. Once again, God swiftly intervened, warning Abimelech of Sarah and Abraham's treachery. When confronted, Abraham justified himself by explaining that Sarah was his half-sister. Terah was the father of both of them, but their mothers were different. Abimelech accepted this explanation, as had the Pharaoh of Egypt before him, and paid them a large sum of money before he sent them away.

Sarah finally believed that God would keep His promises and her faith was rewarded with the birth of her own son, Isaac (see Hebrews 11:11 in the AV, and the footnote in the NIV). Sarah was 90, and Abraham was 100 years old. Sarah again was mocked, this time by Ishmael, and she demanded that Abraham rectify the situation. After assurances from God, Abraham sent both Hagar and Ishmael into the desert, and this time neither returned. Galatians 4 refers to this, emphasising the place in God's plan of both Ishmael (bondage) and Isaac (freedom).

Sarah lived another 37 years (Genesis 23:1), and was buried in a field sold to Abraham by Heth (Genesis 23:3-20 in the AV), the only portion of land that Abraham ever actually owned.

So, what can we learn from Sarah?

Nothing is impossible with God, but we must recognise that His timing is not ours. God has an overall plan for each of us, which we can only see when we look back on our life. Trying to force situations to achieve our own perceived goals –even for His Glory – will backfire, and could even cause harm to others. We each have our role in God's plan, and sometimes we have to practice patience to realise this. Sarah had to wait over 35 years to become a mother, when all around her, others would have become mothers many years before her. Despite this, she became the matriarch of the nation of Israel, and her life has been preserved within the pages of scripture for us to learn from her mistakes, but also to see her ultimate reward.

3. Rebecca

Hazel Stephens

The account of Rebecca in the Bible begins in Genesis 24, when Abraham decided that it was time for Isaac to have a wife. Sarah, Isaac's mother, had died three years previously, and Isaac still grieved his mother's loss. We are not told if Isaac agreed to be wed, but he would have been aware of his place in God's plan for a nation to be created through his bloodline.

Abraham sent his servant to Padan Aram in Mesopotamia (part of modern-day Syria), where his family still lived, as he did not want a Canaanite woman to wed his son. When the servant arrived outside the city where Nahor, Abraham's brother, lived, he offered up a prayer for guidance, and immediately saw a beautiful young woman come to the well, where he was resting with his camels and bride goods.

Rebecca was approached by the servant, and she offered to draw water from the well not only for the thirsty servant, but also for his camels. This showed her willingness to aid a stranger without asking for payment for her work, and he was impressed by her humble attitude. Upon further questioning, Rebecca revealed that her father was Bethuel, who was the son of Nahor, who was a brother of Abraham. She was therefore family. She also told Abraham's servant that there was room for him to lodge at her home. He gifted her with a gold nose ring, which he put on her face (Genesis 24:47) and two bracelets, which she accepted. This interchange was the precursor to the official betrothal of Isaac and Rebecca, and was an acknowledged transaction at the time.

Rebecca went to her family and told them what had occurred. Her brother Laban, seeing the gifts bestowed upon Rebecca, went out to the well to meet with the servant. The servant and his entourage were invited back to their home, and were made welcome. He then relayed the reasons for his journey, and how he had been guided to Rebecca. Laban and Bethuel could therefore see and accept the hand of the Lord in this, and agreed to the marriage in principle. They were aware of Abraham's beliefs, but this did not necessarily mean they were also followers of the Lord themselves. Laban and his mother received the gifts to cement this transaction, and it is generally considered that such gifts were a form of compensation for the loss of a daughter from the family unit. It is interesting to note that her father, Bethuel, was not included specifically in the gift giving, and may suggest that he lived apart from Laban, his mother, and Rebecca. While this might appear that brides were bought and sold by the families involved, the prospective bride had the final say as to whom she married. In this instance, Rebecca agreed to the marriage, and she also received gifts from Isaac through the servant.

Next morning Rebecca was asked if she would leave with the servant straight away, as he had requested. This conflicted with Laban's desire to delay her journey, but Rebecca agreed to the early departure. This decision hints at a determination to be away from her family, and the courage to follow a new path. So, the following morning, Rebecca, her nurse and her maids, together with the gifts already bestowed upon her, left her father's house for her new home in Canaan.

While Isaac meditated in a field, he saw the camel train approach, and walked towards it, probably recognising it as belonging to his family. When Rebecca saw a man walking towards her, she asked the servant about him, and was told that this was his master. When Rebecca realised that he was the man she was betrothed to, she quickly got off the camel, and put on the betrothal veil herself, which showed she made her own decisions freely and independent of others.

She was introduced to Isaac, and he took her to his home, to his mother Sarah's tent, and they began their married life together. In Genesis 24:67 we are told that Isaac loved Rebecca, the first time that such a declaration is recorded in the Bible.

However, for twenty years, Rebecca did not conceive. She, like Sarah before her, was unable to give her husband children, and Isaac prayed to God on her behalf. The barrenness of the second matriarch of the Jews highlights the unique role of these children in the future, as without the Lord's hand in this, these children would never have been born.

Finally, she conceived, but it was a difficult pregnancy. She enquired of the Lord as to why this was, and He responded directly to her. She was told that two nations were within her, that they would both be very different from each other, and that the younger child would be served by the elder.

This overriding of the rights of the eldest son is seen a number of times later in Scripture, for example, when Jacob blessed Joseph's sons, favouring the younger over the elder (Genesis 48), when Gideon was used by the Lord to defeat the Midianites (Judges 6), and when David, who was the youngest of eight brothers, becamc king (1 Samuel 17 and 18). This shows that the order of birth was not important when it came to the Lord's divine purposes.

When her time came and the first baby came out, his body was covered in hair, and was therefore named Esau, which means "hairy". When the second baby came out he was grasping Esau's heel, and was therefore named Jacob, which means "supplanter", or "grasper". Esau grew up to be a hunter, while Jacob preferred home life, living and working in the fields around the tents. Esau had little loyalty to the God of his father, shown by his marriage to two Hittite women, and then to a daughter of Ishmael.

We are told in Genesis 26 that when a famine came on the land, Isaac decided to escape it by going south to Egypt through Philistia. But when he reached Gerar in Philistia, the Lord stopped him going further saying that this area was where he was to live. Abimelech was still the king of the Philistines, the same as in Abraham's time. When the men who were living there asked about Rebecca, Isaac told them that she was his sister as he was afraid he would be killed by them on account of her beauty. He therefore used the same ruse as Abraham had done twice before with Sarah, years earlier, and Abimelech granted Isaac permission to stay in Gerar with Rebecca, just as he had done before with Abraham and Sarah.

However, one day Abimelech, from a window, noticed Isaac caressing Rebecca and he confronted Isaac with his deception. Isaac confessed that he had been afraid of being killed by the local men if they knew she was his wife. Unlike Sarah, Rebecca was never taken into a palace, nor separated from Isaac, and so there was never any potential compromise of God's line of blessing. On the contrary, this time Abimelech ordered that no-one should molest either of them, on pain of death, and so they were protected from harm. Throughout their married life Rebecca had a monogamous relationship with Isaac, unlike Sarah, who shared her husband with Hagar, and unlike Rachel, who shared her husband with her sister and both of their servants.

The final episode with Rebecca plays out in Genesis 27. Each parent showed favouritism to one child. Isaac preferred Esau, who was good at hunting and outdoor activities. However, Esau's choice of wives was a source of sorrow to him.

Rebecca preferred Jacob, who was content to stay within the tents, and used his wits rather than physical strength. Perhaps she deemed Esau as unworthy of Isaac's blessing, as he had previously despised his birth-right (Genesis 25).

In the New Testament, Romans 9:10-16 also comments on this portion of scripture. In verse 13 God states that He loved Jacob, but hated Esau. Rebecca's preference for Jacob was therefore in line with the will of God. However, if she had not deceived Isaac, no doubt God would have brought about the same result, but through different circumstances.

Continuing in Genesis 27 we are told of Rebecca's part in securing the blessing for Isaac. This blessing was more than just a wish for the future. It involved the transfer of property and legal power held by the father to the son, and all decisions made would be legally binding.

Rebecca overheard Isaac tell Esau to bring him some of his favourite venison, upon which he would give his final blessing before he died. So, she told Jacob to get two goats, and prepared a meal for Isaac, so that Jacob could take it into his father, and gain the blessing. While Jacob raised concerns as to how he could be mistaken for his brother, Rebecca had already planned in advance. She prepared the meal, sought out Esau's clothing, and used the skins of the goats that Jacob had brought her to disguise the smooth skinned Jacob into the hairy Esau.

Throughout their marriage, Rebecca comes across as a spirited and intelligent girl who grew to be a wise and shrewd woman. Isaac seems more meditative than Rebecca, and these opposing qualities melded into a strong marriage. We are told that Rebecca's deception fooled Isaac into thinking that Jacob was Esau, and thus secured his destiny as a patriarch in the ancestry of the Jewish people.

When Esau came home and learned of the deception, he was furious. Rebecca was told of his threat to kill Jacob after the death of Isaac, and concocted a plan, which she put to Isaac.

In Genesis 28, we see that Rebecca had already expressed her worry to Isaac that Jacob might follow in his brother's footsteps, and marry a Hittite woman. She suggested that Jacob leave the family holdings and journey to her brother, Laban, in order to choose a more suitable wife. Isaac agreed, and blessed Jacob with the blessings he inherited from Abraham. Jacob left, and the last mention of Rebecca in the Bible is in Genesis 49:31, where she was buried with Abraham, Sarah and Isaac in the cave purchased by Abraham for his family tomb.

So, what can we learn from Rebecca?

She was a woman of faith. She was selected by God at the well, and chose to follow the servant to a new land to wed a husband she did not know. This shows her strength of character.

Isaac loved her, and she had a strong marriage. When she failed to fall pregnant, instead of taking the route of unbelief, and gaining a child by other means, as Sarah and Rachel did, she and Isaac put their petitions to the Lord, and in His timing, she conceived.

She disapproved of Esau's Hittite wives, who worshipped their own gods, rather than the God of Abraham and Isaac (and also her), and she sought a suitable bride for Jacob from her own family instead.

She knew of the promises God had made to Abraham, and did all she could to ensure that these would be fulfilled. God used her failings in His ultimate plan for the nation of Israel.

Like Abraham before them, Rebecca and Isaac owned no land. Still, God blessed them, and enriched them, because material things were unimportant to them, compared with belief in His Word.

4. Rachel

Hazel Stephens

Rachel is first mentioned in Genesis 29, when Jacob, having left his home to escape the fury of his brother Esau, and also to find a wife, arrived in the area of Padan Aram in Mesopotamia, near the city of Haran. Rachel was a shepherdess, and brought her father's flock of sheep to the well where other shepherds gathered to water their own flocks. Smitten by her beauty, Jacob decided to move the stone from the well for her, and then he kissed her, and wept. When Rachel was told of his relationship to her family, she ran home to her father, Laban, who then came out to greet Jacob and offer him hospitality.

In the following month, Jacob spent his time working for Laban and he learned that Rachel had an elder sister called Leah. In Genesis 29:17 the two girls are compared with one another. Leah had weak eyes whereas Rachel was beautiful and lovely in form. During that month, Jacob fell in love with Rachel (Genesis 29:18) and he agreed with Laban he would work for seven years in exchange for Rachel becoming his wife. But Rachel knew nothing of the seven-year agreement between Laban and Jacob. In those seven years Jacob would have been out in the fields, tending the sheep previously watched over by Rachel, and they would have met infrequently, and then only in the company of others. When the seven years were completed, Jacob asked Laban to give him Rachel as his wife.

It was dark when the men began to celebrate the fulfilment of the agreement between Laban and Jacob, and it was probably very late when Jacob went into the tent. As it was dark, and also possibly he had drunk too much wine, he didn't realise which sister was there until it got light the next morning. Being sisters, they may well have resembled each other in the dark, in both size and height, although not in beauty. This similarity would have helped in Laban's deception. The fact that Rachel did not complain about Leah being the first to marry Jacob was also telling. Indeed, the reactions of both sisters showed that neither of them knew of Laban's deceit. It was Jacob who confronted Laban with his trickery, not Rachel, which again implies that she knew nothing of Jacob's intentions toward her.

Subsequently, Laban agreed to give Rachel as Jacob's wife as well, provided Leah's bridal week was completed. Jacob's dismay at finding Leah in his tent, instead of Rachel, must have hurt Leah badly since she must have originally believed that he wanted *her* as his wife. We are not told of Rachel's reaction to being married only seven days after her sister, and to the same man, but it is most unlikely that she wouldn't have realised how badly Laban had deceived all three of them. It must have been a bitter pill for Leah to swallow when Rachel became his second wife after only seven days. This indecently short period of time between marrying both sisters made Jacob's original choice of Rachel obvious, and this began an emotional conflict that continued throughout their lives.

When God saw how Jacob loved only Rachel, He allowed Leah to bear four male children, while Rachel was unable to have any. Genesis 29:32 shows that Leah loved Jacob, and was desperate to have him return her love, but Jacob only ever loved Rachel. It is not stated whether Rachel ever reciprocated Jacob's love. However, Rachel grew ever more jealous with each baby Leah birthed, because she remained childless.

Genesis 30 records Rachel's anguish at not being a mother, and in desperation, she offered her handmaid, Bilhah, to Jacob to be her surrogate. Later when Rachel saw that Bilhah had conceived twice, she acknowledged Jacob's words in Genesis 30:2 that her childlessness was a judgment from God, but that Bilhah's children would be her consolation. However, the rivalry between the two sisters increased with the birth of these babies, and Leah then used the same scheme to increase her own family through her handmaid Zilpah.

In Genesis 30:14, Reuben, Leah's oldest son, found some mandrake plants in a field. These were deemed to be an aphrodisiac. Rachel coveted them, and demanded the mandrakes so that she herself could conceive, but Leah rejected her, revealing that Rachel was already Jacob's beloved; why then should she also help her have his children? Being unable to produce a child in the first ten years of marriage had branded Rachel as barren, which may explain her desperation. A bargain was eventually struck between the sisters, and Leah spent a night with Jacob. What must Rachel have thought when she realised that her bargain with Leah had resulted in yet another male child, whereas she remained childless? And, again, what did she think when Leah produced her sixth son and a daughter after this? All the praying to God, and demanding a child from Jacob, resulted in no children for Rachel. Her self-esteem must have sunk to an all-time low, which allowed even more negative emotions to fester within her.

Finally, after nearly twelve years, Rachel fell pregnant. This infertility mirrored Sarah and Rebecca's lives, once again emphasising the uniqueness of the child in the plan of God. When Rachel's son was born she named him "Joseph", meaning "may he add", revealing that although God had taken away her reproach, she still wanted another son (Genesis 30:22-24). Even after the realisation that her prayers had finally been answered, she was still bitter. After all, Leah had six sons and a daughter of her own, whilst Rachel had only one son. Rachel appears to have spent most of her married life feeling jealous of her fruitful sister, and discontented at her own empty life.

Thirteen years after the marriage deception, Genesis 31:4 states that Rachel and Leah were summoned to a secret discussion with Jacob about their future. Rachel and Leah voiced their anger at never having received any bridal gifts due to them when they married Jacob, and agreed to leave, taking with them the livestock as the sum of Jacob's wages for the previous six years labour.

However, Rachel stole Laban's household idols, without Jacob's knowledge, and then lied about it. Why did she do this? Maybe she wanted something belonging to her family as a keepsake or memorial. Perhaps she thought that stealing his idols would cause him hardship – after all, they would have been valuable to him, both materially and spiritually. Did she think that this was due to her as her portion of her inheritance? Genesis 31:14-16 shows what the sisters thought of Laban and his wealth, but only Rachel seemed willing to take what she perceived to be her rightful portion. After all, Jacob's wages were the livestock he took with him, plus his two wives. Whatever Rachel's motives were, Laban was more upset by his lost idols than the loss of his daughters and grandsons. Jacob promised Laban that if he found his stolen idols with anyone, they would not live, and a search of all the tents was then instigated.

Rachel was probably alarmed by this. However, she thought quickly. The seat from her camel was in her tent, and she placed the idols beneath it. She covered the seat with cushions and blankets and then claimed she was having her period as an excuse for not getting up in her father's presence.

Laban accepted her explanation, and continued to search for his idols in vain. Rachel had succeeded in depriving Laban of his valuables. However, if Jacob's threat of death for whoever had stolen the idols worried Rachel, she kept it to herself. She kept the idols, and the family continued their journey towards the land of their fathers, as directed to by God (Genesis 31:3). On the journey, they saw Esau's entourage heading their way, and Jacob arranged his camel train in order of value, in case Esau's wrath fell upon them all. So, the animals were first, then the two surrogate mothers with their children, then Leah and her children, and finally, Rachel and Joseph. This order showed that Rachel was still more precious to Jacob than all his other family or belongings. Jacob's fear having proved unfounded however, he moved his family to Shechem (Genesis 33:18).

In Genesis 35:1-5 Jacob moved his family away from Shechem, but this time he instructed his entourage to leave all the foreign idols behind. Presumably this would have included the idols that Rachel had stolen, although Scripture does not mention this. The idols were buried beneath an oak at Shechem, and they journeyed on to Bethel. Rachel was by this time heavily pregnant again, and before she reached Ephrath, (i.e. Bethlehem) she went into labour. She died giving birth, and she named her son Ben-oni, which means son of my sorrow (Genesis 35:18). This seems to sum up how she felt about her life. Could this have been a late fulfilment of Jacob's threat of death for the person who had stolen the idols? Her body was buried where she died, not in the ancestral tomb. Later it became a landmark for the Jewish nation (see 1 Samuel 10:2).

So, what can we learn from Rachel?

Rachel prayed to God for children, but God took a long time to answer her prayers. She had Jacob's love, but not his children. Rachel was beautiful, but her beauty could not make her a mother. Her failure to become a mother increased the jealousy and bitterness against her sister. Her last act in naming her son when she lay dying showed how she viewed her life – full of sorrow.

Her life shows us that we can see either the good or bad in situations. Rachel focussed on achieving motherhood by any means, rather than allowing the will of God to prevail, even though it may not have been in line with her own wishes. Her competitiveness with Leah made the family dynamics ever more stressful, resulting in Jacob's rebuke when she demanded a child from him (Genesis 30:2).

Rachel allowed her marriage trials to warp her character. Unlike Hannah (1 Samuel 1 and 2), who remained sweet tempered through similar trials, Rachel grew bitter and jealous. Even when she gave birth to Joseph, she was still demanding another child. We should try to emulate Hannah rather than Rachel when circumstances discourage us, even though it may not be the easy option.

Why did she steal her father's idols? Was this greed fuelled by anger against Laban? Or was it to cause her father difficulties, as she thought he had caused hers? Was her premature death the result of Jacob's threat of death to the thief of the idols? We can't answer these questions definitively, but they are worth thinking about, and we will each come to our own conclusions.

Ultimately, Rachel thought her life was full of sorrow. She could have embraced all that was good, but focussed instead on what she did not have, rather than all that she did.

This is the lesson to us from her life.

5. Rachel, Leah, Bilhah & Zilpah – the four mothers of Jacob's sons

Vicky Wilkinson

Introduction (Genesis 12 – 29)

The promises God had made to Abram are first recorded in Genesis 12:1-3.

> "Get out from your country,
> from your family and from your father's house
> to a land which I will show you.
> I will make you a great nation;
> I will bless you and make your name great;
> And you shall be a blessing.
> I will bless those who bless you, and I will curse
> him who curses you;
> And in you all the families of the earth shall be
> blessed".

These promises were repeated to Abraham's son Isaac (26:1-4), and likewise to Isaac's son Jacob (28:13-15) – whose name was subsequently changed to Israel. One of these promises was that, from Abraham, Isaac and Jacob, would come a great nation, and for that to happen there would need to be many children. And for that to happen, there would need to be wives and mothers. This article is about the four wives of Jacob; the four mothers of the twelve tribes of the nation of Israel.

When the time came for Jacob to take a wife, his father Isaac told him he must do so from their own family in Paddan Aram, rather than from the descendants of Canaan. God wanted them to keep their pedigree pure and untainted from the wicked and evil ways of the Canaanites. So, Jacob travelled to Paddan Aram to his mother's family.

Rachel (Ewe) – Genesis 29-48

When Jacob came near to Haran he stopped by a well in a field and he saw Rachel coming with her father's sheep. When he realised that she was his mother's brother's daughter, he greeted her with a kiss and lifted up his voice and wept. I think that this was indeed love at first sight!

Rachel was a shepherdess, (in Hebrew the name *Rachel* meant "ewe") and chapter 29:17 tells us that she was beautiful in form and appearance. She was the second daughter of Laban, Jacob's uncle. Jacob loved her so much that he was willing to serve Laban for seven years for her hand in marriage. So, an agreement was made. However, when the seven years were fulfilled and Jacob asked Laban to fulfil his promise, Laban deceived Jacob by preparing his eldest daughter Leah and sending Jacob in to her. It wasn't until the morning that Jacob realised what had happened. We could ask the question, was this a reaping of what Jacob had sown? Earlier, Jacob had deceived his brother Esau, and prevented him from receiving the firstborn's blessing, and now Jacob had been deceived by Laban!

Some questions that come to mind are how did both Rachel and Leah feel about this situation? Did they have any say in it? We are not told if Rachel even knew this had happened until after the event. We don't even know if Rachel reciprocated the love Jacob had for her. Personally, I like to think that she did.

The following morning when Jacob challenged Laban, Laban said it was the tradition in their country to give the eldest daughter first in marriage. Well, he could have made this known to Jacob before entering into this agreement. Laban then asked Jacob to wait a full week to fulfil his marriage with Leah and then he could marry Rachel. However, he added he must serve him a further seven years. What an unscrupulous person Laban was! Laban saw how much God had blessed Jacob in the first seven years and wanted more from him. Jacob had no choice but to agree to this if he was ever to have the woman whom he so loved. So, after fulfilling his week with Leah, Jacob received Rachel as his beloved wife.

However, as time went by Rachel remained childless and she became very envious of her sister who by this time had borne four sons to Jacob. Obviously, it is most women's dream, even more so in those days, to bear children for their husband. It was very important for them to have posterity to keep the family name going and Rachel wanted to be part of this. Therefore, she decided to offer her maid to Jacob as a surrogate, which resulted in the birth of two sons, Dan and Naphtali.

Later, God remembered Rachel and listened to her and opened her womb (30:22). Therefore, Rachel conceived and brought forth her very own son whom she named Joseph. She exclaimed "God has taken away my reproach". Rachel the childless wife was enabled to bear a son through divine intervention. Rachel then said, "The Lord shall add to me another son." This eventually happened after Jacob had left Paddan Aram with all his family and livestock to return to Canaan. As they were just leaving Bethel to go to Ephrath (Bethlehem) Rachel went into labour, but very sadly she had a very difficult delivery and she died giving birth. However, her son whom she named Ben-Oni lived but Jacob called him Benjamin (35:16-20). Rachel was buried on the way to Bethlehem and Jacob set a pillar on her grave, which is the pillar of Rachel's grave to this day. The descendants of Rachel that went into Egypt at the time of the famine were fourteen persons (46:22)

Leah (Wearied) – Genesis 29-46

Leah was the eldest daughter of Laban. While Rachel is described as beautiful in form and appearance, of Leah it is said, her eyes were delicate (29:17). I wonder how Leah felt when Laban tricked Jacob by sending him in to her when it should have been her younger sister? Did she have any say in the matter or did she think it was her right being the eldest daughter? We don't know. But what we do know is that this caused a wrestling between the two sisters. However, the Lord took pity on Leah because she was unloved and opened her womb so that she bore to Jacob his first son – Reuben. She said, "the Lord has surely looked on my affliction – now therefore my husband will love me" (29:32). However, it was because she remained unloved that she gave birth a second time to another son – Simeon, followed closely after by the births of Levi and Judah. So, she was blessed by giving birth to four sons to Jacob but then she stopped bearing children. We see here that Leah was constantly working to get her husband's approval and love. No wonder her name meant 'wearied'.

When Leah stopped bearing children she did as Rachel had done and offered her maid as a wife to lie with Jacob! This resulted in the births of two more sons, Gad and Asher. Then there was an incident where Rachel made a deal with Leah to allow her to go in to Jacob if Leah gave Rachel some of Reuben's mandrakes which he had given to his mother. These were fruits that were thought to contain an aphrodisiac ingredient (30:14-15). Leah's words to Jacob were that she had hired him with her son's mandrakes, and he must come in to her that night! God listened to Leah and she gave birth to another son whom she called Issachar. Following this she also bore another son – Zebulun, and afterwards she gave birth to a daughter – Dinah. So altogether Leah bore six sons and a daughter to Jacob.

After Jacob had returned to Canaan with all his wives and offspring, all the descendants of Leah who went into Egypt at the famine were thirty-three persons (46:15). When Leah died she was buried in a cave in the field of Machpelah in the land of Canaan (which Abraham bought) where Abraham, Sarah, Isaac, Rebecca and Jacob were laid (49:31).

Bilhah (Timid) – Genesis 29-46

Bilhah had first been the maid of Laban but when Rachel married Jacob Laban gave her Bilhah as her own maid (29:29). When Rachel became envious of her sister Leah, who had already given birth to four sons to Jacob, she complained to Jacob. He replied, "Am I in the place of God, who has withheld from you the fruit of the womb?" Obviously, Rachel was frustrated in having no children, but then she came up with a plan. She said, "Here is Bilhah, my maidservant. Sleep with her so that she can bear children for me and that through her I too can build a family" (30:3; NIV). After Bilhah gave birth to a son, Rachel said, "God has vindicated me; he has listened to me and given me a son" (30:6; NIV). This happened a second time and

Bilhah bore another son. Rachel named her two sons by surrogacy Dan and Naphtali (30:1-8).

The meaning of the name Bilhah is timid. If this was her nature can you imagine how she may have felt being used in this way. Being a maid, did she have any say in the matter? How did she feel when the children she bore were given to Rachel? Or did she feel privileged to do this for Rachel? There is also another occasion where Bilhah was taken advantage of (see 35:22). The descendants of Bilhah who went into Egypt at the time of the famine were seven persons (46:25).

Zilpah (Dripping of balsam) - Genesis 29-30

As Laban did with Rachel he also gave his maid Zilpah to Leah when she married Jacob. When Leah realised she had stopped bearing children she copied what Rachel had done and gave Zilpah over to Jacob as his wife. This union resulted in a further two sons whom Leah named Gad and Asher. The descendants of Zilpah who went into Egypt were sixteen persons (46:18).

What is interesting is that when Jacob and his wives and family finally left Paddan Aram and returned to Canaan and he was about to meet up with Esau his brother, Jacob arranged his wives in order together with their respective offspring. Therefore, both Bilhah and Zilpah, although only maidservants and surrogates, were given recognition as being the mothers of those they had given birth to (see 33:1-2).

Other observations

There are some similarities in what happened with Jacob and his wives to Abraham, Sarah and Hagar, to Hannah and the birth of Samuel, and to the birth of Samson. While all these stories differ in detail, what lies behind them is the conviction that it is God alone who bestows or withholds life.

While it has always been in God's plan for a man to have only one wife, He allowed polygamy in the Old Testament, in the life of the Patriarchs and also later on. However, it is clear in Jacob's case it wasn't his *intention* to have four wives – he clearly only wanted Rachel! In Acts 17:30-31 it says, "Truly these times of ignorance God overlooked". God was willing to overlook sins done in ignorance; however for sins of intent there was no mercy. Even when the Jews sent Jesus to His death, Peter said they did it in ignorance and urged them to repent (see Acts 3:14-20).

While it appears that women in the Bible often had little choice in their own lives, as we have gone through the accounts of these four women, when it came to having children, it seems they did have some say in this area of their lives.

Conclusion

The twelve sons of Jacob through his four wives were:

Reuben (firstborn)	-	Leah
Simeon	-	Leah
Levi	-	Leah - became the Holy Tribe
Judah	-	Leah - became the royal Tribe
Issachar	-	Leah
Zebulun	-	Leah
Dan	-	Bilhah
Naphtali	-	Bilhah
Gad	-	Zilpah
Asher	-	Zilpah
Joseph	-	Rachel
Benjamin	-	Rachel

These are the 12 tribes of Israel who God chose to be his own, and through whom He worked for the benefit of the rest of mankind. They became a kingdom of priests and a holy nation to the Lord, and a special treasure above all people (Exodus 19:6; Deuteronomy 7:6). Also, through them was the line of descent (through Judah) to the coming Messiah. Despite all their ups and downs, what a privilege these four women of the Bible were given, to become the mothers of God's own chosen nation.

6. Michal

Sylvia Penny

Solomon is well known for his 700 wives and 300 concubines, who turned him astray and led his heart after other gods. However, less well known is the fact that David also had many wives, some of whom we know more about than others. The incident with Bathsheba is well known (2 Samuel 11), but before this David already had many wives and children, six of whom are named in 2 Samuel 3:2-5.

However, the first woman mentioned in connection with David is Michal. She was a daughter of Saul, and had fallen in love with David (1 Samuel 18:20). Saul, with a devious plan in mind to get rid of David, offered Michal to David as his wife if he would kill 100 Philistines in exchange (v25). David went out and killed 200 Philistines instead (v27), and so Michal became his wife. By this episode Saul realised not only did his own daughter love David, but that the Lord was with David as well. As a result he became even more afraid of David, and remained his enemy for the rest of his life.

Michal saves David's life

Apart from this rather unromantic explanation of how they came to be husband and wife, only two further accounts involving Michal are given in Scripture. The first is described in 1 Samuel 19:11-17 where Michal saves David's life. Saul sent men to David's house to watch it, and to kill him in the morning. However, Michal heard of the plot, and warned David to run for his life. She let him down through a window at night. When the men arrived to capture David, Michal told them that David was ill, but when they persisted, and found he had escaped, Saul asked her why she had deceived him and let David escape. She told him David had threatened her life if she did not let him go, and so David got away safely.

Michal despises David

The second episode is described in 2 Samuel 6:16-23 where she despised David in her heart. This happened a number of years later, after Saul had died, and David had become king in his place. The ark was brought back to Jerusalem, and King David was leaping and dancing before the Lord in celebration. When Michal saw this from a window, she despised him in her heart. When David returned home to her, she said to him, "How the king of Israel has distinguished himself today, disrobing in the sight of the slave girls of his servants as any vulgar fellow would" (v20). David replied, "It was before the Lord, who chose me rather than your father or anyone from his house when he appointed me ruler over the Lord's people Israel – I will celebrate before the Lord. I will become even more undignified than this, and I will be humiliated in my own eyes. But by these slave girls you spoke of, I will be held in honour" (vs 21,22). As a result of her attitude to David she never had any children (v23), and in Israel, to have no children was considered a disgrace (Luke 1:25).

Michal was a mixture

Thus we have two episodes described in some detail, both of which paint quite a different picture of the same woman. In one she heroically saved David's life, and in the other she despised him in her heart. Sometimes it is all too easy to hold a cardboard cut-out idea of a person in our minds. They are either "good" or "bad". However, the truth is, we are all a mixture, and it is only the Lord who can truly judge a person overall. Often, we do not have the full picture, or all the facts. If only one of the above episodes involving Michal had been recorded we might judge, either that she was a heroic woman, saving David in the face of adversity, or that she was a proud and snobbish woman who cared more about what people thought than what the Lord thought. We would be wrong in both cases!

An application to ourselves

That everyone is a mixture of good and bad is clearly stated in 1 Corinthians 3:10-15. This refers to how each believer builds their lives on the foundation, which is Jesus Christ. However, each of us builds using a mixture of materials – gold, silver, costly stones, but also wood, hay and straw. On the day of resurrection, when we stand before the Lord, the quality of our work for him will be (symbolically) tested by fire. The wood, hay and straw will be burned up, leaving only the gold, silver and costly stones. Each of us is a mixture, just like Michal was. It is only the Lord, the righteous judge, who will be able to sort this out on the day of resurrection (2 Timothy 4:8).

7. Abigail

Andrea Marple

1 Samuel chapter 25 is where we read about Abigail. The Israelites wanted a king and the Lord gave the prophet Samuel the job of anointing His choice for them; Saul. As Israel's king, he was to be subject to the Law of the Lord and be willing to recognise God as the ultimate power and authority in ruling over the people. King Saul, however, was unwilling to submit in this way, and his disobedience led to the Lord choosing David to be his successor. Samuel, having anointed both Saul and David (Israel's first two kings) had then died. It is during this period of time, in which David is prepared for accession to the throne, that he encounters Abigail who is married to a man called Nabal. She is a courageous and proactive wife. Her actions and words are important in God's preparation of David. As we follow the events, can we perhaps aspire to be like her in some way? Before reading further, you may like to read 1 Samuel chapter 25 first.

David and Nabal

As David evades King Saul's vendetta against him, he and his men move into the Desert of Maon. They are surrounded by a vast number of sheep and goats, which they have been helping shepherds to protect for a wealthy man called Nabal. It is festival time and, hearing that Nabal is nearby shearing his many sheep, David sends ten young men to ask Nabal to be "favourable towards them" in providing food so that they also can celebrate. Nabal is described in verse 3 as being "surly and mean in his dealings", so then, even before David's men arrive, we anticipate him to be harsh and selfish. David's reasonable, courteous request is one that Nabal can well afford. Yet, despite his affluence, Nabal shows no generosity at all. Furthermore, he is rude and dismissive of their request; sending David's men away empty-handed. As David says in verse 21, "He has paid me back evil for good".

Nabal is in the wrong. He isn't willing to listen to David's request for hospitality, instead responding in a provocative and arrogant way. Thankfully, one of Nabal's servants *was* listening and he knew *who* to turn to. Immediate action was needed, and he went straight to Abigail, Nabal's wife, urging her to think what could be done. Nabal's wickedness had surely incurred David's anger and so put him and his whole household in danger.

Abigail and David

Abigail is a complete contrast to her husband. Her name means "source or cause of delight". Verse 3 says, "She was an intelligent and beautiful woman". We've heard the saying that "opposites attract", but in this case we sense that Abigail is not in an easy marital situation. Unlike her husband, when she hears of David's request, she listens and immediately realises how foolish Nabal has been and that steps must be taken to right his wrong. In her role as dutiful housewife, she brings to mind the wife described in Proverbs chapter 31 who is a blessing to her husband and is more than capable of overseeing her household.

Abigail is quickly able to put together bread, wine and lamb alongside raisin and fig cakes. At a festive time, this generosity is what David would have been hoping to be offered. Without telling her husband, Abigail sets off in the hope of saving both him and his household. She *feels* responsible for them all and *takes* responsibility for the problem.

Abigail has correctly sensed that David would seek revenge for Nabal's snub. David's response was to order his men to "put on your swords!" (verse 13) and to go with four hundred of his men towards Nabal's house with the intention of killing every male and obliterating "all who belong to him." (verse 22). Abigail's wisdom, courage and prudence are seen as she waylays David on his way to attack. She hurries down off her donkey to humble herself before him, taking her husband's guilt on herself and making a powerful plea for mercy on his behalf. She asks David to ignore her wicked husband's folly, explaining that his name means Fool, and to forgive the offense Nabal has caused.

David, for his part, was understandably displeased with Nabal. However, his rash way of showing it was wrong. He had initially sent Nabal the greeting of "Long life to you! Good health to you and your household. And good health to all that is yours!" (verse 6). But having been snubbed, he was soon advancing to attack and kill them all.

Abigail courageously confronts David in his anger and gently diffuses it by showing him the sin of his planned bloodshed against Nabal's household. She expresses her trust that God has chosen David to have a lasting dynasty and urges him not to take revenge:

> "When the LORD has done for my master every good thing he promised concerning him and has appointed him leader over Israel, my master will not have on his conscience the staggering burden of needless bloodshed or of having avenged himself." (1 Samuel 25:30-31a)

David listens. He needed to hear this from the Lord via Abigail. He accepts the gifts of food she has brought and praises her bravery and good judgment. Abigail's courage and peace-seeking words have paid off. She has turned away his wrath and helped remind David of what the Lord requires: James 1:20 says "for man's anger does not bring about the righteous life that God desires." Through Abigail, David realises that he would be sinning against God in shedding blood amongst Nabal's household. Peace is restored as David tells Abigail to "Go home in peace. I have heard your words and granted your request."

Abigail and Nabal

On returning home, Abigail might have been forgiven for boasting of her successful mission to ward off disaster to anyone who would listen, but instead she went to speak to her husband. However, Nabal was drunkenly holding a banquet, oblivious both to the danger he had been in and where his wife had been, so Abigail waited until daybreak to see him. In all of these actions - in returning home, in resuming her role and in waiting patiently for the right time, Abigail again acted wisely. When Nabal sobered up, she told him of the gifts of food presented to David and the danger that has been averted. It's *her* role to tell her husband first and so she saves him from further shame.

Now, instead of David, *God* acts to bring judgment on Nabal. As Abigail speaks his heart becomes like stone and fails him, and we read that ten days later "the LORD struck Nabal and he died". The widowed Abigail could have faced an uncertain future, but the Lord intervened. David – impressed by Abigail's wisdom, dignity, and no doubt also her beauty – upon hearing of Nabal's death, sends for Abigail in order to marry her.

Conclusion

Abigail was a housewife. Yet it is in this humble role that her actions and words reveal her many qualities. The Lord was able to use her, even as He prepared David to be His next king. She listened, discerned, organised ... As Christian women, why not ponder on how to imitate Abigail's example of what it means to be dutiful, submissive, and yet proactive. Like Abigail, may we also show courage and wisdom, humbly discerning the way to bring about peace when we can.

8. Martha's Memories (from two days before the crucifixion)

Sylvia Penny

Luke 10:38-42

It's not even a year since I first met Jesus, and yet I feel I've known Him all my life. He first came to my house in Bethany only a few months ago, and yet it feels like a lifetime. Of course, I'd heard of Him before then. I'd heard the rumours of people He had healed, and the people He had fed, but most of all, that He was the most amazing teacher people had ever heard. But just hearing rumours wasn't good enough for me. I was anxious to meet Him for myself, face to face.

At last my opportunity came when I heard He was on his way to Jerusalem, and was passing through Bethany. I invited Him to come for a meal at my home. A number of His disciples were coming with Him, so there was a lot to do. My sister, Mary, and I were busy all day getting everything ready. It was important that everything would be just right. He was an important guest and I wanted to make a good impression. But directly He arrived Mary left the kitchen and sat down with Jesus and His disciples listening to Him – so I was left all by myself to finish all the final preparations. I waited to see if she would come back – but no! So finally, I went to see where she was. I remember feeling pretty upset that there she was, idly sitting down, when there was such a lot to do. She should have been helping me.

I expected Jesus to take my side, and tell her to come and help, and hopefully make her feel ashamed of being so lazy. That was my first big surprise. Not only did He tell *me* that I was too worried about all the work I had to do, He went on to take *Mary's* side completely, and told me she had chosen better, to sit by His feet and listen to His teaching.

At first, I was angry and indignant, and felt totally unappreciated. But after we had eaten, and I listened to Him myself, I slowly began to realise why Mary had sat at His feet from the beginning. He spoke like no other teacher I have ever heard in any of the synagogues I have ever been to. Even in Jerusalem, at the big feasts, I had never heard anyone speak with such authority, and such conviction. And yet at the same time there was a peacefulness and serenity about Him. He was like no man I'd ever met before.

After that He was always welcome at my home. I learned my lesson after that first meeting, and I never tried to impress Him again. It's a waste of time, as I have the feeling He knows exactly what I'm thinking all the time. I'm sure you can't hide anything from Him. Now I'm happy to serve Him without expecting any help, as I know He'll always stay long enough for me to talk with Him later. Our brother Lazarus always comes to join us too, and although we've known Jesus less than a year, He makes us feel as if we are very special friends of His.

John 11:1-44

I would do anything for Him, and we know He will do anything for us. Only three months ago He did the most incredible thing. Our brother Lazarus died, but He raised him back to life. Lazarus had become very sick, and we sent for Jesus to come straight away. But He didn't. It wasn't until Lazarus had been in a tomb for four days that Jesus finally arrived. I went out to meet Him on the road, but Mary stayed at home with the others that had come to comfort us after Lazarus passed away. I didn't want to reproach Him for not coming any earlier, but I couldn't help saying that if He had only arrived sooner, then Lazarus would not have died. I *knew* He could have healed him if He had been there. And in my heart, I still hoped He could do something, even though it seemed hopeless. But it never crossed my mind what an incredible miracle was about to take place.

Jesus told me that Lazarus would rise again, but I thought He was talking about the resurrection on the last day, on the day of judgment. I told Him this, and that I believed that with all my heart. But then He said to me: "I am the resurrection and the life. He who believes in me will live, even though he dies; and whoever lives and believes in me will never die. Do you believe this?" Of course, I told Him I did, *and* that I believed He was the Christ, the promised Messiah, the Son of God who was prophesied to come into the world. After that, Jesus asked me where Mary was, so I went back to the house and told her that Jesus had arrived and wanted to see her. She immediately got up and went to see Him with a group of our friends, and like me, she also told Him that if only He had been there, then Lazarus would not have died.

All of us were still weeping with emotion, not only in grief at Lazarus' death, but also with the thought that if only Jesus had managed to arrive sooner, this would never have happened. We saw Jesus weep too, and thought this showed how much He had loved Lazarus. Little did any of us think that He was about to perform the most amazing miracle in front of us all. Later, when I realised He had *already known* He was going to raise Lazarus from the dead, I realised His tears had really been for all of us standing there. He had felt our loss as if it were His own. Grief at death itself - the last great enemy.

I cannot describe the joy I felt when He finally called in a loud voice "Lazarus, come out!" and Lazarus walked out of the tomb, still wrapped in the grave clothes that had bound him. Mary and I were overjoyed, and the whole group with us were stunned at what we had all just witnessed.

John 12:1-9

Since then, He has visited us a number of times. Only a few nights ago He was here for another meal. Mary anointed His feet with a whole jar full of oil that cost a fortune, but He wasn't at all worried that it was a waste of money. Not like Judas was, who always seems to be concerned about money. Judas asked Mary why the perfume hadn't been sold and the money given to the poor, as it was worth an enormous sum of money – about a year's wages.

I must admit I was surprised at what he said, as privately it had always seemed to me that Judas was more concerned about his own interests rather than those of the poor, but I kept these thoughts to myself.

Jesus told him to leave Mary alone, but the reason He gave Judas troubled me at the time. He said it was right that the perfume should be saved for the day of His burial, because the poor would always be around, but that we wouldn't always have *Him* around. I worried about what He meant. What did He mean about His burial, and that He wouldn't always be around?

Since then I've found it hard not to worry even more. There are rumours that people in high places want Him dead. I'm afraid each day He goes into Jerusalem that He won't come back. It's only two days before we celebrate the Passover, and Jerusalem is always crowded at this time of year. What if He gets arrested? What if He gets falsely accused of some crime? I've told Him that He should be careful, but it seems to me that He knows what is ahead. And has it all planned out. I hope so. He raised my brother Lazarus from the dead. I wonder if He *were* to die, He too would rise from the dead.

That would be the most wonderful miracle of all.

9. Tabitha (Dorcas)

Andrea Marple

"Tabitha, get up." These words are spoken by the Apostle Peter. He was on his knees in an upstairs room, praying over the dead body of a woman. But who was she and what was about to happen?

The book of Acts gives us an accurate account of how Christianity began. The church was growing, and Peter was travelling, visiting believers. The account of Tabitha is the second of two brief stories that involve Peter in Acts 9:36-42. Her name is possibly unfamiliar because "Tabitha" is the Aramaic version. In Greek she is known as "Dorcas."

Peter was visiting the saints in Lydda. Meanwhile, Tabitha was living not too far from there in a place called Joppa. It was an active seaport city on the Mediterranean Sea, about thirty-five miles west of Jerusalem.

Tabitha was part of a community of believers in Joppa. Luke calls her a disciple, so she would have been part of the inner circle of early Christians who followed and had faith in the risen Jesus Christ. Interestingly, this seems to be the only place in the New Testament where the female Greek form of the word disciple is used. Luke uses it here to identify Tabitha.

We know that she followed Jesus' teachings about how to treat others because she "was always doing good and helping the poor" (verse 36). We don't know much about Tabitha's situation and whether, or not, she was a widow. But Luke shows us the role Tabitha had in her Christian community. Transformed by her trust in the Lord, she used the talents and resources she had to meet the needs of those around her. She was able to sew and, in doing so, blessed others by making "robes and other fine clothing" (Acts 9:39).

The impact Tabitha had on her community is seen when, in verse 37, we read that "she became ill and died." Her death is an enormous loss, with many crying and mourning for her. When the disciples heard that Peter was in nearby Lydda, they sent two men there to urge him to "please come at once."

Would Peter have known of Tabitha's impact in her community? Was she prominent? Did he think he was being sent for to add his condolences and encourage the bereaved, and to share in their loss and grief? Or did he realise he was being called upon to act in the Lord's name to perform a miracle? We don't know, but God did, and Peter took the trouble to come.

As he made his way to Joppa, Tabitha was being mourned for by many in an upper room. It is likely some were the very people she had helped during her life. As was the custom, Tabitha's body had been prepared and was awaiting imminent burial. Upon Peter's arrival the mourning widows were able to demonstrate Tabitha's charitable work, done during her life, by showing him some of the garments she had made.

Peter had been preaching boldly and performing many miracles since Jesus' resurrection. And here, in this upper room, he needed the Holy Spirit to empower him again. He sent everyone out, got down on his knees and prayed. When Peter then told Tabitha to "get up", she was brought back to life.

When Peter helped Tabitha to her feet and presented her back, alive, to them, there was joy and amazement. She had been raised from the dead and the good news about what God had done spread quickly "all over Joppa, and many people believed in the Lord."

Even if Tabitha had not been raised back to life, as a believer in Christ, she would have received everlasting life, in the future, on the day of resurrection. But raising her then served to show Peter's authority from God in his ministry, and was a very powerful miracle bringing many more to faith. We can also presume that as Tabitha was restored, her community benefitted as she continued in "doing good and helping the poor."

Her story shows us a life transformed by Jesus. With the Holy Spirit's help, she was able to make a difference in Joppa. She gave of herself to humbly use her gifts in a compassionate and generous way. She loved and helped those in her community, not for her own glory but for God's.

So why not let Tabitha *challenge* you? Can *you* sew? help at a food bank? be a companion? drive a neighbour who needs help? host a coffee morning or lunch? make someone a meal? teach at Sunday school? pray for neighbours? pray for your church? and so on.

Why not let Tabitha *inspire* you. Pray that the Lord will help you to impact your community. We can all witness in some way. We are all given some sort of gift. Remember these words:

> "Only one life, 'twill soon be past.
> Only what's done for Christ will last."
> (C.T. Studd)

10. Lydia, a dealer in purple cloth from Thyatira

Sylvia Penny

Lydia in approximately AD 52

There are only two references to Lydia in Scripture. The first occurs in a passage in Acts 16 and says:

> From there we travelled to Philippi, a Roman colony and the leading city of that district of Macedonia. And we stayed there several days.
>
> On the Sabbath we went outside the city gate to the river, where we expected to find a place of prayer. We sat down and began to speak to the women who had gathered there. One of those listening was a woman named Lydia, a dealer in purple cloth from the city of Thyatira, who was a worshipper of God. The Lord opened her heart to respond to Paul's message. When she and the members of her household were baptised, she invited us to her home. "If you consider me a believer in the Lord," she said, "come and stay at my house." And she persuaded us. (Acts 16:12-15)

The "we" in this passage are Paul and Silas, who were travelling on Paul's second missionary journey, together with Luke, the author of the book of Acts. In Acts, whenever Luke travels with Paul he indicates this by saying "we" to show he was travelling with them. On this occasion, when they travelled to Philippi, there was also a fourth companion with them, a disciple called Timothy, who had joined them at Lystra. Therefore, at this point in Paul's journey there were four of them travelling together - accompanying him on his first venture out of Asia and into Europe. Ironically, we are told in Acts 16:9 that Paul had a vision of a *man* from Macedonia begging him to come over and help them, and yet when he arrives it is to a group of women, gathered at a place of prayer by the river, that he speaks to first.

The second reference to Lydia is in the last verse of Acts 16, at the end of their stay in Philippi:

> After Paul and Silas came out of the prison, they went to Lydia's house, where they met with the brothers and encouraged them. Then they left. (Acts 16:40)

Although there are only these two references to Lydia, we can deduce a fair amount about her from what is said in these two passages.

First, we are told that Philippi was a Roman colony, and that it was the leading city in the district of Macedonia. Lydia was therefore living in an important city. Next, we are told Lydia was a dealer in purple cloth, originally from the city of Thyatira. So, we know that she was a business woman.

Thyatira is also mentioned in Revelation 2:18, as it is one of the seven churches which John was instructed to write to, telling them what was to come. Thyatira itself was a small town, about 40 miles south-east of Pergamum, and was the smallest of the seven cities addressed in Revelation 2 and 3. It was established as a Macedonian colony by Alexander the Great after the destruction of the Persian Empire and it was famous for the manufacture of purple dye. Secular literature of this period has numerous references to the trade guilds which manufactured this particular cloth at the time. Purple dye was expensive, and from this we can deduce that Lydia was a successful and wealthy woman. It is also possible that she moved from Thyatira, across the Aegean Sea to Philippi, because we can see from Revelation 2 that many of those living in Thyatira had turned to immoral and erroneous teaching. Possibly Lydia was one of a small godly remnant who had not followed them, and had instead decided to move away to live in Philippi.

Paul found the group of women on the Sabbath, together with Lydia, at a place of prayer by the river. From this we can deduce that there were not enough men to constitute a synagogue in Philippi (see the New Bible Commentary), and maybe this is why the Lord called Paul to go there in a vision. Certainly, Lydia was very keen to listen to what they had to say. We are told she was a "worshipper of God", (a "God-fearer" as this is translated elsewhere), and as such the Lord knew her heart was ready to hear the message about Christ from Paul. Sure enough, Acts 16:14 records that "the Lord opened her heart to respond to Paul's message" and she and her household were subsequently baptised.

After this, Lydia invited Paul and his companions to stay at her house. Again, this implies she was wealthy enough to afford to run a household, and, in addition, to have enough space to accommodate four more people. She also had a generous nature, as her first thought seems to be to offer to look after them while they are staying in Philippi. Straight away, she showed her willingness to share her wealth to help others.

The rest of chapter 16 describes the incident of Paul casting a spirit out of a slave girl, Paul and Silas being flogged and thrown in jail, the jailer being converted and saved, and Paul and Silas being asked to leave the city. But before they left, as we have seen, verse 40 records that they returned to Lydia's house before they went and "met with *the brothers* and encouraged them." There is no explanation of where these *brothers* came from, or who they were. However, it seems that by this time, Paul and the others had reached a few men as well as the women, and there was the beginning of a small group at Lydia's house. No doubt Lydia was a key person in this swift development of the fledgling church at Philippi.

Lydia in approximately AD 59

Seven years later, in around AD 59, Paul called in at Macedonia on his third missionary journey (Acts 20:1). Although Luke does not record him visiting Lydia, it seems very likely that he would have been to see her. Verse 2 records that he travelled through that area and spoke many words of encouragement to the people there, and so it would be surprising if he had not visited her. Likewise, three months later, Paul returned from his visit to Corinth and we are told in Acts 20:6 that Paul and Luke stayed for an extra five days in Philippi, after the feast of Unleavened Bread. After that, they sailed across to join their other companions in Troas in Asia. Again, it seems possible that they would have spent those five days with Lydia and her household, although Scripture does not record this.

Lydia in approximately AD 64

Five years later, in around AD 64, Paul wrote to the church in Philippi while he was under house arrest for two years in Rome, awaiting trial by Caesar. In Acts 28:30 Luke records that "for two whole years Paul stayed there in his own rented house and welcomed all who came to see him." In his letter to the Philippians, Paul and Timothy start by greeting the saints in Philippi, together with the overseers and deacons. It seems in the interval between Acts 16, when he first visited Philippi, the church in Philippi had developed into a thriving congregation and community of Christian believers. It is a most glowing letter, full of rejoicing and thanksgiving and unity in Christ.

Paul says at the very beginning of this lovely letter,

> I thank my God every time I remember you. In all my prayers for all of you, I always pray with joy because of your partnership in the gospel from the first day until now. (Philippians 1:3-5)

One can only wonder and imagine how much this praise and thanksgiving is due to the influence that Lydia had exerted in this church. It seems to be the first church to have a well-developed system of overseers and deacons. We can see this when we read the letters of Paul to both Timothy at Ephesus and Titus in Crete. Both were written several years later than Philippians, and yet those churches were still in the throes of being given good advice on the type of people who should be leaders and how they should lead the church and how they should conduct themselves.

In verse 1 of chapter 4, the last chapter of Philippians, Paul says he loves and longs for his brothers there. They are his joy and crown. Then, at the very end, in verses 10 to 20 he gives them overflowing thanks for their many gifts. In particular, verses 15 and 16 say,

> Moreover, as you Philippians know, *in the early days* of your acquaintance with the gospel, when I set out from Macedonia, not one church shared with me in the matter of giving and receiving, except you only; for even when I was

> in Thessalonica, you sent me aid, again and again when I was in need.

The generosity of the Philippians was exemplary, and again, although Lydia's name is not mentioned in this letter, it seems most likely that much of this would have come from her *in the early days*. However, in verses 17 and 18 he continues with:

> Not that I am looking for a gift, but I am looking for what may be credited to your account. I have received full payment and even more; I am amply supplied, now that I have received from Epaphroditus the gifts you sent. They are a fragrant offering, an acceptable sacrifice, pleasing to God.

Here Paul refers to a very recent offering, so it seems the Philippians had carried on with their generosity over many years. Whether this was instigated by Lydia, or whether her example had encouraged others to do likewise, we don't know. However, it seems likely that Lydia was a good example of one who was generous, and happy to help others whenever she could. She put into practise what Paul wrote to the Corinthians in 2 Corinthians 9:7, "Each man should give what he has decided in his heart to give, not reluctantly or under compulsion, for God loves a cheerful giver." Paul even mentioned those in the Macedonian churches as an example of rich generosity in 2 Corinthians 8:2 despite their own poverty, and this whole passage from verse 1 to15 is all about encouraging generosity. Clearly, not all the believers in Macedonia were wealthy like Lydia, but they gave according to their means and gave it cheerfully.

Conclusion

Despite only having two short passages that mention Lydia, it seems likely that she was a woman who used her wealth to help others, rather than hoarding it up and keeping it to herself. Most likely she used it to build up the church in Philippi quickly and successfully, and by her example it is likely she encouraged others around her to do likewise.

Christian Living

11. Submission

Sylvia Penny

> *Ephesians 5:22:* **Wives, submit to your husbands as to the Lord.**
> *Colossians 3:18*: **Wives, submit to your husbands, as is fitting in the Lord.**

As Christian wives, how do we put these commands into practice? What do we understand when we read these words? Do these words demand blind obedience, or did Paul have some other meaning in mind?

We may think of Genesis 2:18 where we read: "The Lord God said, 'It is not good for the man to be alone. I will make a helper suitable for him.'" It is clear that woman was originally created in order to help man. However, this does not necessarily involve obedience whatever the circumstances. Sometimes people can be of far greater assistance when they use their own initiative and intelligence, rather than blindly following what they have been told to do. In fact, nowhere in the Bible is there any instruction for wives to obey their husbands. On the other hand, there are numerous occasions on which Christians are told to obey God and His commands. There are also some occasions on which Christians are to obey their earthly masters (particularly referring to slaves), and to obey those in authority (Hebrews 13:17). And there are a couple of references to children obeying their parents (Colossians 3:20; Ephesians 6:1). Admittedly, Sarah is mentioned as obeying Abraham (1 Peter 3:6), but if we read the story of Abraham and Sarah in the Old Testament, we also find God telling Abraham to do as Sarah told him! (Genesis 21:12). If obedience were required in a marriage it seems it was required to be mutual.

We may also think of Genesis 3:16 in which the Lord tells Eve: "Your desire will be for your husband, and he will rule over you." However, this should not be understood as a command from God, but rather as one of the curses which fell upon the whole human race as a result of Adam's sin. In the same way that pains at childbirth were to be greatly increased as a result of sin, so the husband would rule over his wife, *as a result of sin*.

So, if submission is not the same as obedience, and if it is not succumbing to being ruled over, what is it? In *Paul, Women and Wives* by Craig S. Keener, on page 226 the author suggests: "Submission … Is not blind obedience; it is desiring the honour and seeking the blessing of the other person above our own." In Ephesians 5:33 it is also linked with respect: "However, each one of you also must love his wife as he loves himself, and the wife must respect her husband." Just because Paul does not say so, it does not mean that the love, and the respect should not be reciprocated by the other spouse. Of course, a wife should love her husband, and a husband respect his wife. The point is that the relationship should be one of a partnership between two equals, not a hierarchy where one dominates the other.

This is in accordance with the general principle of *mutual submission* given in Ephesians 5:21: "Submit to one another out of reverence for Christ." Included in this general principle are, of course, Christian husbands and wives. This attitude is worlds apart from that of 'demanding equal rights' which is self-seeking, and damaging to relationships. Instead, mutual submission means that each person seeks the other's good, and loves and serves them selflessly. With both marriage partners doing this to the best of their ability, the marriage relationship is likely to go from strength to strength.

The Lord Himself gave a practical example of submission to others while He was on earth. In Luke 22:24-26 we read: "Also a dispute arose among them as to which of them was considered to be greatest. Jesus said to them, 'The kings of the Gentiles lord it over them; and those who exercise authority over them call themselves Benefactors. But you are not to be like that. *Instead the greatest among you should be like the youngest, and the one who rules like the one who serves.*'"

In order to make this lesson clear, John, in his gospel record (John 13:15-17), tells us that after the Lord Jesus had washed the disciples' feet, He said: "I have set you an example that you should do as I have done for you. I tell you the truth, *no servant is greater than his master*, nor is a messenger greater than the one who sent him. Now that you know these things, you will be blessed if you do them." Here,

Jesus made it clear that it was not important to be great, it was not right to exercise authority in a dictatorial manner, and it was wrong to lord it over others. Instead, they should follow His example and serve others. The Lord Jesus is *the* greatest One of all, yet His was a life of service and submission. We should try to follow His example in all our relationships with others, including that between husbands and wives.

So, returning to the two quotations at the beginning of this article, Paul wrote these in a context. The wife's submission to her husband was given as an *example* of the *mutual submission* of all Christians to one another. It refers to mutual respect, honour and service for one another, rather than to blind obedience to a dictatorial ruler.

12. The Will of God

Sylvia Penny

What is the will of God for us? What does God want us to do? Scripture is surprisingly clear and straightforward on this, and yet many of us have great problems with knowing what God's will is for us. Maybe this is because we are looking for direction as to *what* we should do in our lives, rather than direction as to *how* we do those things. According to Scripture, God is more concerned with the way in which we conduct our lives, rather than the specifics of where we go, whom we meet, or what work we do.

There are many verses in the New Testament which refer to God's will. Some of these verses have been selected below, as they not only refer to God's will, but they also explain clearly what this means in practical terms.

> **Ephesians 5:17** says, "understand what the Lord's will is". Verses 18-21 go on to explain what the Lord's will is: do not get drunk; be filled with the Spirit; sing and make music in your heart; give thanks for everything; submit to one another.
>
> **Ephesians 6:6** tells slaves to do "the will of God from your heart". Verse 7 explains that this means they should serve wholeheartedly, and obey their masters in the same way they would obey Christ.
>
> **Colossians 1:9** tells us that Paul kept "asking God to fill you with the knowledge of his will". He explains this meant that they might live a life worthy of the Lord, please him in every way, bear fruit in every good work, grow in knowledge of God, have great endurance and patience, and joyfully give thanks to the Father.
>
> **1 Thessalonians 4:3** says, "It is God's will that you should be sanctified: that you should avoid sexual immorality; that each of you should learn to control his own body in a way that is holy and honourable".

1 Thessalonians 5:16-18 says, "Be joyful always; pray continually; give thanks in all circumstances, for this is God's will for you in Christ Jesus".

1 Peter 2:15 says, "For it is God's will that by doing good you should silence the ignorant talk of foolish men". Peter continues that they should live as servants of God, show proper respect to everyone, love the brotherhood of believers, fear God and honour the king.

Each of these passages is simple to understand, and each gives specific examples of what the will of God is for us. None of them refers to what jobs people should do, nor where they should live or whom they should marry. Instead each of them gives a list of 'dos' and 'do nots' as to how we should behave and how we should treat others.

It seems therefore, that as long as we put God's commands for our behaviour into practice, it is of secondary importance where we are and who we are with. Wherever we go, and whoever we meet, and whatever we do, we should always endeavour to be patient, joyful, thankful, prayerful, and show respect and submission to others. If we can do this, then we can be assured we are carrying out the will of God for us in our lives.

13. Do not judge

Sylvia Penny

Why are we told not to judge one another? Matthew 7:1 says: "Do not judge, or you too will be judged. For in the same way you judge others, you will be judged, and with the measure you use, it will be measured to you." Here, the Lord Jesus gave some sensible advice to the crowd. If they judged one another, they were quite likely to be judged by those others in the same way.

It is a very common human failing, to be able to see all the faults in others, and yet be unable to see our own faults quite so clearly. Hence the next verse, in which the Lord Jesus goes on to talk about removing the plank in our own eye before we try to remove the speck in our neighbour's eye!

However, another reason for not judging others is simply that we are unable to do so fairly. The only way we can judge another person is by what we see, by the outward appearance. 1 Samuel 16:7 says: "…the Lord does not look at the things a man looks at. Man looks at the outward appearance, but the Lord looks at the heart." And again, in Galatians 2:6 we read, "God does not judge by external appearance". God is the only righteous Judge, as it is only He that can look on the heart and determine a person's true motivation for his actions. It is therefore all-important what our motivation is, as this is not necessarily apparent from our actions.

Take, for example, a wrong action. A man murders another man. If we know that the murderer is a husband who killed a man in order to protect his wife from an attack, then we look on the act of murder in a completely different light, compared with the man who commits murder through jealousy, or in order to steal something. So, we judge differently, when we are aware of the motive for an action and when we know the circumstances.

Or, take a right action, where a man donates £1,000 towards a good cause. If we knew he gave generously simply because he was moved to help a person or an organisation then we would praise such an action. On the other hand, if we knew the donor hoped to gain some control over the person or organisation by contributing large sums, then we would look on the action in a completely different light.

However, in reality, we rarely know a person's true motives. That is another reason we are told not to judge one another. We will seldom get it right. We should leave all judgment to God.

The other side of the coin is that although we should not judge others, we should be concerned about our *own* actions, and our motivation for them. One reason is that "the Lord searches every heart and understands every motive behind the thoughts" (1 Chronicles 28:9). We may be able to hide our true motivation from other people, but we can never hide it from the Lord.

Sometimes, due to our powers of self-justification, we may even be able to deceive ourselves as to our true motivation. Solomon wrote in Proverbs 16:2: "All a man's ways seem innocent to him, but his motives are weighed by the Lord." We have to be careful that we do not end up with a conscience that does not work because we have chosen to ignore it so often.

1 Timothy 4:2 mentions "hypocritical liars whose consciences have been seared as with a hot iron". Although this is a fairly extreme state of mind that Paul describes here, it describes how our consciences may become ineffective by being constantly ignored, and by persistent self-justification.

Paul mentions motivation in Philippians 1:18 where he says, "The important thing is that in every way, whether from false motives or true, Christ is preached. And because of this I rejoice." However, Paul did not say this in order to show that motivation was not important. As we have already seen, it is of paramount importance. Paul said this to show that despite the false motives of others, he was able to rejoice in the fact that Christ was preached. The false motives of other people were not his concern. His place was not to judge them, as he knew that the Lord would do that in His own good time.

Paul's attitude towards judgment of himself and others, motivation and conscience is made very clear in 1 Corinthians 4:3-5:

> I care very little if I am judged by you or by any human court; indeed, I do not even judge myself. My conscience is clear, but that does not make me innocent. It is the Lord who judges me. Therefore, judge nothing before the appointed time; wait till the Lord comes. He will bring to light what is hidden in darkness and will expose the motives of men's hearts. At that time each will receive his praise from God.

Paul effectively expands Matthew 7:1, 2. We should not judge others, and we should not even judge ourselves, as we are unlikely to get either of them right. We should leave all judgment to the Lord. We should live according to our consciences, but not judge others according to our own yardstick, or we may become guilty of searching for specks in others, when there are planks of our own in the way.

Finally, although others should not judge us, (in the same way that we should not judge them), we are told in Romans 12:17 that it is still important to be "careful to do what is right in the eyes of everybody". As far as it is within our capabilities, we should try to appear to do the right things. In turn, this should make it easier for others to refrain from misjudging us, and will result in us being better witnesses for the Lord.

14. Riches at Christmas

Sylvia Penny

As another Christmas draws near, we inevitably think of the vast quantities of money spent at this time of year. Spending a lot of money, we are told, is necessary in order to have a good time. The more riches we have, the more we can buy, the more we can possess, and the better our Christmas will be; at least, so the advertisers would have us believe. After all, it's money that makes the world go around.

However, recently I read a thoughtful article by George Monbiot entitled, "What do we really want?" By simple observation, some research and logical reasoning, he came to the same conclusions about wealth and satisfaction that the Bible pointed out thousands of years ago.

> Whoever loves money never has enough; whoever loves wealth is never satisfied with his income. (Ecclesiastes 5:10)
>
> The sleep of a labourer is sweet, whether he eats little or much, but the abundance of a rich man permits him no sleep. (Ecclesiastes 5:12)

The article was summarised in the heading: "Economic growth is seen as an almost universal good, yet it makes many in the rich world miserable." He pointed out that although poverty does not make people happy, there *is* some evidence that wealth causes misery, as apparently, since 1950, 25-year-olds in Britain have become ten times more likely to be affected by depression. And he goes on to say that he considers most of us suffer from subclinical neurosis, anxiety or a profound discomfort with ourselves. I wonder why this is?

Could it be because we no longer have to worry about obtaining the basic necessities of life, we go on to worry about the quality of our life, and the meaning of our life? Here, as Christians, we have a distinct advantage as we experience the love of God in our lives, which gives the quality and meaning to our life that so many rich people lack. We are rich in spiritual blessings, which in our affluent society is a thing lacking in many people's lives. Ephesians 1:7, 8 tells us about these riches: "In Him we have redemption through His blood, the forgiveness of sins, in accordance with the riches of God's grace that He lavished on us with all wisdom and understanding."

George Monbiot went on to say that the rich lock themselves in and lock everyone else out. They become prisoners of their riches. They become fearful of losing their wealth, and suspicious of relationships, as it is difficult to tell a genuine friendship from a false one. They retreat to gated communities, hire guards and install CCTV and movement sensors. In contrast, in southern Ethiopia, in the poorest half of the poorest nation on earth, people relate to each other more freely, smile more often and express more affection than people behind double-glazing, surrounded by remote controls. In other words, people in our society have replaced relationships with material possessions. They buy products to fill gaps in their lives, but ironically the gaps remain.

Christianity is well placed to fill the gaps as our God is One who is concerned with relationships above all else. He is the God of love, not a God of wealth and riches. It is an old cliché, but worth repeating, that money cannot buy love. We are only really fulfilled and satisfied when we have people to love, and people who love us in return. No matter how many cars and televisions we have, they become meaningless if we have no-one to share them with.

The Christmas message of God's love for mankind, of Him coming down to earth and becoming a human being because of His great love for us, so that He could die for us to take away our sins, is surely far more important than this world of affluence and wealth in which many of us in the Western world now live. The riches of God's grace can give far more satisfaction than the riches of this world.

15. How do we spend our time?

Sylvia Penny

There is a time for everything
and a season for every activity
under heaven.
(Ecclesiastes 3:1)

As Ecclesiastes says, there is a time for everything, but do we find time for everything? Is it important how we spend our time as Christians, or is it only how we spend our money which is important? "Time is money" as the saying goes, and although this may only be technically true for those who are in paid employment, the time of those who don't work is still equally as valuable in the Lord's eyes.

Most Christians would agree that it is very important what we do with our money, so is the same true of time? One big difference is that we can bank our money, and then put it to good use some time in the future if we wish. However, *time can never be 'banked'.* We can either use it wisely and well now, or it is lost for ever. So, are we good stewards of our time?

A waste of time

First, we have to decide what activities are a waste of time, and what are a good use of time. Each of us will probably come up with slightly different lists, but my list of top time-wasters would be:

- watching television
- shopping for unnecessary items
- (excessive) entertainment activities

As with many things, there is nothing intrinsically wrong with any of these practices – they are not immoral. It is getting such activities out of balance with the rest of our lives that is wrong. When the average television viewing per week is said to be upwards of 28 hours, one wonders how there is time to fit in anything else at all, except working and sleeping!

A good use of time

What activities would be on our list of ones that are a good use of our time? Possibly our lists would differ more, but at the top of my list would be:

- helping out family and friends
- spending time with family and friends
- being involved in Christian activities (church, Bible study, home-groups)
- being involved in our local community (clubs, societies, volunteering)

Not enough time

Having compiled our two lists, we can then see how our lives measure up to our ideal. If we are the sort of person who always feels "too busy", then maybe we need to stop and think whether our time is filled with more time-wasters than good things. Do we often catch ourselves making excuses for not doing something good because we don't have enough time? If so, have we ever stopped to think *why* we don't have enough time?

It may be that, because of necessary work commitments, we have very little spare time, which makes it all the more important to prioritise what we do with it. Again, to make the analogy with money, if we have very little spare money left after we have bought all the necessities, it is particularly important that we consider very carefully what we do with the extra we have.

Spending our time

Another question we can ask ourselves is, whether we think the Lord would be pleased with the way we are spending our time. What would

He think of our priorities? If we feel He would disapprove of them, then maybe we need to rethink what is most important to us.

Next time we catch ourselves saying, “Sorry, but I haven’t got the time”, perhaps we should stop ourselves and ask instead whether what we mean is, “Sorry, but it’s not very high on my list of priorities”.

16. Gifts and Talents

Sylvia Penny

When we first moved to the USA in 1991, we discovered there was a thriving 'gifted and talented' programme for children in the schools. Much time and effort was spent by teachers identifying and encouraging students perceived as being 'gifted and talented'. These were not just in academic subjects, but in any area from sports, to drama, to art, etc. After returning to the UK in 1999 schools in Britain had followed suit and started 'gifted and talented' programmes for children, in order to encourage their abilities. It has been discovered that the more children's gifts and talents are used, the more they develop. The less they are used, the less they develop, and at worst, disappear altogether.

Do not neglect your gifts

What relevance does this have for us as Christians? We are exhorted by God to use our God given gifts and talents for Him. There is a danger that if we do not, they will diminish, or be taken away completely. Paul advised Timothy not to neglect the gift that he had – "Do not neglect your gift, which was given you through a prophetic message when the body of elders laid their hands on you." (1 Tim. 4:14). Also, he said, "For this reason I remind you to fan into flame the gift of God, which is in you through the laying on of my hands." (2 Tim 1:6). It seems that although Timothy had been given a gift, he was not using it as he should, so Paul encouraged him to do so. Peter advises the same thing in 1 Peter 4:10, "Each one should use whatever gift he has received to serve others, faithfully administering God's grace in its various forms." Here, Peter also gives a reason for using our gifts and talents – it is in order *to serve others*.

Recognise your own talents

However, these passages do not give details of what these gifts, or talents, are. Some may feel they do not have any particular gift, or talent, so they can safely leave these passages of Scripture for others who have. However, Romans 12:6-8 tells us, "We have different gifts, according to the grace given us. If a man's gift is prophesying, let him used it in proportion to his faith. If it is serving, let him serve; if it is teaching, let him teach; if it is encouraging, let him encourage; if it is contributing to the needs of others, let him give generously; if it is leadership, let him govern diligently; if it is showing mercy, let him do it cheerfully." Here we are not only given a list of gifts, we are also told how some of the gifts should be handled.

These examples are given by Paul, not as an exhaustive list, but rather as a selection of those that can be used for serving others. The whole of 1 Corinthians 12 is also about the spiritual gifts of the Acts period, and among the lists given are further examples, such as "those able to help others, and those with gifts of administration" (verse28). Although many of us will not feel able to teach others, or lead others, we can probably see examples of what we could do, such as encouraging, contributing, showing mercy, helping others, or doing administration work. Paul explains in this chapter that all are necessary in the body of Christians. It would be no good having all Christians talented at teaching and leading, but none for helping and administering. Everyone has their place. However, there is a problem if some do not recognise their talents, and do not use them. The body of Christians is then weaker as a whole.

Use them or lose them

There are a number of passages in the gospels that say things like, "Whoever has will be given more; whoever does not have, even what he has will be taken from him." (Mark 4:25). These are all stated in the context of those with light, talents, minas, knowledge, etc, but who have not shared them or used them. Mark 4:21 says, "Do you bring in a lamp to put it under a bowl or a bed? Instead, don't you put it on its stand?" In other words, we should let our lights shine. We should share the gospel with those we come into contact with, and not be ashamed of our faith. Similarly, in Luke 8:18 it talks about putting a lamp on a stand, so those who come in can see the light.

Matthew 13:12 says, "The knowledge of the secrets of the kingdom of heaven has been given to you, but not to them. Whoever has will be given more, and he will have an abundance. Whoever does not have, even what he has will be taken from him." In this context those who wanted knowledge and understanding (His disciples) were to be given more, whereas those who were not particularly interested (the large crowds) would lose even the little they had.

Matthew 25:14-30 tells the parable of the five talents, the two talents and the one talent. Luke 19:11-27 tells a similar parable of the ten minas, the five minas and the one mina. Both end up with the person given the one talent (mina) having it taken away and given to the one with the most. The reason given is that they did not use it. Both are concluded with the same words, "to everyone who has, more will be given, but as for the one who has nothing, even what he has will be taken away." Although there are details in both these parables that are not easy to understand, the gist of both is clear. If people do not use what gifts God has given them, it is likely they will lose them.

How can we serve others?

Maybe we should spend a little time thinking about where our particular talents lie. What are we good at doing, and how can we use this ability to serve others? It does not have to be spectacular, but it *does* involve deciding to do *something* in service for the Lord. If we do not do this, we may be in danger of losing the abilities we already have, through a continued lack of motivation and commitment. At the end of the day, we would all like to hear the words that the men with the five and the two talents heard from their master on his return:

> "Well done, good and faithful servant! You have been faithful with a few things; I will put you in charge of many things. Come and share your master's happiness!" (Matthew 25:21)

17. Christianity in Society

Sylvia Penny

An article included in *The Times* was headed "Societies worse off 'when they have God on their side'". The article was reporting on a study produced by Gregory S. Paul in the *Journal of Religion and Society*, a US academic journal. In this he refutes the popular assertion that belief in a creator is instrumental towards providing the moral, ethical and other foundations necessary for a healthy, cohesive society. What does he base his conclusions on? Statistics! He looks at a selection of various social ills in different societies throughout the world, and correlates them to how secular, or how religious that society is. His conclusion is that the more religious a society, the more societal distress it experiences. Conversely, the more secular a society the more superior is its societal health. It seems that today more and more people are trying to find ways to do without God. Anything that negatively impacts Christianity is reported in the secular press and given serious consideration.

The article looks at such things as murder rates, abortion, STDs and suicide. It compares the rates in relatively secular countries, including Britain, with the US, where the majority still believe in a creator. The article then states that, in general, higher rates of belief in and worship of a creator correlate with higher rates of homicide, juvenile and early adult mortality, STD infection rates, teen pregnancy and abortion.

Comparison of USA with Europe

However, when the article is read in detail, it is clear that the conclusion is based mainly on comparing the societal ills in the USA with those of secular Europe. The USA is the world's only prosperous democracy where murder rates are still high, rates of gonorrhoea in adolescents in the USA are up to 300 times higher than in other countries, and it suffers from uniquely high adolescent and adult syphilis infection rates and adolescent abortion rates. The article then jumps to the conclusion that *the reason for this is the higher rates of belief and worship of a creator!* This seems to be a prime example of human 'wisdom'. When people wish to do away with God, they seem able to use any sort of justification or argument with impunity. This is then reported on by the national press, where it does further widespread damage, by spreading an idea that had not previously been thought of by the general population.

Why does Gregory Paul correlate higher homicide rates with belief in God, when surely it would be far more logical to correlate them with the phenomenal level of private gun ownership in the USA – unique in the world! Why does he correlate higher rates of STDs with higher levels of worship of a Creator, rather than with the fact that 25% of the USA population have no health care and antibiotics are not easily available to them. The secular European countries that he compares with all have national health care systems. Why did it not occur to him that this may be the reason for the improved levels of health, and nothing to do with how secular the population is?

Battling the media

Christians today are battling against a media that seems determined to denigrate Christianity. Suggesting that belief in God is bad for society goes one further step down the slippery slope towards a totally godless society where anything is acceptable. Despite Gregory Paul's attempts at statistical correlation, many people (at the moment) still believe that the reason for the fall of many great civilisations of the past has been their slide into secular 'wisdom' and godless immorality.

What difference can we, as individual Christians, make? We can make sure that everyone we come into contact with sees the difference between a Christian and a non-Christian lifestyle. When people see true Christianity in practice this is the most potent answer to any allegations of society being better off without it. If Christians are busy feeding the poor, helping the disadvantaged, loving their neighbours, being faithful to their spouses, caring for their children, spending their money wisely, talking respectfully and behaving decently, then it is difficult to argue that such behaviour is bad for society.

The Apostle Paul's advice

The Apostle Paul's words in Romans 12:17-21 are very pertinent to today, just as they were in Roman society 2,000 years ago:

> Do not repay anyone evil for evil. Be careful to do what is right in the eyes of everybody. If it is possible, as far as it depends on you, live at peace with everyone. Do not take revenge, my friends, but leave room for God's wrath, for it is written: "It is mine to avenge; I will repay," says the Lord. On the contrary: "If your enemy is hungry, feed him; if he is thirsty, give him something to drink. In doing this, you will heap burning coals on his head." Do not be overcome by evil, but overcome evil with good.

The Apostle Paul saw what went on in secular Roman society in his day, and gave solid advice to the Christians living then as to how they should conduct themselves and how they should behave in society, so they would be good witnesses for Christ. What a shame that today, people like Gregory Paul not only try to belittle the good that Christians do in society, but in addition imply that they are actually a force for evil. It seems we have gone full circle from Roman times, when Josephus described Christianity as "that pernicious sect". We have similar problems today when evil is accepted, and good is denigrated. No wonder Paul had to write "Do not be overcome by evil, but overcome evil with good."

18. Believers and Atheists

Sylvia Penny

Some years ago I was heartened to read a short article in the Guardian Weekly by Roy Hattersley with the caption heading "We atheists have to accept that most believers are better human beings." It surprised and pleased me, as, firstly, the media are usually so negative towards Christianity, and secondly, atheists seldom admit that believers are better than them. I was surprised that the paper had printed it, and pleased that Roy Hattersley had written it!

It was written in the context of observing how the Salvation Army was given special status as provider-in-chief of American disaster relief. He pointed out that its work was augmented by all sorts of other groups – almost all of them of a religious character. He went on to say "notable by their absence are teams from rationalist societies, freethinkers' clubs, and atheists' associations – the sort of people who not only scoff at religion's intellectual absurdity but also regard it as a force for evil". He went on to conclude that good works are most likely to be performed by people who believe that heaven exists. Finally, he tried to come up with a reason as to why this should be. His conclusion was that "faith comes with a packet of moral imperatives, that, while they do not condition the attitude of all believers, influence enough of them to make them morally superior to atheists like me."

This is an interesting conclusion for an atheist to come to. He concedes that believers feel morally obliged to do good, whereas non-believers feel no such duty, and therefore, as a group, are less inclined to do so. As a non-believer however, he has missed out one vital ingredient from the equation. Every believer experiences the indwelling of the Holy Spirit – a deposit guaranteeing his inheritance (Ephesians 1:14). It is the Holy Spirit Who can enable us to act in generous and unselfish ways. Galatians 5:22 tells us that "the fruit of the Spirit is love, joy, peace, patience, kindness, goodness, faithfulness, gentleness and self-control". It is the Holy Spirit within each of us Who empowers us to such great effect, and Who, at the end of the day, sets us apart from the unbeliever.

"It ought to be possible," Roy Hattersley wrote, "to live a Christian life without being a Christian" – but he admitted that, for some reason, it isn't. The missing piece to his puzzle is the Holy Spirit. It is this key difference that leads to the result which he observed – that as a group, Christians are morally superior to atheists.

19. How to be Happy!

Sylvia Penny

When I was browsing through a holiday/leisure magazine I came across a page headed up "Health Tips" and entitled "100 ways to be happy!" Curiosity got the better of me and I read through the list, only to be struck by the very strange assortment of advice given. No wonder people are mixed up and muddled about things today if they ever follow such advice. The very first one was "Never put yourself last." It didn't quite say, "Always put yourself first", but being the first piece of advice in the list gave it a special significance. The very last one was "affirm all the good things about yourself". Having read the first and the last, and both being opposite to Biblical teaching, I went through the list and found the following:

- Send yourself a kind message.
- Pamper yourself.
- Live your life according to what is right for you.
- Accept compliments from others so you can see the truth about yourself.
- Don't condemn yourself for your imperfections.
- Admit your wrongdoing and forgive yourself for it.

All of these sound nice on the surface, but are in fact empty and meaningless. No wonder no such advice appears in the Bible. Rather, we have in Job 5:17 "Blessed (happy) is the man whom God corrects, so do not despise the discipline of the Almighty". None of the 100 tips included happiness coming from correction and discipline! That does not sound so "nice".

Man's wisdom is not God's wisdom. Often, they are diametrically opposed to one another. Proverbs 3:13 says "Blessed (happy) is the man who finds wisdom, the man who gains understanding." We will not find wisdom from secular literature or atheistic philosophers. We will only find it from our Creator, our Lord and our Saviour, given to us through the Scriptures. Only by reading them and meditating upon them will we gain the wisdom and understanding to make us truly happy.

The "kind message" we find in Ephesians 1:3 which says we are "blessed in the heavenly realms with every spiritual blessing in Christ" is far more effective than "sending a kind message to ourselves".

Proverbs 29:18 says "… blessed (happy) is he who keeps the Law". If we keep God's rules we will end up being happier than if we don't. However, living our lives in accordance with what *we* think is right is a recipe for disaster. Many people have totally different ideas on what is right and what is wrong. Many people who live their lives according to what *they* think is right for them end up being some of the unhappiest people, with broken relationships, broken marriages, and permanent family rifts.

As for forgiveness, it is the Lord's forgiveness of our sins for our salvation that is important, not our forgiveness of ourselves. The majority of people seem very able to forgive themselves for all sorts of actions. Self-justification is a natural human self defence mechanism employed to preserve our sanity. Our main problem is being unable to forgive others, rather than not being able to forgive ourselves. The Scriptures give us plenty of advice on forgiveness of others, for example Colossians 3:13 says "Bear with each other and forgive whatever grievances you may have against one another. Forgive as the Lord forgave you."

Strange ways to be happy

There were also some rather bizarre suggestions included in the list, such as:

- Always own a pair of old, faded jeans.
- Burn the candle that has been in storage for the last two years.
- Eat something green.
- Go fly a kite.
- Sit on the lawn without worrying about grass stains.

Maybe these were sprinkled throughout the list in order to bring the total to 100, or maybe they were included for comedy value, or maybe they were supposed to be serious suggestions. Fortunately, throughout the Bible we have nothing but sane, sensible and God-given advice. We can rely on the Scriptures completely, and know that if we put it into practice we are far more likely to end up happy and contented with what we have.

Sensible suggestions on how to be happy

Finally, to be fair, there were a few suggestions given that are in accordance with Christian principles:

- Count your blessings every day.
- Diminish your wants instead of increasing your needs.
- Rejoice in other people's triumphs.
- Do a kind deed for someone else.
- Forgive anyone you've been holding a grudge against.
- Say a prayer.
- Remember that you are a spiritual being in a physical body.
- Stand up for what you believe in.
- Tell someone you appreciate them.

These are excellent advice for everyone. Proverbs 14:21 says "... blessed (happy) is he who is kind to the needy." To be kind and generous to others not only makes the Lord happy with us, it also has the effect of making us happy too. It is a win-win situation.

Not included in the list

However, there are many verses in the Bible that describe ways to be happy that are not included in the list at all:

> Psalm 146:5 Blessed (happy) is he whose help is the God of Jacob, whose hope is in the Lord his God.

> Proverbs 16:20 ...blessed (happy) is he who trusts in the Lord.

Proverbs 28:14 Blessed (happy) is the man who always fears the Lord.

If our hope is in the Lord, our trust is in Him, and we fear (are in awe of) the Lord, then this will lead to a happy and fulfilled life here on earth. The choice is ours.

Mixed advice

With such mixed advice given in magazines and popular literature today, no wonder people are confused as to what to do and how to live their lives. There is no consistency, and no knowing which advice to follow, and what advice to ignore. Without a yardstick to guide us we can end up in the exact opposite state to the one promised by the article – unhappy and discontent. Fortunately, the Lord has provided the Scriptures "which are able to make you wise for salvation through faith in Christ Jesus" (2 Timothy 3:15).

20. Let us Love one Another

Sylvia Penny

> If anyone says, "I love God," yet hates his brother, he is a liar. For anyone who does not love his brother, whom he has seen, cannot love God, whom he has not seen. And he has given us this command: Whoever loves God must also love his brother. (1 John 4:20,21)

These words were written by the apostle John who is described a number of times as "the disciple who Jesus loves" in John's gospel. If we hate our brother, (that is, our fellow Christians) then he states we cannot love God. These are strong words. Yet they strike at a very fundamental human weakness. It is all too easy to glibly declare that we "love God", but so much harder to show by our actions that we love our fellow Christians. But if we do not do this, God says, how can we say in all honesty that we love Him?

> "Dear children, let us not love with words or tongue but with actions and in truth." (1 John 3:18)

Again, this puts the finger on another very common failing. We may have managed to train ourselves to *say* the right things, but do we put our words into action, and do our words match what we really feel and think about people? Or do we merely copy secular society – do we say the right things to the right people at the right times, but when their backs are turned, do we tell a different story, and act in a different way? If we do, then can we honestly stand up and declare that we love God?

The prayer of Jabez

Some time ago a book called *The Prayer of Jabez* by Dr. Bruce Wilkinson came out. This exhorted people to use two verses in 1 Chronicles 4:9-10 as a prayer for themselves on a daily basis. All sorts of criticism has been levelled at this, from comparing it to the "prosperity gospel" (God blesses good living Christians with material wealth), to its extreme commercialisation, with all that entails. However, if I was asked to recommend just one passage of Scripture to be repeated every morning by every Christian before they got out of bed it would be 1 Corinthians 13, rather than the prayer of Jabez, without a doubt. This is for the simple reason that in verse 13 it tells us "And now these three remain: faith, hope and love. *But the greatest of these is love.*" 1 Corinthians 13 tells us how God wants one Christian to love another, and ends by telling us that this love is the greatest quality of all. Without such love, we are nothing.

What is true Christian love?

> If I speak in the tongues of men and of angels, but have not love, I am only a resounding gong or a clanging cymbal. If I have the gift of prophecy and can fathom all mysteries and all knowledge, and if I have a faith that can move mountains, but have not love, I am nothing. If I give all I possess to the poor and surrender my body to the flames, but have not love, I gain nothing.
>
> Love is patient, love is kind.
> It does not envy, it does not boast, it is not proud.
> It is not self-seeking, it is not easily angered, it keeps no record of wrongs.
> Love does not delight in evil but rejoices with the truth.
> It always protects, always trusts, always hopes, always perseveres.
> Love never fails. (1 Corinthians 13:1-8a)
>
> And now these three remain: faith, hope and love. But the greatest of these is love." (1 Corinthians 13:13)

It is clear from this passage that Christian love is a quality of character which results in always treating others well, *no matter what their response is*. There is no suggestion that our love should be withdrawn if it is not reciprocated. In fact, it does not depend on the other person at all. It depends totally on us. However, we are not totally alone in trying to achieve this seemingly impossible command. We were sealed with the Holy Spirit when we believed the gospel of salvation (Ephesians 1:13), and if we let Him (Ephesians 4:30) we can display the fruit of the Spirit which is love (Galatians 5:22) manifested as "joy, peace, patience, kindness, goodness, faithfulness, gentleness and self-control."

Emotional love

However, should there not be some emotion involved in Christian love? I would answer "yes", but not the sort of romantic emotion normally associated with love in our present society. Rather, it is the sort of emotion that "does not delight in evil, but rejoices with the truth".

There is an expression "cold as charity", and it is possible to do the right things, and to say the right things, but with a cold and dispassionate attitude. I am not sure it is possible to love others in the way described in 1 Corinthians 13 without any sort of emotion or feeling of well-being towards them. There should be joy and rejoicing when we help others, for our Lord said, "It is more blessed (happy) to give than to receive" (Acts 20:35). We sense the difference between those people who are acting dutifully and those who are acting whole-heartedly, and we also know the difference when we are acting likewise.

God also notices the difference. 2 Corinthians 8:7 says "Each man should give what he has decided in his heart to give, not reluctantly or under compulsion, *for God loves a cheerful giver*." It is important to God for us to be cheerful when we do the right things. Again, 1 Timothy 6:6 says "Godliness *with contentment* is great gain." Our attitude towards living a godly life is important to God. It should not be reluctant or grudging or self-congratulatory. Instead, it should be done with contentment.

Christ at home in our hearts

Thus, God prefers whole-hearted actions, springing from pure motivation and true emotions. Without the help of the Holy Spirit working within our lives, this would be totally impossible, but as Paul says in Ephesians 3:16-17, He can strengthen us with power through

His Spirit in our inner being, so that Christ can feel at home in our hearts. He will feel at home if we are content and cheerful and love our fellow Christians in the way described in 1 Corinthians 13.

21. Motivation is important

Sylvia Penny

Some of the comments made in 1 Corinthians 13 are quite surprising, and counter intuitive. Humanly speaking, if we saw someone give all their money to the poor, or give themselves up for martyrdom by burning, we would assume that such acts would be highly valued by God. Yet this passage tells us that even if a person did this, but had no love for others, they would be nothing, and gain nothing in the eyes of God.

Maybe Paul had in mind here the hypocritical and Pharisaic attitude that prevailed during the gospel period, where some openly gave large sums of money to the temple treasury, but had no brotherly love towards those who they considered inferior to themselves. And perhaps he also had in mind the sort of person who would even die for their faith, and yet faced with a fellow believer in need would not lift a finger to help them. Mark 7:6-13 describes the Lord's attitude towards these hypocritical Pharisees who "honour me with their lips, but their hearts are far from me." They gave gifts to the temple, and said that this relieved them of any duty to help even their own mother or father. The Lord's comment on this was "Thus you nullify the word of God by your own tradition that you have handed down. And you do many things like that."

Ananias and Sapphira also come to mind, in Acts 5:1-11, where they were struck dead for lying about the sum of money they gave to the apostles for work with the poor and needy. Although they did a good thing in giving a large sum of money for a very good cause, their motivation was to receive praise and honour from men, and as a result they lied to the Holy Spirit about the sum they received from the sale of their property. This was unacceptable to the Lord.

Putting on an act

God therefore requires our good acts to be motivated by thoughts which are pure and honourable. Our acts do not stand in isolation.

Although self-sacrificial acts usually do result from self-sacrificial thoughts, it is clear that this is not always so. It is possible to "put on an act" and be hypocritical like the Pharisees, or like Ananias and Sapphira, but God sees right through such acts, even if fellow human beings do not. Thus, our motivation is very important to God. This is confirmed in Proverbs 16:2 which says, "All a man's ways seem innocent to him, but motives are weighed by the Lord." Also, 2 Corinthians 8:7 says, "Each man should give what he has decided in his heart to give, not reluctantly or under compulsion, for God loves a cheerful giver." The Lord likes people to give, but he also likes them to give cheerfully. It detracts from the good act when it is done reluctantly or compulsorily. We often cannot tell if someone is doing something begrudgingly or willingly, but the Lord can always tell.

Solomon

In the OT, when David spoke to his son Solomon about the future building of the temple for the Lord, David advised him, "Serve him with wholehearted devotion and with a willing mind, for the Lord searches every heart and understands every motive behind the thoughts" (1 Chronicles 28:9). It would do Solomon little good if he built the most wonderful building for God, only to fall into idolatry. Unfortunately, this is exactly what happened later in Solomon's life, when he turned astray under the influence of his many foreign wives (1 Kings 11:1-13). His heart was no longer wholeheartedly devoted to the Lord. Despite having built the most wonderful Temple for the Lord, and despite having been rewarded for this by the Lord with untold wealth and splendour, Solomon was led astray –sadly never to return to his former ways. Presumably it is because of this that he is not listed among the OT faithful in Hebrews 11.

Judgment

1 Corinthians 4:4-5 says, "It is the Lord who judges me. Therefore judge nothing before the appointed time; wait till the Lord comes. He will bring to light what is hidden in darkness and will expose the motives of men's hearts. At that time each will receive his praise from God." We are not to judge one another for the very good reason that the motives of other people are hidden from us. If we do judge, we

can only judge from outward appearances, and are quite likely to jump to the wrong conclusions about a person. This is one of many reasons that judgment should be left to the Lord alone.

Do false motives really matter?

However, there is one verse that appears to say that a person's motives are *not* important. When Paul wrote to the Philippians he referred to two different groups of people. One group preached Christ out of love and goodwill, whereas the other group preached Christ out of envy and rivalry. Although it is difficult to understand why anyone would do such a thing, Paul then says in Philippians 1:18, "But what does it matter? The important thing is that in every way, whether from false motives or true, Christ is preached. And because of this I rejoice." Here Paul is saying that the false motivation does not matter to the *recipients* of the gospel message. He is *not* saying that it did not matter to the Lord. It did, as we have already seen from the other passages quoted above.

However, some may argue that if this is the case, then we should not do any good acts until we are completely sure our motivation is totally pure and laudable. Perhaps we should never volunteer to do anything, never give any money to a good cause, never help anyone else, unless we are absolutely sure that we are doing it for the right reasons, rather than the wrong ones. However, adopting this attitude could stop us doing anything, because many of us, if we are totally honest, do things for mixed reasons, both good and bad. This is surely not what Scripture is saying. I believe that we should not let *worrying* about our motives stop us doing a good thing. Rather, we should recognise that there is probably something wrong if the only reason we want to do something is one that the Lord would *not* find praiseworthy. Maybe an example of this would help.

Sunday School helpers

A person may volunteer to help with teaching Sunday School. This is something that is good, worthwhile and honourable, and something that could please the Lord very much. However, there could be very different motives for volunteering. One person may want to do this as they are very keen to help young people come to know the Lord as their Saviour at an early age, before they are led astray by the bad influences in our society. A second person may think the church is short of volunteers, and feel they ought to do this out of a sense of duty, and even a little reluctantly. A third person may volunteer because they know lots of people in the church will think they are a really good person, and they will get plenty of praise. A fourth person may be a paedophile who has joined the church hoping to have access to children. Each of these four may well act in the same way. It may be impossible for us to tell the difference. It is only the Lord who knows. 1 Corinthians 3:10-15 explains how, in eternal life, the Lord will reward people differently depending on the quality of their work for Him. Thus, each of these people will be treated differently by the Lord, depending not only on their outward acts, but also their inward thoughts and motivation. We have already quoted 1 Corinthians 4:5 above, which confirms this, where it says when the Lord returns he will expose the motives of men's hearts and they will receive their praise from God.

The point is, each of us in ourselves knows what the right motivation should be. It is obvious. However, if we are aware of this struggle and are trying to do something about it, we are already on the right pathway. If we are not, maybe we need to stop and think again. Ironically, it is those who never think about their motives that are likely to be those in the greatest need of doing so as, for example, the Pharisees in the Lord's day. But, when we do stop and think about our motives, it should not be with a view to stopping what we are doing in case our motives are wrong, but rather with a view to changing and improving our motivation. How can we do this?

How to improve our motivation

It is clear from many passages of Scripture that God is very interested in our state of mind, and gives many instructions and advice on how to keep our minds pure. One of my favourites is found in Philippians 4:8-9:

> Finally, brothers, whatever is true, whatever is noble, whatever is right, whatever is pure, whatever is lovely,

> whatever is admirable – if anything is excellent or praiseworthy – think about such things. Whatever you have learned or received or heard from me, or seen in me – put it into practice. And the God of peace will be with you.

First, we are given advice for helping us set our minds right, and if we follow this, our motivation is far more likely to be pleasing to the Lord. *Next,* we are given advice for putting our faith into practice.

Finally, as a result of doing this, we are given the promise that the God of peace *will* be with us.

22. Life is so daily!

Laura Kestly

In this earthly world, as the saying goes, *Life is so daily!*

There are always dirty dishes and dirty laundry to wash, personal finances to attend to, meals to cook and homework to help your children with. Dust seems to ever be accumulating so vacuuming and sweeping must be done. What about that job you need to keep getting up for each day? The mundane and tedious chores…the routine obligations of our day can really wear us out!

We seem to forget that sorrow, toil and pain are all part of our sinful fallen world. The moment Adam and Eve disobeyed God, they gave up the power God had given them to take care of and preserve the Garden. They were supposed to keep it safe, (Genesis 2:15) but, as the Scriptures tell us, they believed and succumbed to the serpent's 3 lies (Genesis 3:1-6) and all this toil, pain and suffering (Genesis 3:16-19) came into the world. Even worse than all that was our separation from God – our death sentence that would return us to the ground. But, thankfully, God had already made other plans.

The plans, as Hebrews 2:9-18 basically say, involve Jesus, Who was to be made a little lower than the angels – *by the grace of God.* He would taste death for *every* man. He was to come down and wear flesh and blood clothing, just like us. He was to share the same things as us. Through His death He would end the reign of the one (speaking of the Devil) who has the power of death, and so set us free from the fear of death and our return to the ground. Mind you, He wouldn't be taking on an angelic form to save the fallen angels, (from which Satan came), but, as verses 16-17 say, He came and took on Him the seed of Abraham, to save fallen man.

Jesus spoke the following words to His disciples shortly before His crucifixion: "*In the world you shall have tribulation: but be of good cheer; I have overcome (conquered) the world*" (John 16:33).

We should also be of good cheer with these assuring words – but even knowing this we still fall into the trap of listening to the lies of the temporary ruler of this world.

Paul, in chapter 6, warned the Ephesians of this very thing, telling them that they wrestle *not* against flesh and blood (the seen – as the Devil would have us believe) *but* rather against the authorities, the world's rulers of the darkness of this age and against the spiritual powers of evil in the heavenlies (the unseen). Obviously, we can't resist and stand with that kind of power against us!

Do not fret

Now we don't need to fret because here's the important part that we always need to keep in mind. When we accept Christ as our Lord and Saviour, as it says in Colossians 3:1-3, we become raised with Him and so we should seek the things above, where Christ is sitting at the right hand of God. We should mind the things above, *not* the things on the earth because we have died and our life is now hid with Christ in God. That's where our protection and strength comes from. When we wear the armour of God, that Paul talks about in Ephesians 6, we *can* stand against the wiles of the Devil – not in our own strength, but in the powerful and mighty strength of the Lord!

When all the armour pieces of the Lord Jesus Christ cover us the enemy won't be dealing with us (because we are hid) but he'll have to go toe-to-toe with the Lord. The Lord *will* fight our battles for us. God does desire us to live a balanced, ordered life of simplicity. Life *is* daily but God's grace and mercies *are* daily too! As we rely and trust in Him (daily), from the mundane chores to the frightening events in our life, we will find peace and joy.

Our enemy, the Devil, wants us to focus on what we see – the piles of laundry, the unpaid bills, the messy house, the toils of this earth – and be discouraged and depressed. He wants us to listen to *his* lies as he tells us how unproductive and unsuccessful (in the shallow worldly sense) our lives are; how we need to work harder by doing, doing, doing…to keep up with "*the Joneses*" and be slaves to this world and its ways.

Who do we listen to?

We need to actively listen to the *Voice of Truth and Hope*, getting it through our thick, fleshly skulls that God loves us, in spite of what we do or do not do. And I want to encourage us all to find the courage to die to every other story line that the enemy is telling us. We must embrace a story that is greater than that. We must believe that the one God is telling us, the one of love and hope with an ending that is really a beginning of *Happily ever after*.

We need to recognize the purposeful beauty of our weaknesses and make peace with the fact that we *don't* have all the answers, but rejoice in the fact that we *do* have a loving, living God who does! His grace is sufficient His strength ***is*** made perfect in weakness (2 Corinthians 12:9).

I'll close with encouragement from a man in the Old Testament who was familiar with sorrow. After reading the book bearing his name Jeremiah, you'll understand the title of his follow up book, Lamentations. In the midst of all the sorrow, he said in Lamentations 3:22-24,

> It is of the Lord's mercies that we are not consumed, because His compassions fail not. They are new every morning: Great is thy faithfulness ... The Lord is my portion … therefore I will hope in Him.

Let us trust and rely on His sufficient, daily dose of grace and mercy.

23. Balance

Laura Kestly

> See, I have set before you this day life and good, and death and evil. (Deuteronomy 30:15)

Just like it was in the Garden of Eden, so it is today – the choice is between God's way and man's way We live in a time and society where we are deluded into thinking that we can have it all ... a little of God's way and a little of man's way. In fact, *balance* is a popular word in today's society. We try and *balance* many things, from cheque books and credit cards to diets and schedules. We reason that if we attend church on Sunday and Bible study on Wednesday, perhaps we're okay to go our own way the rest of the week.

The Bible is very clear on what will happen if we rely only on our own will, wisdom, drive and purpose, to sustain ourselves and keep our lives in so-called *balance*. We will eventually stumble and fall. The book of Proverbs is full of teaching in this area. Consider the following quotations from Proverbs:

- The wise in heart will receive commandments; but a prating fool shall *fall.* (10:8)
- Where no counsel is, the people *fall.* (11:28)
- Pride goes before destruction, and a haughty spirit before a *fall.* (16:18)
- The wicked shall *fall* into mischief. (24:16)
- He that hardens his heart shall *fall* into mischief. (28:14)
- He that is perverse in his ways shall *fall* at once. (28:18)

Real balance can only come into our lives when we see and seek things through God's perspective and by keeping our focus consistently on Him. Our enemy Satan has one goal for the child of God, and that is to distract him from the course God has set and to throw him *off balance* so he *falls*. Be continually aware of your thoughts, because it is Satan whose words are laced with discouragement and accusations.

Self and a spirit of pride

Let's look at some of the ways the enemy will distract us from Christ and tempt us to fall. When we focus on 'self' – *a spirit of pride* sets in and we see things in a way that only benefits ourselves, whether in position, possessions or power. This is the thinking where 'we' are self-sufficient and can handle everything and do not need God or anybody else's help. This is a big problem and examples from the Bible range from Satan (Isaiah 14:12-15) to Adam and Eve (Genesis 3) to Uzziah (2 Chronicles 26) to Nebuchadnezzar (Daniel 4).

Insecurity and fear and lack of trust

In another area (at the other end of the scale) is 'insecurity' – *fear and lack of trust*. This occurs when we look and focus on our circumstances instead of trusting the sovereignty and strength of our infinite and all-powerful God.

This is illustrated best in Matthew 14:22 onwards. After Jesus miraculously fed the 5,000 with 5 loaves of bread and two fish, He directed the 12 disciples to get into the boat and go before Him to the other side, while He sent away the crowds. After Jesus did this He went up into the hills by Himself to pray. In the meantime, the boat that the disciples were in was miles away from land, out on the sea. The wind was against them and so the boat was beaten and tossed by the waves. Between about 3:00 and 6:00 a.m., Jesus came to them, walking on the sea. Seeing this, the disciples were terrified, thinking it was a ghost. Instantly, Jesus spoke to them and said, "Take courage! I AM! Stop being afraid." (See also Exodus 3:14.)

Peter said, "Lord, if it is You, command me to come to You on the water." Jesus said, "Come!" So Peter got out of the boat and walked on the water, and he came toward Jesus. "But when he perceived and felt the strong wind, he was frightened, and started sinking …" The moment Peter became more aware of his circumstances (the boisterous wind of the storm) than of Jesus he was overwhelmed by the sea and sank.

Insecurity leads to jealousy

Insecurity can also take other shapes and forms - such as jealousy. The moment we begin to think about who has got more than us or is getting ahead of us, we set ourselves up for trouble. We can become so caught up in what another person has that we lose sight of what God has given us. When we focus on having more or receiving more, on "keeping up with the Joneses," we begin to lose our sense of peace.

God really does not want us to compare ourselves to anyone else as this leads to a competitive spirit and results in a fear of losing control which will result in an *imbalance* in our lives. When we put unnecessary pressure and expectation on ourselves (that God never intended for us) we can become frustrated, apathetic and depressed. Remember, as Ephesians 2:10 says, "We are His workmanship, created in Christ Jesus for good works, which God prepared beforehand so that we could walk in them."

God loves us and has a great purpose for our lives, but as He has created each of us uniquely, so are His purposes for us. So, keep your gaze upward and focus not only on the Lord but also on the great love and purpose He has for you and the wonderful hope of eternal life He offers you, through the blood of His precious Son, Jesus. "Delight yourself in the Lord and He will give you the desires of your heart." (Psalm 37:4)

24. Love

Laura Kestly

When we think of *love* we usually think of warm, fuzzy, and sweet things. However, when we search the Scriptures we find a much more extensive and complete definition, rather than the shallow one that the world offers us. The popular verses of 1 Corinthians 13:4-8 have been recited at many weddings, but is their meaning acted out after the vows have been said?

> Love is Longsuffering. Love is kind
> It does not envy, it does not boast, it is not proud.
> It is not rude, it is not self-seeking,
> It is not easily angered, it keeps no record of wrongs.
> Love does not delight in evil but rejoices with the truth.
> It always protects, always trusts, always hopes, always perseveres.
> Love never fails.

What tops this list, definition-wise, of love? Longsuffering! The definition of longsuffering includes: bearing injuries; forbearance; patience of offence; not easily provoked; to spare. Longsuffering is an aspect of God Who is love. He proclaims it of Himself in Exodus 34:6:

> And he passed in front of Moses, proclaiming, "The Lord, the Lord, the compassionate and gracious God, *slow to anger*, abounding in love and faithfulness."

A companion to longsuffering is being *slow to anger* and is again an attribute of Who God is and what He is like. In the verses below, it is coupled with showing great mercy:

> The Lord is *slow to anger*, abounding in love and forgiving sin and rebellion. (Numbers 14:18)

> The Lord is compassionate and gracious, *slow to anger*, abounding in love. (Psalm 103:8)

> The Lord is gracious and compassionate; *slow to anger* and rich in love. (Psalm 145:8)

Longsuffering is also one of the fruits of the Spirit (Galatians 5:22-23).

Paul, in his letter to Timothy, refers to longsuffering when speaking of his manner of life (2 Timothy 3:10). And in his first letter to Timothy (1:12-16) Paul writes how thankful he is that Christ Jesus came into the world to save sinners of whom he was chief; and that because he had received mercy, he was an example, through Jesus Christ, who showed forth God's longsuffering.

For Christians, longsuffering should be associated with their walk and it is an important factor in keeping the unity of the Spirit, as in Ephesians:

> Walk worthily of the calling in which you were called, with all humility and meekness, *with longsuffering, bearing with one another in love,* being eager to keep the unity of the Spirit in the bond of peace. (Ephesians 4:1-3)

Colossians links longsuffering with joy, and says:

> Walk worthily of the Lord to all pleasing ... being empowered with all power according to the might of His glory, to all patience and *long suffering with joy.* (Colossians 1:10-11)

Such is the modern mentality that it is not too hard to see how this mind-set has spilled over into our relationships as well. The divorce rate is soaring and even among believers we are quick to switch churches, sever friendships and family relationships over petty disagreements, instead of doing the real work of persevering patiently with truth in unconditional love. Please do not misunderstand. I am not negating legitimate circumstances where change is necessary, but we will not be able to endure with longsuffering (especially with joy) if we do not renew our earthly way of thinking. Allowing the old man to be '*put off*' and the new man to be '*put on*' as Ephesians 4:22-32 and Colossians 3:12-14 commands us, will enable us to think with the mind of Christ. It still takes time (and trusting in God) to learn to speak the truth in a kind way. Whether we're a teacher, parent or in any form of leadership where we are ministering to either students, children or employees, if we take the time to correct in a patient and loving way, we'll bear more fruit than when we do it in a hasty and harsh way. Why *do* we get so easily annoyed and angered at others who are struggling, making mistakes or just plain doing it differently from us?

Also, it truly is hard when someone we love, or have invested our time in, lets us down or hurts us. It's easy to hold a grudge and become bitter about the way some things are sometimes handled, or we are treated. At such times we should remember, "Love suffers long and is kind".

If we really believe what God's Word tells us we need to acknowledge our own sinfulness and easily forgive others as God has forgiven us (Ephesians 4:32). God has not asked us to be a doormat to those who abuse us, but He does ask us to love each other (being kind even to our enemies, Luke 6:27,35), while still setting healthy and godly boundaries. This is what He wants, rather than us just '*writing someone off*' when disagreements arise or when they become harder to love.

> Speaking the truth in love, we may grow up into Him in all things, who is the Head, the Christ. ... producing the growth of the body to the building up of itself in love. (Ephesians 4:15-16)
>
> Love each other as I have loved you. (John 15:12)
>
> Therefore, as God's chosen people, holy and dearly loved, clothe yourselves with compassion, kindness, humility, gentleness and patience. Bear with each other and forgive whatever grievances you may have against one another. Forgive as the Lord forgave you. And over all these virtues put on love, which binds them all together in perfect unity. (Colossians 3:12-14)

25. Thankfulness

Laura Kestly

> In everything give thanks: for this is the will of God in Christ Jesus concerning you. (1 Thessalonians 5:18)

Isn't it easy to be grateful and thankful to God when things are going well and times are good? We actually start taking them for granted, whether it be in the form of our health or wealth, but just ask Job. He went from having everything to having it all taken away. He was sifted like wheat, through a challenge Satan presented to God: would Job be faithful to God without all his blessings? In the end it wasn't Job's wisdom, good works, merit or even his repentance; but "The Lord gave" (Job 42:10) and "the Lord blessed" (42:12).

Job had been brought to the end of himself; and was in the right position to see the "end of the Lord". Although God is very "great", He is also "full of compassion and mercy", which explains the verse in James 5:11, "As you know, we consider blessed those who have persevered. You have heard of Job's perseverance and have seen what the Lord finally brought about."

Suffering and Crises

It seems that it is only through personal crises and suffering that we are led more deeply into a living trust of the personal God we are so eager to proclaim. In fact, we will not experience true inner transformation until whatever it is we really live for is shattered, and we are willing to die and give up everything we have loved, casting ourselves completely on the Lord.

> In retrospect, even my misfortunes were in some ways fortunate, for they taught me things that would be hard to understand otherwise, and they presented reality from an angle not given to those, among intellectuals especially, whose career have followed a more straight-line path in familiar grooves. I lived through experiences which they can

> only theorize about. (From Preface in *A Personal Odyssey* by Thomas Sowell)

When we face loss, we are then struck by how temporal, broken and incomplete everything in this world is. It is only then that we can really experience an awakening hunger and start to grasp a shadow of the transcendental and eternal.

I can speak from my own experiences the truth of these words. Seven years ago, shortly after 9/11 and about ten months after a college roommate of mine had lost her battle with breast cancer, my big and strong, former college football player and head high school football coach father, was diagnosed with an aggressive brain cancer. My family and I saw his body atrophy rapidly to a shell of the man he was in just three short months and then … he was gone.

And while that event totally reshaped our family dynamics in a way that I still grieve, it was in that time that the Scriptures truly came alive for me and I started to grasp how much God loved me and was there for me. Oddly, I long for that closeness that I experienced during that period of sorrow and brokenness (the truth of Psalm 34:18). I love Sara Grove's song "What I thought I Wanted" which includes these lines:

> What I thought I wanted,
> and what I got instead,
> leaves me broken and grateful.

I appreciated and treasured motherhood more after my first pregnancy ended in a miscarriage. I cherished good health more after both my sons struggled with theirs in their early years. If we can just trust God through our suffering and trials we can become *better* instead of *bitter.*

Pain and Hardship

For those of you who are parents, like me, who sometimes like to intervene in your children's lives so that they do not experience any pain or hardship, be careful! Many times you will deprive them of the very thing that will teach them what is truly important in God's economy, and lead them to be dependent on the Lord.

I get deluded (so easily) into thinking that anything good in my life, or the life of my family, has *anything* to do with me. And I seem to teeter so quickly when the least bit of trouble, or even inconvenience, comes my way.

My prayer is to be able to truly trust in the Lord *at all times* and be like Paul, who said this in his letter to the Philippians in 4:11-13:

> I am not saying this because I am in need, for I have learned to be content whatever the circumstances. I know what it is to be in need, and I know what it is to have plenty. I have learned the secret of being content in any and *every* situation, whether well fed or hungry, whether living in plenty or in want. I can do everything through him who gives me strength.

Strength and sufficiency

It is only through the almighty strength and sufficiency of God that we can make it through our valleys. Wow! If only we could really grasp who God is ... and what He has indeed done for us and then be ever mindful of that in our "now".

26. Summertime

Laura Kestly

When we romantically think of summer we may think of:

- lazy days laying on a hammock,
- the smell of wildflowers & newly cut grass,
- the chirping of birds and the buzzing of bees,
- spending time with a friend on a sunlit day,
- sipping a cool glass of lemonade or
- enjoying the majesty of a warm starlit night.

There is no event so commonplace that God is not present

Although hidden from our eyesight He is as near and as available as the summer breeze blowing through our hair. Do you sense His presence as He waits to have fellowship with you? Do you hear Him? Or is the volume too loud on the stereo or TV, or is it the constant chatter of your mind that is drowning out an awareness of the presence of God?

His ever-present friendship can bring peace and joy to the heart and mind even amidst a busy and troublesome day

What friend knows you better – your strengths and weaknesses – and still unconditionally loves you? We get glimpses of this type of love through good friends and family but when we do, it should point us back to The One Who created us in Whom we live and move, and have our being (Acts 17:28). Communing with God should be as natural and as regular as breathing.

Prayer means keeping company with the God Who is already present

Henri Houwen once said that "*to pray is to walk in the full light of God, and to say simply, without holding back, 'I am human and You are God.'*" To know God is to know His sufficiency. He provides for our every need (even if it comes in a form that we did not desire or expect).

"Be Still and know that I am God." (Psalm 46:10)

Peace should follow if you can be still *and* you realize that you aren't God, and that only God is God, so your dependency is on Him.

Singer Steven Curtis Chapman's chorus of his song, *Declaration of Dependence* says,

> This is my declaration of dependence.
> This is my declaration of my need.
> This is my declaration of dependence.
> On the One Who gave His life to me.

Psalm 139 says,

> How precious also are Your thoughts to me, O God! How great is the sum of them! If I should count them, they would be more in number than the sand; when I awake, I am still with You! (Psalm 139:17-18)

These types of statements are contrary to many new age philosophies that keep resurfacing in different shapes and forms but essentially purport the same lies. The book, *The Secret* is just the latest. This book claims that power and energy are within ourselves to channel as we choose. This is the antithesis of biblical truth that encourages prayerful humble submission to God and His will, which keeps us dependent on Him, not on ourselves.

Our worth is tied up in our relationship with Jesus Christ

Our worth, joy and peace is not tied up in whether we can convert our negative energy into a positive form. Our worth is tied up in our relationship with Jesus Christ and accepting what He did for us at the cross at Calvary. The *gift* of salvation He offers is a gift that can only be received – it cannot be earned, willed or achieved (Ephesians 2:8-9). Believing in what Jesus Christ did gains us righteousness, not what we earn through position, salary, good grades or accomplishments – neither what we do on the golf course, in a painting or by logging in a certain amount of volunteer hours.

We need God, and we reach God through Christ. We need to get to know Him through His living Word and communicate/talk to Him through prayer – seeking His will and submitting to His ways, which at times are very contrary to what we may think or feel, or how the world perceives things. (See Proverbs 3:5-6; 2 Corinthians 10:5; Galatians 2:20; Ephesians 2:10; Colossians 1:10.)

Knowing Christ becomes our priority. We can find a real completion in Him alone (Philippians 3:8-10; Colossians 2:10; 3:13).

While Jesus was on earth, He demonstrated an attitude of humility and submission to His Father's will, (John 5:19, 30, 6:38; Philippians 2:5-8). The Bible teaches about suffering and that suffering can bring about growth in Christ – because in our weakness, we glorify the Lord, (Matthew 5:12; Romans 5:3; 2 Corinthians 6:4-10, 12:9-10; 2 Timothy 1:8, 3:12). This is yet another truth that contradicts with *The Secret* and other new age philosophies and false religious ways of thinking.

Come to Him, all those labouring and being burdened

He will give you rest. Take His yoke upon you and learn from Him, because He is meek and lowly in heart, and you will find rest to your souls. For His yoke is easy, and His burden is light (Matthew 11:28-30; Jeremiah 6:16). His rest is given. Ours must be found in His gift. We have none to give.

Can one find a friend so faithful, loving, merciful and true as Jesus?

Then be humbled under the mighty hand of God, that He may exalt you in time; cast all your anxiety onto Him, because it matters to Him concerning you (1 Peter 5:6-7).

Relax this summer

Relax this summer and rest, not only in a hammock with a glass of lemonade, but in the knowledge of a faithful friend – the Lord and Saviour Jesus Christ. Through it all, He will never leave you nor forsake you (Hebrews 13:5).

27. Rise above on eagle's wings

Karen Bismark

> But those who trust in the Lord for help will find their strength renewed.
> They will rise on wings like eagles;
> they will run and not get weary;
> they will walk and not grow weak.
> (Isaiah 40:31)

I can relate to the last part of that verse. Every morning I walk with my two children to school, we take a picturesque walk through Forfar, the lovely little town that we live in. My son and I first leave my little girl at her school and then walk with my son about three quarters of the way to his school. When we part I usually walk straight home.

Physical strength

The journey to these two schools is downhill, so that means the return journey is uphill, and a fairly steep hill at that. Sometimes on the way home I do a little shopping or run a few errands. This adds more distance to the journey. When I reach the unit of flats in which we live I have to scale three flights of steep stairs before I reach my doorway. By the time I close the door behind me I am very weary and tired from the long walk and the steps.

If I have had no time to eat before leaving, or even taken time to swallow a cup of coffee, I feel faint. This is my daily routine. It is a difficult one, but the longer I keep it up the stronger my body becomes and therefore I am physically more equipped to handle the fainting feeling. My body even gains the extra strength to ward off any flu bugs or other ailments which can creep up on us.

Spiritual strength

It is the same with spiritual strength which needs to be exercised as well; the first line of the verse says, "But those who trust in the Lord for help will find their strength renewed". Here again there is a part for me to play. Strength does not just come upon us; ask any gym enthusiast. It takes regular training and determination to reach a required goal.

If I neglect to wait upon my Lord and serve Him faithfully by a daily reading of His Word, and then putting into practice what He says I must do, I cannot expect to be a strong Christian. He gives me guidelines in His Word to help me. It is like any manual but if I toss it aside, how do I grow spiritually? Where would my strength come from?

Those who wait upon the Lord shall have their strength renewed, and only then can we stand against the enemy's attacks. Our enemy, the devil, waits patiently for us to become weak before he attacks.

They will rise on wings like eagles

Eagles spend much of the day soaring, especially where high hills and sheer cliffs provide strong thermals. Golden Eagles are typically seen soaring high above mountain peaks, alone or in pairs, looking for prey. With his super vision, the eagle scours the big picture below him, and when he spots his prey, he focuses on that one thing and forbids anything to distract him.

Have you ever seen an eagle unsure of himself? He takes off from his perch, or nest and doesn't look back, he is not afraid to fall because he is confident of his ability to rise again. When he leaves his perch, he knows what his aim is. When he is at his highest, he is *free*, all trouble is below him. The only thing on his mind is achieving his goal. He does not worry about his food and where it will come from. It is out there.

This helps me understand Matthew 6:31-13, which talks about not worrying. Jesus is teaching us to set our eyes on the Kingdom of God and what He requires of us. Though we, like the eagle, can see the big picture because of our sight range, our eyes should really be focused on one thing: what God requires of us, and that is what we must strive to accomplish every day. And when we do this, we experience that feeling, 'They will rise on wings like eagles", for without worry, and with the proper focus, we are free to soar on wings like eagles.

When I do my best to obey the teachings Christ gave, I too can be more confident within myself knowing I will be able to defend myself when the enemy attacks. Also, my problems become a tiny speck beneath me.

New every morning

When I wake every morning, I ask my Heavenly Father to take care of whatever I will face during the day, and then I must practice my faith by leaving the day in His hands. Soon I begin to realise that my mountains which were tormenting me, no longer seem so big.

Galatians 6:9 tells us not to become tired of doing good. When you are in service to the Lord, do not give up and exclaim, "I am tired", or "I am too old", or "let someone else do the work". Our Father never gets tired of working for our good. He is also the one who rewards us.

When you are daily working for the Lord, it somehow does not seem as tiring as when you are doing work for personal or financial gain. In fact, once you start experiencing all the blessings reaped from a busy Christian life, you will experience true joy and you will be glad that you made the effort. You will feel the benefit of "those who trust in the Lord for help" and who "soar on wings like eagles".

The Lord Jesus Christ

28. The final journey

Vicky Wilkinson

Reading: John 19:16-30

In the frustration of modern day living no doubt we can tell a tale of an unfavourable journey by car, train or bus.

The reading above begins with Jesus being led on the final lap of a journey that is comparable with no other. This journey out of Jerusalem, which was a relatively short one because John describes it as being near to the city (v. 20), led Jesus bearing His cross to a place outside the walls of Jerusalem called "the place of a Skull", namely Golgotha (Hebrew) or Calvary (Greek). Even before this journey He had been subjected to a scourging that almost preceded crucifixion, which meant that His body was stripped naked and flogged until the flesh hung down in blooded shreds. He had been crowned with platted thorns, struck and mocked and now He was led as a lamb to the slaughter.

Nearly two thousand years earlier a similar journey took place in that location. Even as God the Father led His only begotten Son to Calvary's hill, so did the patriarch Abraham lead his only son whom he loved to a mountain in the land of Moriah to be offered as a burnt offering. Can you imagine the sufferings of the father Abraham as he did this? But even more so, the sufferings of God the Father, because in this case there was no substitute to be found. This was no picture or pattern. This was the real thing.

Jesus was led to a death that is described as being "the most cruel and most frightful means of persecution" (Cicero) or "the most pitiable of all forms of death" (Josephus). Even so this type of death was not unique to Jesus. In fact two malefactors were crucified on either side of Him. Over and above the excruciating physical sufferings of the cross and of the abuse and insults from the crowd, the great agony that made Jesus' death unique was, I believe, the following:

- This man, who was described as being *holy, undefiled and separate from sinners* (Hebrews 7:26) was accused of blasphemy against God the Father and deemed worthy of death by His own people (John 19:7; Leviticus 14:16).
- He was to become a curse (Galatians 3:13; Deuteronomy 21:23).
- Most degrading of all, and the reason He was brought to this place outside the holy city, was that His soul was to be made an offering for sin. He who knew no sin was made to be sin for us (2 Corinthians 5:21), and in this He suffered the abandonment of His Father – and the darkness of sin covered the whole land.

And yes, *He did it for us.*

29. The Ascension

Vicky Wilkinson

Forty days after His resurrection, Jesus met with His disciples one last time. On the Mount of Olives the disciples witnessed the ascension of Christ, as He was taken up from the earth before their eyes, and a cloud received Him out of their sight (Acts 1:1-11).

Traditional Christianity makes much of the birth, death and the resurrection of Christ, by the Christmas and Easter celebrations, and this rightly so. However, Ascension Day seems to have been forgotten, which is a shame because it is a very important event. This was when Christ actually ascended into heaven itself, and presented Himself to God the Father as our sin bearer (Hebrews 9:24-28). Although His work of redemption was finished by His death and resurrection, His ascension filled up God's purpose concerning this.

When Hebrews 4:14 speaks of the ascension, it states that Jesus, the great High priest, passed through the heavens to present Himself to the Father, after which He sat down at the right hand of God (Hebrews 9:24, 10:12); a way of demonstrating that His work of redemption was fully completed and would never need to be repeated.

This place to which Christ ascended, and is now seated, is in the heavenly places, far above all principality and power and might and dominion, and every name that is named (Ephesians 1:20-21); far above all heavens (4:10). When Christ ascended, He passed through the heavens, and He gave a witness of His victory over sin and death to all the principalities and powers (spiritual forces both good and evil) in the heavenly places (Ephesians 6:12; Colossians 2:15). Christ has now been exalted to the highest pinnacle of glory, with all things under His feet, and also given a name which is above every name, that at the name of Jesus every knee shall bow (Philippians 2:9-10).

Christ now sits at the Father's right hand as our intercessor, and He can sympathise with all our weaknesses because He has been tempted ever as we are. Not only this but a further title has been given to Him in His ascended capacity, which is as Head of the Church, which is His Body (Ephesians 1:22-23). This aspect has far reaching consequences for us today who put faith in the Lord Jesus as our Saviour.

Christ is the Head of the Church which is His Body

It was the ascended Christ who called the Apostle Paul to be His minister, particularly to the Gentiles (Acts 26:16-17; 1 Timothy 2:7). However, at the end of the Acts period, when it became evident that Israel, as a nation, was not going to repent and turn to Christ, the Holy Spirit instructed Paul to turn his attention wholly to the Gentiles (Acts 28:23-31).

It was at this time that the ascended Christ, who had sat down at the Father's right hand, revealed that he was Head of the Church which is His Body (Ephesians 1:20-23). Paul was under house arrest at Rome, and so speaks of himself as a prisoner of Jesus Christ for *you* Gentiles (Ephesians 3:1). This was when the ascended Christ revealed new truths connected to His purpose for the Gentiles (that is ***us***), contained especially in Paul's last seven letters: Ephesians, Philippians, Colossians, 1 & 2 Timothy, Titus and Philemon.

By revelation God made known to Paul and others the knowledge of a mystery (or secret) that had previously been hidden in God. Paul was now commissioned to make known the fellowship of this mystery to the Gentile world (Ephesians 3:3,9). What was this mystery that was now the subject of Paul's preaching? This mystery is tied up in Christ who is the Head, and His church which is His Body (Ephesians 3:8-10, 5:32, Colossians 1:24-27), and of the fellowship of equality amongst all believers of all nationalities.

First, Paul made clear that from that time forward, because of their unbelief, Israel were no longer the channel of God's blessing, and all who believe in Christ were one in Christ – Jew or Gentile are equal (Ephesians 3:6). The Jew no longer had the priority, status or privilege, as previously in the Acts period (see Romans 1:16; 2:9-10;

3:1-2) All who believe were made equal members of this church in which there exists no national privileges.

But the most wonderful thing of all that Paul made known was the hope of inheritance to which those who become members of this church are called. Addressing the Gentiles (Ephesians 2:11), Paul told them that because God is so rich in mercy and loved us with a great love, He raised us up and made us to sit together in the heavenly places in Christ (Ephesians 2:6).

When we believe in Christ as our Saviour we are made members of His Church, the Body of Christ. We are therefore seated with Him in the heavenly places, at God's right hand, far above all. We share His place of glory! What a wonderful privilege!

Seated with Christ in heavenly places

The Apostle Paul's letters to the Ephesians and the Colossians deal with the subject of Christ and His Church of the ascension, the Body of Christ. Whilst Colossians considers Christ and His position as Head of that Church, Ephesians gives thought to the believer's position as a member of that Church.

Colossians 2:9 tells us that in Christ dwells all the fulness of the Godhead bodily and, in comparison, the Church is described as being the *fulness of Him who fills all in all* (Ephesians 1:23). Each member of the Church is complete (filled full) in Christ. Therefore, the church is the fulness of Christ and Christ is the fulness of God.

When the Apostle Paul wrote about the truth of the mystery which he received in a revelation from the ascended Christ, and which is so relevant to this church, he first made plain the foundational truths with respect to our salvation. These are redemption through Christ's shed blood, salvation by God's grace, forgiveness of sins, sanctification and reconciliation. All these rest on Christ and do not change. He is the centre of our hope and of God's purpose.

We will now consider more things, some of which did change when this new church was revealed. These are related to our hope. Consider Ephesians 1:

- *God has blessed us with every spiritual blessing in the **heavenly places** in Christ* (v. 3). Nothing that is spiritual is held back from us in this heavenly sphere.
- *He chose us in Him **before** the foundation of the world* (v. 4). Even before the Genesis creation, God chose us to be a people with whom He would work out His heavenly purpose in Christ.
- *We should be holy and without blame before Him in love* (v. 4). The object of the church.
- *Having predestined us to adoption as sons by Jesus Christ to Himself* (v. 5). This was not by promise but according to the good pleasure of His will.
- *We are accepted in the Beloved (v. 6). This being to the praise of His glory!*
- *We have obtained an inheritance* (v. 11). This was when we were sealed with God's Holy Spirit of promise, which is also a guarantee of our hope to come (v.13-14).

We sit in the heavenly realms as a witness, to all the dignitaries there, of God's great love and mercy to us. What a privilege! What a blessing! No wonder riches and glory are the characterisation of our hope in Christ (Colossians 1:27).

30. The Miracle Baby – God and Man

Sylvia Penny

It was a miracle that Christ was ever born. How can God, Who is infinite, immortal, invisible and all-powerful, become a human being who is finite, mortal, visible and weak? That is just one of the mysteries of godliness. 1 Timothy 3:16 says: "Beyond all question, the mystery of godliness is great: He appeared in a body …"

It is not surprising that ever since this miracle took place, over 2,000 years ago, people have questioned the authenticity of this event. John 1:10 tells us that "though the world was made through Him, the world did not recognize Him". Few of those living in His time recognized that God Himself was living among them. Even His own disciples had great difficulty understanding and believing that He was, indeed, God. However, by contrast, after His death some people had difficulty believing that He was ever truly human.

The problem was (and still is), that people found it impossible to accept that God could truly and fully become a human being. So, either they accepted that Jesus was a man, a human being, and the greatest prophet the world had ever seen, but not that He was God manifest in the flesh; or they accepted that Jesus was indeed God, but that He was never a true human being, He only looked like one, just as the angels did occasionally. Either way, it was easier to believe.

However, Christianity involves believing things which are sometimes impossible to understand. How can we ever fully understand that when Jesus lay weak and helpless in that manger in Bethlehem, there lay God Himself, the centre of the universe, totally dependent upon Mary and Joseph for His care and upbringing? Somehow our minds boggle at such a thought. Our conventional ideas of Who and What God is, conflict with our conventional ideas of what a baby is. One is a wonderful and powerful Being on Whom we are totally dependent. The other is a weak and helpless infant totally dependent upon human adults. The two are seemingly incompatible and yet the impossible happened! They combined, and God became a baby.

But how could God the Son give up His "place" in glory (John 17:5) and come to earth as a human being? And why would an all-powerful Being want to do such a thing?

Mary asked the first question: "How will this be"? What was the answer given to her? "The Holy Spirit will come upon you, and the power of the Most High will overshadow you. So the holy one to be born will be called the Son of God" (Luke 1:34,35). The unique combination of God the Holy Spirit and a human egg from Mary resulted in the greatest miracle ever performed – God being born as a man. The fact itself is very easy to grasp, but very difficult to accept, which is why so many people reject this very basic doctrine of Christianity.

The second question: "Why did God want to do such a thing?" is answered in John 3:16: "For God so loved the world that He gave His one and only Son, that whoever believes in Him shall not perish but have eternal life." The answer to the question is therefore enigmatic: He was born to die. He loved us in such a way that He wanted to become human, so that He could die in our place. Without His sacrificial death, there would have been no payment for our sins (Romans 6:23).

God loves us and wants us to share eternity with Him. We cannot, because He is Holy and we are sinners, and the wages of sin is death. We are all sinners, and without Christ's sacrifice on the cross, without His payment of our wages, we would not be redeemed, not be justified, not be made righteous, and not receive eternal life (Romans 3:23, 24). It was necessary for God, the all-powerful Being, to die so that we could be saved from our sinful state. In order to make this sacrifice, He had to become human.

Thus, what we celebrate every Christmas came about. God became a weak and helpless baby. For a little while He became "lower than the angels" (Hebrews 2:7). Let us stop and think again this Christmas about what this means to us. How much do we appreciate all that God has done for us and what do we think of the “miracle baby” born in Bethlehem over 2,000 years ago?

31. Jesus' life in danger

Sylvia Penny

The time of year when we think most about the death and resurrection of our Lord Jesus Christ is at Easter. But do we ever stop to think about how often His life was in danger throughout His three-year ministry? Many times during this period there was a very real threat to His life, which was often averted by miraculous means. It is very easy to read these passages and hardly notice them.

First occasion

One of the first occasions this happens is recorded in Luke 4:28-30: "All the people in the synagogue were furious when they heard this. They got up, drove him out of the town, and took Him to the brow of the hill on which the town was built, in order to throw Him down the cliff. But He walked right through the crowd and went on His way." This was at the very beginning of His ministry after He returned to Galilee from the Jordan. He infuriated the Jews in the synagogue when He reminded them of Gentiles in the Old Testament who were more favourably treated by God than the Jews. It was not the sort of message they wished to hear, or be reminded of. As a result they tried to throw Him off a cliff. However, although they drove Him out of town and up to the brow of a hill, we are told He walked right through the crowd and went on His way. In a miraculous way they were unable to harm Him because it was not yet the time for Him to lay down His life. Until His time had come (John 17:1), His life was miraculously preserved, not just once, but many times.

In John 10:18 Jesus clearly stated that He had total control over His life and death, "No-one takes it from me, but I lay it down of my own accord." When He died on the cross we should be in no doubt that He allowed Himself to be crucified. He laid down His life so that the penalty for our sins would be paid. If He had not purposely succumbed to His arrest, mock trial, and crucifixion, nobody would have been able to force Him to it. "He humbled Himself and became obedient to death – even death on a cross" (Philippians 2:8).

Second occasion

Some time after the incident in Luke 4, Jesus returned to Jerusalem for a feast (John 5:1). Here He healed a man on the Sabbath, which led to more Jews persecuting Him. John 5:18 records, "For this reason the Jews tried all the harder to kill him; not only was He breaking the Sabbath, but He was even calling God His own Father, making Himself equal with God." Again, His life was in very real danger.

Third occasion

After this, it was more dangerous for Him in Jerusalem and Judea than it was in Galilee, and so John 7:1 tells us, "After this, Jesus went around in Galilee, purposely staying away from Judea because the Jews there were waiting to take His life." Later however, He returned to Jerusalem for the Feast of Tabernacles, and confronted the Jews directly, "Has not Moses given you the law? Yet not one of you keeps the law. Why are you trying to kill me?" When the crowd denied this accusation, Jesus ignored their denial. Instead of trying to placate those who were intent on killing Him, He continue to speak out boldly and openly. "At this they tried to seize Him, but no-one laid a hand on Him, because His time had not yet come" (John 7:19-30). His life was protected until His message was complete.

Fourth occasion

On the last day of the same feast, once again they wanted to seize Him, but were miraculously prevented from doing so – "Some wanted to seize Him, but no-one laid a hand on Him" (John 7:44).

Fifth occasion

A day later, He returned to the temple courts and when challenged by the Pharisees He silenced them with His answers, but John 8:20 tells us "no-one seized Him, because His time had not yet come". Jesus openly confronted them with their murderous intent, "you are ready to kill me" (John 8:37), and "you are determined to kill Me, a man who has told you the truth" (John 8:40). He continued by telling them they belonged to their father, the devil, a murderer and liar. He certainly did not mince His words, nor did He endear Himself to the Pharisees. When He finished by telling them "before Abraham was born, I am" (John 8:58) verse 39 continues, "At this, they picked up stones to stone Him, but Jesus hid Himself, slipping away from the temple grounds." The more Jesus spoke the truth about Himself, and about the Pharisees, the more strongly they wanted to get rid of Him. Time and again Jesus confronted them, and time and again they either wanted to kill Him, or tried to kill Him, but were prevented from doing so by miraculous means.

Sixth occasion

It was possibly about a year later, when Jesus once again returned to Jerusalem for a feast, this time the feast of Dedication, in the winter, that He stated, "I and the Father are one .... The Jews picked up stones to stone Him" (John 10:30,31). They condemned Him for blasphemy, for claiming to be God. They did not believe His claims, and did not want others to believe His claims either. Jesus told them they should believe the testimony of His miracles, even if they didn't believe His words, but their response was that "again they tried to seize Him, but He escaped their grasp" (John 10:39).

Seventh occasion

Shortly after this, Jesus performed His greatest miracle – raising Lazarus from the dead, after he had been in the grave for four days. When the word spread about this, the Sanhedrin had a special meeting at which they officially plotted together to take Jesus' life (John 11:53). Seven days later, Jesus was crucified. Humanly speaking, this was the result of their evil plans, but spiritually speaking it was the time foreordained for His sacrifice for the sins of all mankind.

Jesus went willingly and obediently to His death. The time, at last, was right (John 17:1). He did not slip away, nor did He not evade their grasp. It was Passover, and He was to be the perfect Passover lamb, sacrificed for the sins of the world.

Jesus' three-year period of ministry was fraught with danger from beginning to end, but maybe this is one aspect of His life we do not think about very often. We think of His teachings, His miracles, the many who did believe in Him, and sometimes forget, or don't notice, the enormous amount of opposition He suffered, not only at the end of His ministry but throughout the whole period from His baptism to His crucifixion.

32. The Resurrection

Sylvia Penny

The bodily resurrection of Christ is one of the most important parts of the Christian gospel. "For what I received I passed on to you as of first importance: that Christ died for our sins according to the Scriptures, that He was buried, *that He was raised on the third day…*" (1 Corinthians 15:3,4). Then Paul goes on to say, in verse 14, "And if Christ has not been raised, our preaching is useless and so is your faith." The resurrection of Christ is essential to our Christian faith. Yet are we able to explain to others why it is reasonable to accept that this is a historical fact and not just an unsubstantiated belief of ours?

Only two alternatives

We only need to take a couple of logical steps. Jesus claimed that He was the Christ, the Messiah, the Son of God, and as such was God Himself, come to earth in human form. He also predicted His own death and subsequent resurrection three days later. There are therefore only two alternatives we can adopt:

1. Jesus was a liar or a deluded mad-man, and He never did rise from the dead.
2. He did rise from the dead and was all that He claimed to be – none other than God incarnate.

However, many people will take a middle option. They deny His resurrection, and say it could never have taken place, but accept that Jesus was a great prophet, on a par with other prophets in the past. This, however, is not a viable option. No sane person, let alone a great and inspired prophet, has ever claimed to be God Himself. Prophets have always been sent by God, spokesmen on God's behalf, used by God, but never claimed to be God Himself. Jesus is unique in this claim. If Jesus did not rise from the dead, all His claims to Godhood were in vain, and He should instead have gone down in history as an unfortunate, deluded mad-man. However, He did not. Why not? The short answer is because He *did* rise from the dead.

The eleven disciples return to Jerusalem

At the time of His crucifixion, Jesus was deserted by all His followers save John, His closest disciple, and a handful of women including His mother. Ten of the disciples fled in fear for their lives, and the eleventh, Judas, had betrayed Jesus and then hanged himself in remorse. Humanly speaking, that would have been the end of the story, a sorry end to a powerful and miracle-filled three-year ministry. Peter went back to Galilee and started fishing again (John 21:3). Probably each of Jesus' followers would have eventually returned to the lives they had led before they met Him. However, they did not. Instead, they returned to Jerusalem and formed the beginning of Christianity. Why did they do this? Because Jesus really did rise from the dead. In doing so, He not only did what He had said He would do (John 2:19-22), He also confirmed that He was God Himself (John 10:33).

Jesus' half-brother James became a believer

It is recorded in the gospels that Jesus was not believed by His own family: "For even His own brothers did not believe in Him" (John 7:5). His brothers and sisters thought that He was mad (Mark 3:21) and sometimes tried to take charge of Him. Yet we find soon after His death that His brother James was a leader of the Christian movement in Jerusalem (Acts 15:13; 21:18), and His other brothers, including Jude (writer of the New Testament letter), became staunch believers. Why was this? Because Jesus rose from the dead and appeared to them (1 Corinthians 15:7).

Joy and enthusiasm

Not only did the disciples quickly turn around from despondency to joyfulness after the crucifixion, their enthusiasm was so infectious that, after the feast of Pentecost, many thousands of Jews were converted to Christianity within a short time. This enthusiasm, this hope, this joyfulness, can only be explained by the resurrection. No pretence of Jesus' resurrection, no hiding of the body, no deceitfulness on the part of the disciples, or a small group of them, could have achieved this dramatic and sustained turn around in their emotions and behaviour. That Christ literally rose from the dead is the only explanation.

Perhaps Jesus never died on the cross

Some, in an attempt to get around the implications of the death and subsequent resurrection, have suggested Jesus never died at all. It is suggested instead that He was unconscious on the cross, and revived in the tomb. However, it has been demonstrated beyond doubt that no-one who had gone through what Jesus suffered could have survived. The final sword thrust in His side was proof enough. Roman soldiers were experts at crucifixion. They did not make mistakes.

Even supposing He had miraculously survived, He was bound tightly in grave cloths, and would not have been able to escape from the tomb. If, as some suggest, the disciples had freed Him from the grave cloths, why would they have remained so joyful and intent, over many years, on preaching Christ's resurrection from the dead, knowing all along that it was a lie? Why would they all, without exception, suffer a martyr's death for a faith which was based on a falsehood, a deception of the greatest magnitude? In addition, how could a group of people maintain the truth of such an incredible deception for so many years without there ever being a single hint as to its falsehood? And also, why is there no record of Jesus Himself living on to a ripe old age? The answer is because none of this happened. The disciples' faith was based instead upon a solid fact of history – the fact of the resurrection of Christ.

The empty tomb

There is no getting around it. If Jesus died on the cross, and was placed in the tomb as recorded, then His body should have been there when the women went to the tomb. That the tomb was empty is a historical fact. The body could not have been stolen for both practical and psychological reasons. The tomb was guarded by soldiers who were threatened with death if they deserted their posts. A huge rock was rolled in front of the opening. It was effectively sealed. If the Jewish leaders had stolen the body in order to disprove the resurrection story, all they had to do was to produce the body. Neither the women, nor the disciples could have stolen the body, for the reasons given above. And no unknown, impartial third party would have stolen the body, for the simple reason that they would have had no reason to, and wouldn't know where it was anyway. Yet the tomb was empty.

Again, the only logical explanation is that Jesus did indeed rise from the dead.

Paul Althaus of the University of Erlangen, Germany says: "The resurrection could not have been maintained in Jerusalem for a single day, for a single hour, if the emptiness of the tomb had not been established for all concerned" (quoted in *The Resurrection Factor* by Josh McDowell, an excellent book giving an overwhelming number of reasons and evidence for the fact of Christ's resurrection).

Belief without seeing

We read that Thomas was not with the disciples when Jesus first appeared to them after His resurrection. So he refused to believe that they had really seen Jesus. However, when Jesus again appeared among them one week later, and Thomas was there to see it, he fell down and worshipped Him, and called Him "My Lord and My God" (John 20:28). Jesus told him that he had believed because he had seen, but "blessed are those who have not seen, and yet have believed" (John 20:29).

We are among those who have believed without seeing, although we do have the testimony of many who did, and the benefit of recorded history. When all the details are studied, when all the alternatives are considered, there is only one logical conclusion. Christ is risen! Praise the Lord.

33. The Son of God

Sylvia Penny

Some people question whether Jesus Himself ever claimed to be God. After all, it is an amazing truth that a human being, Who was born, lived, and died among other human beings, was actually God Himself living among mere mortals for over thirty years. As this was so, why was it not spectacularly obvious to everyone around Him that He was God? Why did He not say so clearly? Why did He not do things which made it obvious? The answer of course is that it was obvious, He did say so clearly, and He did do things which made it obvious! However, human beings have always been excellent at ignoring the obvious when it suits them, and this was no exception.

He made people feel uncomfortable if they were self-satisfied, He questioned their motives for doing things, and He pointed out their failings. This did not go down well with those that were self-righteous, those that held high opinions of themselves, and those that were high up in the social hierarchy. None of these *wanted* to accept that He was God, as this would mean having to accept all that He taught, and worse still, having to accept all He said about their own failings. It was much better to ignore, argue against, and ultimately get rid of Him.

Reason for writing John's gospel

John's gospel was written specifically so that people would believe that Jesus was the Messiah, the Son of God. It starts out in chapter 1 explaining that the "Word was God" (verse 1), and that "The Word became flesh" (verse 14), referring to Jesus being born as a human being, thus being both God and man rolled into one. The gospel then finishes by saying, in John 20:31, "But these (miraculous signs) are written *that you may believe that Jesus is the Christ, the Son of God*, and that by believing you may have life in his name."

The phrase "the Son of God" is used of Jesus throughout the gospels. To the Jews, this emphasised His deity – it did not detract from it. To be the Son of God was to be fully God, in the same way that to be a son of a human being was to be fully human. Jesus was, uniquely, both. Vine's *Expository Dictionary* says of the title "Son of God", "*absolute Godhead*, not Godhead in a secondary or derived sense, *is intended in the title*". It also states that when the disciples, and others, addressed Him as the "Son of God" they probably meant that He was a manifestation of God in human form. Quite often the context makes it clear that they were so overawed with what He has just said or done, that an incredible realisation that He was God Himself flooded over them.

People overawed by Jesus' words and deeds

For example, when Jesus told Nathaniel He had seen him sitting under a fig-tree before Philip had called him to come and see Jesus, he exclaimed "Rabbi, you are the Son of God…" He realised there was no other explanation for Jesus' knowing about him (John 1:49).

Another time, when the disciples were in a boat together, Jesus walked across the water to reach them. Peter impulsively asked Him to let him walk on the water too, which he did until he saw the wind, and was afraid that he would sink. Jesus immediately caught him by the hand and helped him to the boat. The disciples in the boat worshipped Jesus there and then and said "Truly, you are the Son of God" (Matthew 14:33). By worshipping Him, they showed their complete acceptance of Him as the one and only true God. Jews at that time refused to worship anything other than God (thus causing much trouble to the occupying Romans who tried on a number of occasions, unsuccessfully, to get them to worship Caesar as a god).

Even the Roman centurion, sent to guard Jesus at the foot of the cross, realised in the end that Jesus was God. Matthew 27:54 says, "When the centurion and those with him who were guarding Jesus saw the earthquake and all that had happened, they were terrified, and exclaimed, "Surely he was the Son of God!" Time and time again people were convicted of His deity just by being with Him and witnessing what He said and what He did.

Believing *without* seeing

Some people seemed to have no trouble accepting that Jesus was God. They did not have to see great proofs or miracles. They accepted Him for Who He was. John the Baptist said "I have seen and I testify that this is the Son of God." (John 1:34). This was before Jesus had performed a single miracle, and before He had called a single disciple to follow Him. Simon Peter said, "You are the Christ, the Son of the living God", (Matthew 16:16), and Jesus commended him for this. Peter did not doubt or question this, like some, but accepted Him wholeheartedly. Martha was similar. She said simply, "I believe that you are the Christ, the Son of God" (John 11:27). She said this even though her brother Lazarus had just died, and despite the fact that she believed that Jesus could have saved his life if He had only turned up a little earlier.

Testimony of Spiritual Beings

Spiritual beings, whether angels, demons or evil spirits often referred to Jesus as the Son of God. They never questioned His position or His authority. They knew Who He was, and why He had come to earth. For example, the angel Gabriel said to Mary "He will be great and will be called the Son of the Most High" (Luke 1:32). He also said, "So the holy one to be born will be called the Son of God" (Luke 1:35).

Evil spirits and demons were obviously in awe of Him. Mark 3:11 says, "Whenever the evil spirits saw him, they fell down before him and cried out, "You are the Son of God!" and in Luke 4:41, "demons came out of many people, shouting, "You are the Son of God". One, called Legion, was in fear of Jesus. "He shouted at the top of his voice, "What do you want with me, Jesus, Son of the Most High God? Swear to God that you won't torture me!" (Mark 5:7, Luke 8:28). It is clear that whatever else they knew about Jesus, they also knew that He was God, and had power and authority over them.

Jesus' own testimony

Jesus Himself clearly stated that He was God. That was ultimately the reason the Jews wanted to get rid of Him. For a human being to claim that they were God was the ultimate blasphemy, which is why they picked up stones to stone him on a number of occasions. If He had not clearly stated that He was God, they would never have reacted in this way. John 10:30-33 is very clear:

> 30 "I and the Father are one."
> 31 Again, the Jews picked up stones to stone him.
> 32 But Jesus said to them, "I have shown you many great miracles from the Father. For which of these do you stone me?"
> 33 "We are not stoning you for any of these," replied the Jews, "but for blasphemy, *because you, a mere man, claim to be God*."

Jesus continues His arguments against them in the next few verses, and states again in verse 36, "Why then do you accuse me of blasphemy because I said, 'I am God's Son'?" He never denies that He claimed to be God, but instead He clearly confirms it, and challenges their accusation of blasphemy.

It is this very point which eventually leads to His crucifixion. It is so crucial that it is one of the very few details that is included in all four gospels. When Jesus stands accused, Matthew 26:63,64. Mark 14:61,62 and Luke 22:70 record that:

> The high priest said to him, "I charge you under oath by the living God: Tell us if you are the Christ, the Son of God." "Yes, it is as you say," Jesus replied.

In John 19:7 the Jews insisted, "We have a law, and according to that law he must die, because he claimed to be the Son of God."

Today

The testimony that Jesus is God is quite clear. His actions and words proved that to those around Him on many, many occasions. Those that met Him and then wrote about Him showed that in their writings. People were persuaded either by His authority, or His words, or His actions. Everyone is different, and comes to belief and acceptance by a different route. However, many refused to be persuaded or convinced. Despite the evidence, and the proofs performed before their very eyes, they decided to deny the truth, and to get rid of Him instead.

People are not so very different today. There are those that accept Jesus as their God and Saviour without having to seek constant reassurance and proofs. There are those that look for evidence to support their beliefs. And there are those that ignore what they see and what they hear, argue against any evidence in support of Christianity as a reasonable faith based upon a firm foundation of facts, and prefer to continue living in the way they always have. At the end of the day they are not so very different from the Jewish leaders 2000 years ago.

34. A Child is born ... and he will be called ... Everlasting Father

Sylvia Penny

> For to us a child is born, to us a son is given,
> And the government will be on his shoulders.
> And he will be called Wonderful Counsellor, Mighty God,
> Everlasting Father, Prince of Peace.
> (Isaiah 9:6)

These well-known words from Isaiah 9 appear on many Christmas cards each year, and this is one of the many familiar Christmas readings in services in different churches in the weeks leading up to Christmas Day. As such, it is very easy to read over these words, and not take in their full meaning.

First and foremost, they are a wonderful testimony to the deity of Christ, as they make clear that the "child", the "son", is also "Mighty God". This is similar to Hebrews 1:8 which says,

> But about the Son he says, "Your throne, O God, will last for ever and ever".

It is clear the Son is God.

However, the verse in Isaiah also adds that one of the titles of the Son is "Everlasting Father". So, in what sense is the Son also the Father? The Lord Jesus addressed this particular question in John 14:9-10, when Philip asked Him to show them the Father.

> Jesus answered: "Don't you know me, Philip, even after I have been among you such a long time? Anyone who has seen me has seen the Father. How can you say, 'Show us the Father'? Don't you believe that I am in the Father, and that the Father is in me? The words I say to you are not just my own. Rather, it is the Father, living in me, who is doing his work".

Here Jesus equates Himself with the Father. They are One. However, it was a difficult concept for the disciples to understand, hence Philip's request to see the Father.

When Jesus was speaking to some unbelieving Jews at the Feast of Dedication at Jerusalem, he told them:

> My sheep listen to my voice; I know them, and they follow me. I give them eternal life, and they shall never perish; no-one can snatch them out of my hand. My Father, who has given them to me, is greater than all; no-one can snatch them out of my Father's hand. **I and the Father are one.** (John 10:27-30)

When Jesus said this, the Jews picked up stones to stone him, because they accused Him of blasphemy; He was claiming to be God. Of course, if He was not God, they were correct in this. Their mistake was not to believe that He was. Here again, Jesus equated Himself with the Father.

Maybe it is also a difficult concept for us to understand completely, but there are a number of Scriptures written after the Lord's resurrection and ascension that also talk about the nature of the Son that can help us understand in what sense they are One and the same.

Hebrews 1:3 tells us that "The Son is the radiance of God's glory and the exact representation of his being, sustaining all things by his powerful word".

2 Corinthians 4:4 says "Christ … is the image of God", and Colossians 1:15 says the Son is "the image of the invisible God" followed by verse 19 that says, "For God was pleased to have all his fulness dwell in him".

Whether we fully understand this or not, it is clear that the Father and the Son were, and are, intricately linked one with another, and that although we don't fully understand the nature of God now, there is a time in the future when "we will know as we are known".

Now we see but a poor reflection as in a mirror; then we shall see face to face. Now I know in part; then I shall know fully, even as I am fully known. (1 Corinthians 13:12)

35. Jesus, Firstborn from among the Dead (Colossians 1:18)

Sylvia Penny

Firstborn over all creation

When we think about the Easter message of resurrection, it is good to revisit what the Apostle Paul says in Colossians 1. Not only does Paul remind us that Christ is the image of the invisible God, but he tells us He is "the *firstborn* over all creation". This means that He is the pre-eminent One, the One Who is above all others. The reason for this is that He is Creator, and as such is greater than His creation. "He is before all things, and in him all things hold together." (Colossians 1:17)

Firstborn from among the dead

However, he then goes on to tell us that Christ was also the "*firstborn* from among the dead". What does this mean? Jesus was certainly not the first man to be raised from the dead, but He was the first to be raised to eternal life, *never to die again.* We have a number of examples of people who were raised from the dead, both in the OT and the NT, but none of these remained alive. In the natural course of time, each of these died again. In fact, John 3:13 makes this very clear. It says "No-one has ever gone into heaven except the one who came from heaven – the Son of Man". This must of course include Enoch, despite the fact Genesis 3:24 tells us that "God took him away", and Elijah, despite the fact that 2 Kings 2:11 tells us that "Elijah went up to heaven in a whirlwind". Both of these men must have subsequently died. Christ is the only One who has been raised from the dead, and remained alive ever since. This is what Paul meant when he described Jesus as being the firstborn from among the dead.

Without resurrection our faith is futile

1 Corinthians 15 is the great resurrection chapter of Scripture, in which Paul points out that "if Christ has not been raised, our preaching is useless and so is your faith." The resurrection of Christ is of paramount importance, as without this "your faith is futile; you are still in your sins".

Paul then confirms again that "Christ has indeed been raised from the dead, the firstfruits of those who have fallen asleep." It is *because* Jesus has been raised from the dead that we can have confidence that, one day, we too will be raised from the dead by the same power that raised Jesus from the dead. Ephesians 1 refers to this great power in verses 19 and 20 where it tells us that the Father's incomparably great power works for us in the same way it worked in Christ when He raised Him from the dead and seated Him at His right hand in the heavenly realms. Then Ephesians 2:6 tells us that "God raised us up with Christ and seated us with him in the heavenly realms in Christ". So, it is made clear that in our resurrection life we will be together with Christ in the heavenly realms.

When will this happen?

When will this happen? If we go back to 1 Corinthians 15 it gives us the answer:

> For as in Adam all die, so in Christ all will be made alive. But each in his own turn: Christ, the firstfruits, *then when he comes, those who belong to him.*" (1 Corinthians 15:22,23)

Our resurrection will take place "when Christ comes". This will be at some time in the future. This is also referred to in 1 Thessalonians 4 where Paul writes about what will happen to the dead when the Lord returns. In verse 14 he says, "We believe that Jesus died and rose again and so we believe that God will bring with Jesus those who have fallen asleep in him."

Those "who have fallen asleep" is the way Scripture often refers to those who have died. It is the way God has chosen to refer to death, as death is not a permanent state. It is like a sleep and will not last for ever. It is only temporary until the day of resurrection. We can take comfort in this thought when we lose loved ones, as we can think of them being "asleep in Christ" (1 Corinthians 15:18), and that one day we will see them again – on the day He returns to wake us all up. On the day of resurrection.

The Person of God

36. Only God is Good and Holy

Vicky Wilkinson

Reading - Mark 10:17-22

Recently, I was asked to give my comments on a booklet the subject of which was a refutation of the Deity of Christ. One of the many sections of Scripture used by the author, as support for his doctrine, was the above reading – particularly verses 17-18. I can well understand his use of these verses to validate his argument, as it appears on the surface that when Jesus said to the rich young ruler, "Why do you call me good? No one is good but One, that is, God", He was denying His equality with God, who is indeed good.

However, it is to be noted that on many occasions during Christ's ministry, when He was confronted by a question, instead of giving a direct answer He instead asked another question, as if He were trying to provoke deeper thought on the subject. I personally believe that when Jesus answered the rich young ruler this way, He was more or less saying that yes, he had addressed Him correctly and was asking him if he recognised who indeed it was he was speaking with.

Only One is good - God (Psalm 25:8), even as "there is none holy like the Lord" (1 Samuel 2:2). As God the Father is infinitely good and holy, so likewise Jesus Christ the Son who said, "I am the good shepherd" (John 10:11; compare Psalm 23). Also, He (Christ) is called the Holy One and the Just (Acts 3:14) – the One who knew no sin, who was without sin and without spot, holy, harmless, undefiled and separate from sinners (Hebrews 7:26).

In the beginning God created the heavens and the earth and all that was in them and when He saw everything that He had made He saw that it was very good indeed. However, because of what happened as recorded in Genesis 3, mankind fell from God's goodness and became spoilt and lost. But because of God's great love for His creation, He provided the way, through Jesus Christ the Holy One of God, as the Good Shepherd who gave His life for the lost sheep, by which they could be saved. Can we therefore forego the riches of this world, take up our cross and follow Him? If we can, not only will we have treasure in heaven, but we will taste and see the Lord is good indeed (Psalm 34:8).

37. Omnipresence of God

Vicky Wilkinson

If we were asked the question "Who is God?", how would we answer? If we are Bible believing Christians we have the wealth of Scripture at our fingertips to aid us in our answer, as well as our own experience of how God has worked in our lives. In an attempt to answer this question in a short series, I shall look at only four different aspects of the Person of God that make up His substance and being. However, as we do this, we must to so humbly, keeping in mind the following:

> Oh, the depth of the riches both of the wisdom and knowledge of God! How unsearchable are His judgments and His ways past finding out! (Romans 11:33)

The four attributes of God that I would like to consider are as follows:

- His omnipresence
- His eternality
- His omnipotence
- His omniscience

In this article we will begin with the first – His omnipresence – followed by the three others in subsequent articles.

His Omnipresence

The Oxford dictionary gives the meaning of the above as follows: *To be everywhere at the same time.* If God is a person, how then could He be everywhere at the same time? The answer to this question is found in John 4:24 which tells us that God is 'Spirit' (Greek, *pneuma*).

Another meaning of this same Greek word is 'wind'. Therefore, in the same way that the wind can be everywhere at the same time, so can God, but with a difference: God is a being, a Divine Being.

The Bible

Do the Scriptures enlighten us on this attribute of God? The answer to this question is 'Yes!' Consider the following:

Psalm 139:7-10 (NKJV) - a psalm of David

> Where can I go from Your Spirit? Or where can I flee from Your presence? If I ascend into heaven, You *are* there; If I make my bed in hell, behold, You *are there. If* I take the wings of the morning, *And* dwell in the uttermost parts of the sea, Even there Your hand shall lead me, And Your right hand shall hold me.

1 Kings 8:27 - the prayer of Solomon at the dedication of the temple

> But will God indeed dwell on the earth? Behold, heaven and the heaven of heavens cannot contain You. How much less this temple which I have built!

Acts 7:49 - Stephen quoting from Isaiah 66:1-2

> "Heaven is my throne, and earth is my footstool. What house will you build for me?" says the Lord. "Or what is the place of my rest? Has not my hand made all these things?"

When we consider the words of the above Spirit filled men of God, we can definitely ascribe *omnipresence* to our unfathomable God.

However, what about Christ Jesus, God's Son? As Christians we believe that He also is a Divine Being who shares God's Deity, being part of the Godhead. Consider what He has to say:

Matthew 18:20 - Jesus' words to His disciples

> For where two or three are gathered together in my name, I am there in the midst of them.

Matthew 28:19-20 - Jesus' words to the eleven apostles

> Go therefore and make disciples of all the nations, baptizing them in the name of the Father and of the Son and of the Holy Spirit, teaching them to observe all things that I have commanded you, and lo, I am with you always, even to the end of the age.

And Paul says of our risen and glorified Saviour:

Ephesians 3:17, 4:9-10

> That Christ may dwell in your hearts … He who descended is also the one who ascended far above all heavens that He might fill All things.

The above Scriptures tell us that the risen and exalted Christ, like God, through His Spirit, can be everywhere at the same time. He can be in and with believers wherever they may be.

Even though Christ had a human body when He came down from heaven, and now has a glorified body as He sits at the right hand of God, just like God the Father He can come to us by His Spirit. 1 Peter 1:11 speaks of the *Spirit of Christ*, who was in the prophets of old and who is now in us, bringing us God's grace and salvation.

Therefore, we can ascribe omnipresence to both God the Father and God the Son alike, because they are ***one*** (John 10:30). This also enables us to start answering our question 'Who is God?' We can say that God is The Divine Spirit who, at any moment in time, is everywhere.

38. Eternality of God

Vicky Wilkinson

In this second article on 'The Person of God' we will consider the eternality of God. Genesis 1:1 says, "In the beginning God created the heavens and the earth". The *beginning*, marked by creation, is for the benefit of us, His finite creatures. But note, in the beginning God was already in existence. Psalm 90:2 states that: "Before the mountains were brought forth, or ever You had formed the earth and the world, even from everlasting to everlasting, You *are* God". Consider the following:

Habakkuk 1:12	Are you not from everlasting, O Lord my God....
Romans 16:26	But now has been made manifest, and by the prophetic Scriptures has been made known to all nations, according to the commandment of the everlasting God.
Deuteronomy 33:27	The eternal God is your refuge, and underneath are the everlasting arms.
Isaiah 57:15	For thus says the High and Lofty One who inhabits eternity, whose name is Holy...

The above gives substantial Scriptural backing that the God of the Bible is from eternity and has always been and always will be in existence. Therefore, He is a God in whom we can put our trust, not only in any place but also at any time, knowing He will be around to hear and support us. He said to His people, "I am the Lord, I do not change" (Malachi 3:6).

But what about God's Son, Jesus Christ? Even though Jesus had a human beginning when He was born in Bethlehem, He also, according to the Scriptures, is from eternity. Consider the Scriptures below. These show without doubt that Jesus Christ, the Son of God, is from eternity.

He was One with the Father in the beginning when the heavens and the earth were created, and will always be. For this reason, He is given the title of the *Everlasting Father* in Isaiah 9:6 and also the *Alpha and Omega* (the beginning and the end) in Revelation 21:6. Jesus Christ is the same yesterday, today and for ever (Hebrews 13:8). God the Father, Jesus Christ the Son, and likewise the Holy Spirit, (Hebrews 9:14) are from eternity.

John 1:1-2, 14	As the living Word of God who became flesh, He was already in existence in the beginning with God.
Colossians 1:17	And He is before all things and in Him all things consist. (This refers to both time and His pre-eminence.)
Micah 5:2	In this prophecy of the coming Messiah Christ is referred to as being from everlasting.
Hebrews 1:10-12	God said to the Son, "You, Lord in the beginning laid the foundation of the earth…You are the same and your years will never fail."

Who is God? We can now build on our answer. The God of the Bible is not only the Divine Spirit who is omnipresent, i.e. everywhere at the same time, but He is from everlasting to everlasting. He was in existence in the beginning and will still exist at the end. He is omnipresent and He is eternal, and we can also add to this the fact that He is immutable. He never changes!

39. Omnipotence of God

Vicky Wilkinson

In this third article on 'The Person of God' we will consider the omnipotence of God. *The Oxford Dictionary* defines this as 'of great or absolute power'. The question is, can we ascribe absolute power to the God of the Bible, the Christian's God?

God, speaking to Moses, said: "I am the *Almighty God*" (Genesis 17:1; see also Exodus 6:3; Revelation 4:8). However, the first demonstration of God's absolute power is seen in the creation. Jeremiah 32:17 says, "Ah, Lord God! Behold you have made the heavens and the earth by your great power and outstretched arm. There is nothing too hard for you." See also Jeremiah 10:12 and consider the following:

Psalm 62:11	Power belongs to God.
2 Samuel 22:33	King David said, "God is my strength and power. He makes my way perfect."
Job 42:1-2	Job answered the Lord and said, "I know you can do everything and that no purpose of yours can be withheld from you."
Romans 1:20	For since the creation of the world His invisible attributes are clearly seen, being understood by the things that are made, even His eternal power and Godhead, so they are without excuse.

We also read that God is clothed with power (Psalm 65:6), is excellent in power (Job 37:23) and when He brings in His kingdom rule, He will rule by His power (Psalm 66:7).

We have touched upon God's absolute power revealed in creation but the next Scripture introduces God's second mighty work, which is redemption, centred in the Lord Jesus Christ. Ephesians 1 contains a prayer of the Apostle Paul on behalf of his fellow believers at Ephesus.

In verse 19 he prays that they would come to know "the exceeding greatness of His (God's) power towards us who believe, according to the working of His mighty power, which He worked in Christ when He raised Him from the dead and seated Him at His own right hand".

Speaking of the resurrection, the Apostle Paul said that Christ was declared to be Son of God with power, according to the Spirit of holiness, by the resurrection from the dead. It was the risen and ascended Christ who was able to give His power to those who put their faith in Him by means of the Holy Spirit. This enabled them to do the mighty works of God (Romans 15:19). Even before His death and resurrection Jesus had said, "*all power* has been given to me in heaven and on earth": Matthew 28:18 KJV and Mark 2:10. See also the following which are applicable to Christ Jesus:

Isaiah 9:6	In this prophecy He is given the title of the *Mighty God*
Luke 9:43	And they were all amazed at the mighty power of God…they wondered everyone at all things which Jesus did. (KJV)
Luke 21:27	Then they will see the Son of Man coming in a cloud with power and great glory.
Hebrews 1:3	Speaking of the Son – He upholds all things by the word of His power.

The above verses show that the mighty power of God was likewise possessed by His Son. Even when He was here in the flesh and confined in a human body, He demonstrated this: He even had power over the wind and sea (Mark 4:35-41). And at His return His power will be displayed to the full when He defeats all the enemies of God and brings in His heavenly rule upon this earth. Then it will be said: "Alleluia! For the Lord God Omnipotent reigns" (Revelation 19:6).

Who is God? The God of the Bible is omnipresent. He is from everlasting, He will always exist, and He never changes. We can now build further on this picture by adding He is omnipotent. He is the God who possesses absolute power.

40. Omniscience of God

Vicky Wilkinson

We continue with our attempt to describe 'The Person of God'. In the previous three articles we have considered His Omnipresence, His eternality, and His omnipotence. Now we come to the last of the main attributes of God in this series - His Omniscience.

Again, we turn to the *Oxford Dictionary* for the meaning of this word and it states 'knowing everything'. This poses the question, "Does God, the God whom Christians serve and worship, know everything?" What do the Holy Scriptures have to say on this aspect of God's being?

In Isaiah 46:9-10 it says, "I am God and there is none like me, declaring the end from the beginning, and from ancient times things that are not yet done."

Even at the beginning before anything took place, God knew the end. Consider the following:

Daniel 2:21-22	He gives wisdom to the wise and knowledge to those who have understanding. He reveals deep and secret things. He knows what is in the darkness and light dwells with Him.
Psalm 44:21	Would not God search this out? For He knows the secrets of the heart....
Psalm 94:11, 103:14	The Lord knows the thoughts of man ... For He knows our frame and remembers that we are dust.
Psalm 139:15-16	My frame was not hidden from you when I was made in secret ... your eyes saw my substance being yet unformed and in your book they were all written.

The above texts show that God is all knowing. He knew in the beginning how things would turn out and that is why His plan and purpose to save mankind, in and through His Son, Jesus Christ could be put into motion the minute it was needed.

As we have gone through this series we have seen that Jesus Christ also possesses the same attributes of God. Is this so in this instance? Is Jesus omniscient? In Colossians 2:2-3 we read that all the treasures of wisdom and knowledge are hidden in Him. Consider the following:

John 1:47-48	Jesus knew Nathaniel before He met him.
John 2:24	Jesus knew all men.
John 16:30; 21:17	Jesus' disciples perceived that He knew all things.
John 11:14	Jesus knew Lazarus was dead even before He set off for Bethany.
Matthew 9:4	Jesus knew their (the Scribes) thoughts.

Even though Christ Jesus may have relinquished His full omniscience when He came to the earth in human likeness (see Matthew 24:36), He still knew and understood the reason why God the Father sent Him to the earthly home of mankind and made Him like us. He predicted and prepared His disciples for this course of action (Mark 9:30-32). He knew that He must fulfil the Father's will to redeem us and carried it out faithfully to the end, despite the shame and suffering.

To summarise: as we have considered these four attributes. We have seen that the God of the Bible is:

- **omnipresent** (everywhere at the same time)
- **eternal** and **immutable** (from everlasting to everlasting and never changes)
- **omnipotent** (all powerful)
- **omniscient** (all knowing)

Whilst the above attributes paint a picture of a mighty and powerful God, for me the all-consuming attribute of God is found in 1 John 4: 8 which says, "God is Love". Verse 9 continues, "In this the love of God was manifested towards us, that God has sent His only begotten Son into the world, that we might live through Him."

Such love! Therefore, an all-embracing answer to the question *Who is God?* Is

GOD IS LOVE.

41. Why is the Universe just right for life?

Sylvia Penny

Many highly intelligent, educated people ask the above question and some spend years of their lives trying to answer it. They imply that it is really difficult to understand why the universe sustains life, and more importantly, human life.

The Goldilocks Enigma: Why is the Universe Just Right for Life?

Paul Davies, a theoretical physicist, produced a book entitled *The Goldilocks Enigma: Why is the Universe Just Right for Life?* in which he explored this question. In it he suggested a number of theories, including:

a) the multiverse theory (where we inhabit just one of an infinite stream of universes),
b) a *Matrix* type hypothesis (where we live in a type of computer simulation as in the film *The Matrix*), and his favourite,
c) the self-organising universe. This is where the universe so structures itself that it can ask (through the emergence of intelligent life – human beings), "Why is there a universe, rather than nothing?"

Intelligent Design is considered, but only in the sense of a designer of laws rather than individual species, and one where no miracles are involved.

The answer is clear!

However, the answer to this question is clear to Christians! The universe is just right for life because God created the Universe so that it *could* sustain human life. The corollary is that if it *couldn't* have sustained human life, He would never have created it in the first place. This is known as the *anthropic principle.* (The universe was created with man in mind.) Einstein remarked that the most incomprehensible thing about the universe is that it is comprehensible. The fact that the universe is comprehensible implies the emergence of an entity to do the comprehending – i.e. man.

The Bible says that it should be clear to human beings from the Creation that there is a Creator. For example, Psalm 19:1 says "The heavens declare the glory of God; the skies proclaim the work of his hands." It should not be a conundrum or something to puzzle over for years, as to why the Universe and we are here. It should be obvious!

In similar fashion, Romans 1:18-20 says:

> "The wrath of God is being revealed from heaven against all the godlessness and wickedness of men who suppress the truth by their wickedness, since what may be known about God is plain to them, because God has made it plain to them. For since the creation of the world God's invisible qualities – his eternal power and divine nature – have been clearly seen, *being understood from what has been made,* so that men are without excuse."

In this passage, the Apostle Paul makes it quite clear that men are without excuse when it comes to believing in God as Creator, because God's eternal power and divine nature are made plain to men through His Creation.

Making God unnecessary

There are some people who wish to find an alternative explanation for Creation so that God is then unnecessary. They wish to have an intellectually satisfactory way of explaining Him away. If they can do away with a Creator, they can do away with any obligation or responsibility to such a Being. However, when individuals and society decide they can do away with God, society begins to degenerate as a whole.

Returning to the passage in Romans 1, the Apostle Paul describes the type of people who disregarded God:

> "For although they knew God, they neither glorified him as God nor gave thanks to him, but their thinking became futile and their foolish hearts were darkened. Although they claimed to be wise, they became fools …" (verses 21, 22)

> "Furthermore, since they did not think it worthwhile to retain the knowledge of God, he gave them over to a depraved mind, to do what ought not to be done. They have become filled with every kind of wickedness, evil, greed and depravity. They are full of envy, murder, strife, deceit and malice. They are gossips, slanderers, God-haters, insolent, arrogant and boastful; they invent ways of doing evil; they disobey their parents; they are senseless, faithless, heartless, ruthless." (verses 28-31)

In this passage Paul describes a society that ignored God. Much of his description can also be applied to our secular society today. Our intellectuals and philosophers claim to be wise, and yet according to the Bible, they are fools – "The fool says in his heart, 'There is no God'" (Psalm 14:1). The result of such a philosophy is devastating to society, and we can see the evidence of it all around us. We have broken families, child abuse, sexually transmitted diseases, violence, drugs, and the list goes on.

A bleak view of the world

Paul Davies paints a bleak view of the place of humanity within the universe as a whole, and indeed, if there were no God he would be right to do so. Answering the question of what would happen if the human race were destroyed in a forthcoming cataclysm he says, "It may never happen again. The universe may endure for a trillion years shrouded in total mystery, save for a fleeting pulse of enlightenment around one average star in one unexceptional galaxy, 13.7 bn years after it all began." In other words, to him, the whole of the human race is pointless, meaningless, and insignificant. In the grand scheme of things, we are worthless.

Blessings in Christ

Fortunately, as believers, we know better. Ephesians 1-3 makes our blessings in Christ very clear, and very certain. In Christ's eyes we are not worthless – we are priceless, for He bought us with His own life.

> Praise be to the God and Father of our Lord Jesus Christ, who has blessed us in the heavenly realms with every spiritual blessing in Christ. For he chose us in him *before the creation of the world* to be holy and blameless in his sight. In love he predestined us to be adopted as his sons through Jesus Christ, in accordance with his pleasure and will – to the praise of his glorious grace, which he has freely given us in the one he loves. (Ephesians 1:3-6)

Since God had a plan for us *before* He even created the world, it is clear that, to Him, we are not meaningless and insignificant. The universe is just right for life because human beings were in mind *before* God created it. When we know and believe that, what a difference it makes!

The Bible

42. Reading the Bible

Sylvia Penny

When you are a new believer it's hard to know where to start reading the Bible without someone telling you. It's mind-boggling when you first approach it – wondering how it all fits together, working out which bits are relevant for us today, and what to do with the bits that don't seem quite so relevant. It's difficult to know where to start.

It's similar for long-standing believers who, for whatever reason, may have never read much of the Bible. Although bits and pieces are familiar from here and there, sometimes it is still difficult to put it all together. It's like a jigsaw. It may be difficult to know where to start without having someone to point us in the right direction.

And what about long-standing believers who have read and studied the Bible for many years? How should they approach reading the Bible? There is not only one, right, answer to that question. It is different for different people. However, it is often helpful to know what other people do, and how they change throughout their lives, as it may help us in what we do. That has been true for me throughout my life. Learning from other people's experiences has been really helpful.

My story

Years ago, I started by listening to talks on selected books of the Bible – invariably the New Testament - which prompted me to re-read some of these sections of the Bible for myself. At the time, these were mainly Paul's letters to people in different churches, helping them to sort out their faith, their beliefs, and their practical way of living.

After a while, I realised I didn't know much about the gospels, although I knew many of the stories contained in them, as I had learned all about them in Sunday School when I was a child, brought up in the Church of England. However, putting them all together, and knowing where they came from in the Bible was another matter. So,

I decided to read through the whole of the New Testament from start to finish, which meant I started with the gospels. For the first time I found out where all the "stories about Jesus" came from, and how they fitted together.

Because I had listened to many talks on Paul's letters by this time, and also on the historical book of Acts, I was able to follow through the rest of the New Testament fairly easily, as much of this was by then familiar territory. Then I reached Revelation!

Prophecy

Revelation I found fascinating. In my teens, it seemed totally incomprehensible! So, I got side-tracked into studying it "in depth". First though, I was advised to study Daniel, as this gives lots of background to Revelation, and without this I would be sunk! So, looking at Daniel was one of my first detailed looks at the Old Testament. Although, I hasten to add, this isn't the Old Testament book I would recommend anyone else to read first! Again, I found it fascinating, and as a result, became very interested in Biblical prophecy. So much so I did a complete course on Daniel and Revelation provided by the Seventh Day Adventists. I learned a lot, but I also learned that different people had many different views on prophecy. So, from very early on, although very interested in prophecy, I always approached it with caution, knowing it was easy to come to very different conclusions based on the same passages.

Having looked at Daniel, (and then Revelation), I decided it would be sensible to start the Old Testament from the beginning and work through. So, I read a chapter every night, and then carried on and went through the New Testament again. There was much in the Old Testament I didn't understand, but reading it through in the light of what I already knew about the New Testament helped a little. I didn't *study* the Old Testament. I just read it through to get an idea of everything the Bible said. Even though I couldn't remember it all, I knew that, at least, I had read everything the Bible had to say.

Daily Bible reading notes

By this time, a number of Christian friends had mentioned "daily Bible reading notes". So, over the years I embarked on a number of different ones. Some were more helpful than others, but I often found that they were "bitty". They would focus on a small portion of Scripture, but I always wanted to know what the context was. Not having time to do this, I gleaned what I could, but ultimately found many of these unsatisfying.

I then discovered that another Christian friend had decided simply to read through the whole Bible continuously. He read a chapter or so a day, and just kept going. Once he got to the end of Revelation, he went back to Genesis and started again! Having already done this once, I thought maybe I needed to revisit this idea. I have never looked back! Each time I do it (and it can sometimes take three or more years, depending on my other commitments) I see new and different things I have never seen before.

A few years later, I was tempted to start the "reading through the Bible in a year" programme, but having already read right through the Bible I found it took me a lot longer than a year to do this. I didn't want to set an artificial deadline for myself. I decided it didn't matter how long it took as long as long as I got to the end. No one was going to check up on me as to how long that took!

All Scripture is useful

It is surprising, even when you have a fairly good knowledge of Scripture and have grasped the overall plan of God as it unfolds throughout the Bible, how you often notice new things you never noticed before while you are reading through. 2 Timothy 3:16-17 says:

> All Scripture is God-breathed, and is useful for teaching, rebuking, correcting and training in righteousness, so that the man of God may be thoroughly equipped for every good work.

Therefore, although it may not all be written to us, or about us, all Scripture is useful, especially when it is to do with the practical issues of how we should live out our Christian lives. None of us are above and beyond being able to learn more about how God wishes us to live our lives and carry out His wishes.

We, rightly, spend a lot of our time as Christians within our different churches and denominations looking at the New Testament and its teachings. However, by reading through the Bible, chapter by chapter, regularly throughout our lives, we can also become familiar with what the Old Testament has to say, and the stories that would have been familiar to the Jews living at the time of Jesus. Often, if we know the New Testament well, a passage may well come to mind while we are reading through the Old Testament. Jesus often referred to the Old Testament, and he quoted from, or alluded to almost every book we find there.

Using a cross-reference Bible

I have a very useful "wide-margin" bible with plenty of space for my own notes, together with a central column of Bible references. These often point me to other relevant Scriptures linked with the ones I am reading, so if I want to, I can gain a fuller understanding of what is being said while I'm reading through. Because I have no programme to follow, sometimes I stop and spend more time on a particular verse, or phrase, or chapter, that takes my attention. And now and again I make notes of thoughts, or cross references, which are particularly meaningful. Other times I may read three or four chapters without stopping.

The Bible is up-to-date!

As I've got older, I have found I have appreciated the "wisdom" section of the Old Testament more and more – Job, Psalms, Proverbs and Ecclesiastes - and have been struck by how modern and up-to-date many of the sentiments expressed there are. It is amazing how accurately they describe the human condition today, as if they are describing the present world around us. People, it seems, do not change over the centuries. If we are to change, we need the Lord to do this for us.

Meditation

Apart from reading the Bible through, and studying the Bible in detail, another way we can let the Bible help us in our daily walk with the Lord is by meditating on certain verses, or phrases, or chapters. The book of Psalms particularly lends itself to this sort of approach. We can spend some time thinking about what is said and how it can help us. However, it is best to do this once we understand which parts can be applied to ourselves. We need to have a good understanding of the overall plan of God laid out in Scripture, *before* we start to do this, or we may find that, if we take verses out of context, we apply them to ourselves incorrectly. However, with this in mind, meditation on any book of the Bible can be helpful and uplifting. It can help us in our daily walk and it can help us to get to know the Lord, and his plan for us, better and better.

Finally, no matter *how* we approach reading the Bible, there is no doubt that, just like a daily exercise routine, the more we keep to it, the more we benefit.

43. What does the Bible say to *me*?

Sylvia Penny

> All Scripture is God-breathed and is useful for teaching, rebuking, correcting and training in righteousness, so that the man of God may be thoroughly equipped for every good work (2 Timothy 3:16).

We know from the above verse that the whole Bible is useful for us to read, so that we can understand God and learn how to live our lives in accordance with His will. However, does the whole Bible *apply* to each of us? Most of us realise it doesn't! There is a big difference between saying the whole Bible is *useful* and that the whole Bible *applies* to us.

The Old Testament

The Old Testament is easy when we consider whether something applies to us or not. We realise that it relates to Israel, (apart from the first eleven chapters of Genesis), and it is easy to explain why we don't need to sacrifice animals, why we don't have to cast lots, and why men don't have to be circumcised. However, we recognise that adultery and murder are still wrong. In fact, the moral aspects of the Old Testament are still very much applicable to today.

The New Testament

The problem comes when we start looking at the New Testament. Although we know (intellectually) that the vast majority of the New Testament also relates to Israel, we tend to think that most of it, especially the Lord's own words, must also apply to ourselves, Gentiles. Although His sacrifice for sin was for the world, Jesus made it quite clear His earthly ministry was to Israel, so should we take all His words and apply them to ourselves?

Words such as, "Do not go among the Gentiles, or enter any town of the Samaritans. Go rather to the lost sheep of Israel" (Matthew 10:5,6) and "I was sent only to the lost sheep of Israel" (Matthew 15:24) which were spoken by our Lord tend to be forgotten. And in Romans 15:8 Paul clearly states that Jesus was a servant and minister to Israel.

Sometimes more emphasis is placed on the words of Jesus when He was a man walking on earth, rather than on those of our risen Saviour and Lord, after He had ascended to heaven, when He spoke through His chosen apostle to the Gentiles, Paul. However, the reverse should be true. God's revelation in the Bible is progressive and thus greater emphasis should be put on the later parts. Also, we are clearly going to find letters like Hebrews more difficult to understand, as it was written to Christian Jews, during the Acts period.

The seven letters written by Paul to the Gentiles, after the end of the Acts period, are more relevant to us today than some of the things our Lord said to the Jews while He was on earth. These letters are:

1. Ephesians
2. Philippians
3. Colossians
4. 1 Timothy
5. 2 Timothy
6. Titus
7. Philemon

These we can read and are much easier to understand. We can apply almost all of them to ourselves, so that we "may be equipped for every good work". The main problem is trying to put them into practise on a daily basis.

But, what about the rest of Scripture, and particularly the rest of the New Testament? "All Scripture is God-breathed", but we have to be careful not to assume that everything we come across relates to us Gentiles today.

Sell your possessions and give to the poor

One example can be used to demonstrate this. Luke 12:33 says, "Sell your possessions and give to the poor." Jesus said this to His disciples, so why should we also not have to carry this out? After all, in the Acts period the faithful disciples *did* carry this out. "Selling their possessions and goods, they gave to anyone as he had need" (Acts 2:45). However, very few, if any, Christians today carry out this instruction. This is because we not only read Scripture, we also interpret Scripture. We decide what it means in its context. It is only after the correct interpretation of Scripture is made that we can then consider if any of it applies to us today.

In this case, this instruction was made at a time when there was the possibility of the imminent second coming of Christ (Acts 3:19-21), in which case He would have supplied their every need. There was therefore no need to keep hold of their earthly possessions at that time, as when the Lord returned, He would provide for them. Today this is not the case, and so this instruction is no longer applicable. We may however take *some* of the sentiments expressed as an *application* for ourselves. Giving to the poor is a good work at *any* time, so being generous and setting aside some of our money for work with the poor is an excellent idea, and undoubtedly the Lord will bless such an action.

Interpretation is important

It is therefore important when we read the Scriptures to first determine what the interpretation is. What did it mean to those people to whom it was directed and why did the Lord want them to do it? After we are sure of this, we can then look at the application, and see if there is any way we can use what is said to guide us in how we live today. However, if we get the interpretation wrong, it is possible we will end up trying to do something which is no longer required of us today.

So, to answer my question, "What does the Bible say to me?" the easiest answer is to start with Paul's last seven letters, listed above, as the vast majority of what is said in these can be safely applied to us Gentiles today. Once we have got to grips with these, then we can progress on to the gospels, and then on to the rest of the New Testament. Finally, we can go back to the Old Testament, and although much of this will not apply to us today, we *can* learn many lessons from the way God dealt with Israel as a nation and individual Jews during that time.

44. Genesis – Should we take it literally?

Sylvia Penny

Sometimes you hear Christians say that you don't have to believe everything written in Genesis, particularly the earlier chapters of Genesis 1 to 11. To the modern mind, some of what is written is questionable, if not totally unbelievable. So, it is suggested that the themes of Genesis are true, even if the details are not.

For example, was Adam really the very first (and only) man? Was Eve literally created from Adam? Did they really start out in a place called the garden of Eden? And so on. We are led to believe it all sounds a bit like a far-fetched fairy story.

One problem with this view is that in the New Testament the Lord Jesus Himself endorses much of what is said in Genesis, and so does the Apostle Paul and other New Testament writers. The Lord Jesus quotes from Genesis 2 and refers to the Creation account, to the Fall, to Satan, Abel, Noah, the flood, to Lot and the destruction of Sodom. General or specific references are made to Genesis chapters 1,2,3,4,5,6 to 9 and 11, together with other references to the lives of Abraham, Isaac and Jacob.

Below are a few examples to illustrate this.

1. Matthew 19:4,5 says, "Haven't you read," he replied, "that at the beginning the Creator 'made them male and female', and said, 'For this reason a man will leave his father and mother and be united to his wife, and the two will become one flesh'? These are direct quotes from Genesis 1:27 and Genesis 2:24. Here the Lord endorses the special creation of human beings. The reason given in Genesis for the man and woman becoming one is that the woman was 'taken out of man' in the first place. Although the word 'rib' is used, the note in the NIV says alternatively 'part of the man's side'. Some believe that God may have used Adam's DNA to create Eve, but that this would

have been impossible to explain scientifically until now. Whatever the science involved, the fact remains that the Lord Jesus refers to this, and thus confirms what is written.

2. John 8:44 says, "You belong to your father, the devil, and you want to carry out your father's desire. He was a murderer from the beginning, not holding to the truth, for there is no truth in him. When he lies, he speaks his native language, for he is a liar and the father of lies." Here the Lord Jesus clearly alludes to Genesis 3:4 where the serpent speaks to Eve. "You will not surely die," the serpent said to the woman, "For God knows that when you eat of it your eyes will be opened, and you will be like God, knowing good and evil". This is the first recorded lie in the Scriptures, and leads to the fall of mankind. Eve was deceived by Satan's lie (Genesis 3:13), but Adam was not (1 Timothy 2:14). Adam deliberately disobeyed God and thus sin entered the human race. When the Lord refers to Satan, He makes it clear he is a being who exists, and one who is a murderer and a liar. If the 'devil' should be understood to be a concept, a force for evil, a vague idea of anything that isn't 'good', then certainly the Lord Jesus did not make this clear. Rather, He once again endorses what was written in Genesis.

3. Luke 11:50,51 says, "Therefore this generation will be held responsible for the blood of all the prophets that has been shed since the beginning of the world, from the blood of Abel to the blood of Zechariah, who was killed between the altar and the sanctuary." Here the Lord refers to the murder of Abel by Cain, thus endorsing Genesis 4:8 which says, "Now Cain said to his brother Abel, 'Let's go out to the field.' And while they were in the field, Cain attacked his brother Abel and killed him." According to the Lord Jesus these were real people who actually existed.

4. Luke 17:26,27 says, "Just as it was in the days of Noah, so also will it be in the days of the Son of Man. People were eating, drinking, marrying and being given in marriage up to the day Noah entered the ark. Then the flood came and destroyed them all." Here, the Lord refers to Noah and the flood as a fact, told

in Genesis 6 to 8, not as an ancient myth grown up over years of time, embellishhed by each re-telling.

5. He continues in Luke 17:28, "It was the same in the days of Lot. People were eating and drinking, buying and selling, planting and building. But the day Lot left Sodom, fire and sulphur rained down from heaven and destroyed them all." The account of the destruction of Sodom and Gomorrah, and the escape of Lot, is given in Genesis 19, and again the Lord refers to this as a fact of history, not as a story to prove a point.

6. John 8:56 says, "Your father Abraham rejoiced at the thought of seeing my day; he saw it and was glad." Here, not only does the Lord refer to Abraham, He also says He saw Abraham! As a result of this claim the Jews picked up stones to stone Him for blasphemy (John 8:59), but somehow Jesus managed to slip away unharmed. Not only does Jesus endorse Abraham as a historic figure, He claimed to have met him. Genesis 18:22-33 records this encounter, where the two of them discuss the fate of Sodom and Gomorrah. Genesis 11:27 is the first occurrence of Abraham (then Abram), and is included as part of a genealogy that links Shem to Abraham. If Abraham is accepted to be a historic figure, it is difficult to separate him from the genealogical links back to Noah.

So, as we can see, the Lord Jesus confirms much of what is written and recorded in the very early chapters of Genesis. Added to this, there are many other references to these events made by the Apostle Paul and the other New Testament writers. Some of these have been listed below in order to illustrate how detailed is the confirmation of the literal truth of Genesis in the New Testament.

- Acts 14:15 - the living God, who made heaven and earth and sea and everything in them
- Acts 17:24 - the God who made the world and everything in it
- Col 1:16 - for by him all things were created: things in heaven and on earth

- 2 Peter 3:5 - long ago by God's word the heavens existed and the earth was formed out of water and by water
- Hebrews 4:4 - on the seventh day God rested from all his work
- 1 Cor 11:8,9 - for man did not come from woman, but woman from man
- Romans 5:14 - death reigned from the time of Adam to the time of Moses
- 1 Cor 15:22 - as in Adam all die, so in Christ all will be made alive
- 1 Tim 2:13 - for Adam was formed first, then Eve
- 1 Tim 2:14 - Adam was not the one deceived; it was the woman who was deceived
- 1 John 3:12 - Do not be like Cain, who belonged to the evil one and murdered his brother
- Jude 14 - Enoch, the seventh from Adam
- Hebrews 11 - mentions Abel, Cain, Enoch, Noah, Abraham, Isaac, Jacob, and so on
- 2 Peter 3:6 - By these waters also the world of that time was deluged and destroyed (the flood)

Some *may* argue that these other New Testament writers simply wrote from the viewpoint of their day, and that they didn't know any better. However, Scripture tells us that these men's writings were inspired by God and so what we have above is an endorsement of the early chapters of Genesis. Also, when we come to the Lord Jesus' *own* words, we cannot argue this way. We have to accept that what He said was so. If the Lord knew that these people did not exist, and that the events He referred to never actually took place, then we would effectively be accusing Him of dishonesty.

In conclusion then, although it may be hard for some to accept that the very early events in Genesis actually took place as described there, and to accept that the people there actually existed, it is equally difficult to explain why they are confirmed as *facts* by the Lord Jesus Himself if this is not true.

45. Genesis 2 – The Two Trees

Sylvia Penny

We are all familiar with the two trees mentioned in Genesis 2 – the tree of life and the tree of the knowledge of good and evil. There are only a few verses that mention these trees. These are given below.

> And the Lord God made all kinds of trees grow out of the ground – trees that were pleasing to the eye and good for food. In the middle of the garden were the tree of life and the tree of the knowledge of good and evil. (Genesis 2:9)

> And the Lord God commanded the man, "You are free to eat from any tree in the garden; but you must not eat from the tree of the knowledge of good and evil, for when you eat of it you will surely die." (Genesis 2:16,17)

> The woman said to the serpent, "We may eat fruit from the trees in the garden, but God did say, 'You must not eat fruit from the tree that is in the middle of the garden, and you must not touch it, or you will die.'" "You will not surely die," the serpent said to the woman. "For God knows that when you eat of it your eyes will be opened, and you will be like God, knowing good and evil." When the woman saw that the fruit of the tree was good for food and pleasing to the eye, and also desirable for gaining wisdom, she took some and ate it. (Genesis 3:2-6)

> And the Lord God said, "The man has now become like one of us, knowing good and evil. He must not be allowed to reach out his hand and take also from the tree of life and eat, and live for ever." (Genesis 3:22)

> After he drove the man out, he placed on the east side of the Garden of Eden cherubim and a flaming sword flashing back and forth to guard the way to the tree of life. (Genesis 3:24)

Literal or figurative

One question that comes to mind is, are these literal trees, or are they figurative – symbolic of truths that the Lord wished to convey to humankind. One of the best ways to answer this question is to look at other places in Scripture that mention either of these two trees. We will immediately find, looking at a concordance, that the tree of life occurs several times, but the tree of knowledge of good and evil occurs nowhere else in Scripture. A list of the verses that mention the tree of life, in addition to those above, is given below … they all occur in Proverbs or Revelation.

Prov. 3:18	She (wisdom) is a tree of life to those who embrace her; those who lay hold of her will be blessed
Prov. 11:30	The fruit of the righteous is a tree of life, and he who wins souls is wise.
Prov. 13:12	Hope deferred makes the heart sick, but a longing fulfilled is a tree of life.
Prov. 15:4	The tongue that brings healing is a tree of life, but a deceitful tongue crushes the spirit.
Rev. 2:7	To him who overcomes, I will give the right to eat from the tree of life, which is in the paradise of God.
Rev. 22:2	On each side of the river (of the water of life) stood the tree of life, bearing twelve crops of fruit, yielding its fruit each month. And the leaves of the tree are for the healing of the nations.
Rev. 22:14	Blessed are those who wash their robes, that they may have the right to the tree of life and may go through the gates into the city.
Rev. 22:19	And if anyone takes words away from this book of prophecy, God will take away from him his share in the tree of life and in the holy city, which are described in this book.

The trees in Proverbs

Each of the four references to the tree of life in Proverbs is obviously figurative. Wisdom, the fruit of the righteous, a longing fulfilled, and a tongue that brings healing are each in turn likened to a tree of life.

Therefore, using Scripture to understand Scripture, it seems likely that the tree of life in Genesis is also symbolic or figurative. Some may object that in Proverbs there is no definite article, "the". However, in his book *In the Beginning,* Henri Blocher states that in Proverbs "The article is not used before *life*, but that difference is scarcely significant because the construct state implies that the absolute is definite, and in any case the article is often dropped in poetry." In other words, although Proverbs refers to 'a' tree of life, rather than 'the' tree of life, he considers this does not detract from the argument that the tree of life in Genesis is also figurative.

The trees in Revelation

Revelation 2:7 tells us that those who overcome will have the right to eat from the tree of life. The *New Bible Commentary Revised* states that "to eat of the tree of life" is to partake of the fullness of eternal life." Other verses in Revelation that refer to these overcomers are below:

Rev. 2:10	Be faithful, even to the point of death, and I will give you the crown of life.
Rev. 2:17	To him who overcomes, I will give some of the hidden manna. I will also give him a white stone with a new name written of it, known only to him who receives it.
Rev. 2:26-28	To him who overcomes and does my will to the end, I will give authority over the nations – "He will rule them with an iron sceptre; he will dash them to pieces like pottery" - just as I have received authority from my Father I will also give him the morning star.
Rev. 3: 5	He who overcomes will … be dressed in white. I will never erase his name from the book of life, but will acknowledge his name before my Father and his angels.
Rev. 3:12	Him who overcomes I will make a pillar in the temple of my God. Never again will he leave it. I will write on him the name of my God and name of the city of my God, the new Jerusalem, which is coming

	down out of heaven from my God; and I will also write on him my new name.
Rev. 3:21	To him who overcomes, I will give the right to sit with me on my throne, just as I overcame and sat down with my Father on his throne.

These verses clearly portray what is given to the overcomers as figurative, each of the figures symbolising something fuller and greater than eternal life itself. The overcomers have not only eternal life but will also receive a reward; i.e. partake of the fullness of eternal life as the *New Bible Commentary Revised* puts it. Also, referring to Rev. 22:2, it states "as in the case of the water of life, the healing powers of the leaves are taken in a purely spiritual sense." Similarly, the verses in Rev 22:14 and Rev 22:19 may also be understood symbolically as representing eternal life in all its fulness.

The trees in Ezekiel

The descriptions of the river of life and the tree of life in Rev 22:1,2 are reminiscent of Ezekiel 47:6-12, which also refers to the river and the trees, but does not specifically call them "the tree of life". However, the similarity is inescapable. Verses 6-7 and verse 12 are quoted below:

Ezek. 47:6-7	He asked me, "Son of man, do you see this?" Then he led me back to the bank of the river. When I arrived there, I saw a great number of trees on each side of the river.
Ezek. 47:12	Fruit trees of all kinds will grow on both banks of the river. Their leaves will not wither, nor will their fruit fail. Every month they will bear, because the water from the sanctuary flows to them. Their fruit will serve for food and their leaves for healing."

Ezekiel 31 also describes trees in the "garden of God" and "the trees of Eden" and these trees are very obviously figurative. A quick read through these eighteen verses will make this clear. A few of the statements made in this chapter are, "Consider Assyria, once a cedar in Lebanon … the cedars in the garden of God could not rival it …

the envy of all the trees of Eden in the garden of God … I brought it down to the grave … then all the trees of Eden were consoled … you will lie among the uncircumcised, with those killed by the sword." Here nations are symbolised by trees. It is nations and people who experience rivalry and envy, being consoled and being killed by the sword – not trees.

Trees are also used symbolically in many other places; e.g. the fig tree and the olive tree are frequently used as symbols of Israel.

The trees in Genesis

So, to return to the trees in Genesis, I would argue the meaning is to be taken figuratively, rather than literally, as in Ezekiel, Proverbs and Revelation. If this is the case, then we need to understand what the meaning of the symbolism is. We have already seen that the tree of life in Revelation is considered to be symbolic of the fullness of eternal life. It represents close communion with God Who is the inexhaustible source of life and so, at the beginning, Genesis 2:16 suggests that Adam was free to eat from the tree of life, symbolising this relationship. However, after the fall, he no longer had this close communion with God and he was sent out of the garden and barred from the tree of life (Genesis 3:24). The gift of the never-ending fullness of life, symbolised by the tree of life, was withdrawn, and Adam was doomed to die in punishment for his disobedience.

The tree of the knowledge of good and evil

If the tree of life symbolises the fullness of eternal life, then what does the tree of the knowledge of good and evil represent? Genesis 3:5 gives us a clue, when Satan says, "For God knows that when you eat of it your eyes will be opened, and you will be like God, knowing good and evil." In grasping at the fruit of this tree they grasped at equality with God, knowing good and evil. This is confirmed by the Lord God in Genesis 3:22 when He says, "The man has now become like one of us, knowing good and evil." By contrast, the Lord Jesus Who is described as the last Adam in 1 Corinthians 15:45, gave up equality with God when He came to earth as a man. Philippians 2:6,7 says Christ Jesus, "Who, being in very nature God, did not consider equality with God something to be grasped, but made himself nothing, taking the very nature of a servant, being made in human likeness." So, the first Adam sought to grasp something that was *not* his and make it his own (equality with God), resulting in the fall of mankind, whereas the last Adam (Christ) did not grasp at something that *was* His, but was prepared to humble Himself in order to save mankind.

So, the tree stands for equality with God and the fruit for knowing what is right and wrong independently of God. At the heart of sin lies man's claim to autonomy, rather than recognising his total dependence upon God. In other words, we should recognise our total dependence upon God for everything, and not presume to be in control ourselves, deciding what is right and what is wrong. It is clear that if man is left to his own devices, each person ends up doing what is right in his own eyes, rather than what is right in God's eyes, and the result is a moral wilderness.

Literal trees

[1]

To return to our original question as to whether the two trees in Genesis are literal or figurative, we have argued that they have a figurative meaning. We have seen that this is true in other parts of Scripture and it avoids the idea that these trees in the garden of Eden were capable of bestowing life and knowledge on anyone that ate their fruit. Nowhere else in Scripture is there an example of trees having such powers. Rather, these two trees symbolised very deep and real truths that run throughout Scripture. It is only through God that we can receive the fullness of eternal life, and if we presume to do without His direction, the results are disastrous for individuals and for society.

Later in time, the Lord went on to use multiple such symbols with the people of Israel and, on many occasions, they were themselves likened to an olive tree. Literal objects were used as symbols of the

---

[1] For more on this see *Trees and their Symbolism in the Bible* by Vicky Wilkinson, published by The Open Bible Trust.

many Spiritual truths that they were to learn about. Moses was taught how to set up an entire system of worship, with a full priesthood, together with rules on how they were to conduct themselves, both morally and practically, in their day-to-day living. The tabernacle and all the objects within it were given as symbols to help them understand, more fully, the Spiritual reality which lay behind everything that the Lord wanted to share with mankind. The high priest himself symbolised the future Messiah, the Lord Jesus Christ, and everything within the Tabernacle was a copy and shadow of what is in heaven. (See Hebrews 8:1-6.)

In this context, we can see that, in Genesis, the groundwork for the symbolism the Lord was going to use in the future was laid down from the beginning.

46. Ecclesiastes and the meaning of life

Sylvia Penny

Meaningless! Meaningless!" says the teacher.
"Utterly meaningless! Everything is meaningless."
(Ecclesiastes 1:2)

This statement starts the book of Ecclesiastes, written by King Solomon, the wisest man who ever lived. His was a God-given wisdom, and God Himself told Solomon that there had never been anyone like him, nor would there ever be in the future (1 Kings 3:12). So we have to accept that what he wrote in Ecclesiastes is a true and accurate view of the world in which we live.

His view was that everything in this world is meaningless, and that the only way for man to find satisfaction is for him to enjoy his work. He did not arrive at this view lightly, nor after a short time. He had lived a full and immensely rich and varied life, met and talked with many types of people, high and low, rich and poor, and experienced everything that a wealthy person at that time could experience. Despite all that, his conclusion was that nothing satisfied him, and all was meaningless, because in the end, no matter what we achieve, we all die.

For with much wisdom comes much sorrow; the more knowledge, the more grief. (Ecclesiastes 1:18)

It seems the more Solomon understood about the world and the people in it, and the more he found out about what really went on, the more sorrowful he became. He did not like what he discovered, and he became totally disillusioned with life. He tried all sorts of activities. He tried pleasure, laughter, wine, and folly as "I wanted to see what was worthwhile for men to do under heaven during the few days of their lives" (2:1-3). Yet when he had tried everything imaginable, his conclusion was the same, "everything was meaningless" (2:11). Whether a man was wise or foolish made no difference for, "I came to realise that the same fate overtakes them both" – "Like the fool, the wise man too must die!" (2:14,16).

What does a man get for all the toil and anxious striving with which he labours under the sun? All is days his work is pain and grief; even at night his mind does not rest. (Ecclesiastes 2:22,23).

The answer to this is "nothing". It is all meaningless. We become anxious and troubled about what we do, and dwell on problems at night and yet, in the end, what does it all signify? "Whoever loves money never has money enough; whoever loves wealth is never satisfied with his income. This too is meaningless. As goods increase, so do those who consume them. And what benefit are they to the owner except to feast his eyes on them?" (5:10, 11). These comments came from the wealthiest man who had ever lived, who had as much money and riches and possessions as he wished. He knew only too well that no matter what he had, he could always wish for more. No matter how many possessions he had, they never brought any lasting satisfaction as all you can do with possessions is look at them. They didn't bring him any happiness or contentment.

He might as well have written these words yesterday, they are so relevant to our modern western affluent society. So many of us have more than we need, and yet there is so much discontentment and dissatisfaction with life. There is a constant striving to accumulate more wealth and possessions and status, in the mistaken belief that in the end it will lead to happiness. If only people read and believed Ecclesiastes before they jumped on the bandwagon, they could save themselves a lot of heartache and suffering.

Older people tend to talk about "the good old days". Solomon has a word for even these: "Do not say, "Why were the old days better than these?' For it is not wise to ask such questions" (Ecclesiastes 7:10).

As we get older it is tempting to look back to earlier days and imagine things were better when we were younger, for whatever reason. Solomon dispels that myth. All that has changed is our perception. Younger people tend to be more optimistic than older people, and maybe simply because they lack the wisdom and knowledge of older people, which, as we saw earlier, leads to sorrow and disenchantment.

We gradually realise the truth of what Solomon realised and expressed thousands of years ago.

There is something else meaningless that occurs on earth: righteous men who get what the wicked deserve, and wicked men who get what the righteous deserve. This too, I say, is meaningless. (Ecclesiastes 8:14)

Some people, mistakenly, believe that life will be good to good people, and that the wicked will eventually get what they deserve in this life. Yet by simple observation Solomon, and we today, can see that this does not happen. This is very demoralizing, and another reason why Solomon comments, "This too … is meaningless."

Solomon's answer to the meaninglessness of life

Does Solomon offer any sort of comfort, or answer, in all this gloom? He does, but whether we take comfort in what he has to say will depend on our own expectations of life, and how we believe God should be acting in our lives.

Solomon's answer, in a nutshell, is expressed in Ecclesiastes 8:15: "So I commend the enjoyment of life, because nothing is better for a man under the sun than to eat and drink and be glad. Then joy will accompany him in his work all the days of the life God has given him under the sun."

Maybe this answer is a little unexpected, especially to the Christian. Basically we are told we should "eat, drink and be merry" and enjoy life. We should not spend our time worrying about the past or the future, neither of which we can do anything about. We should live in the present, and enjoy each moment as it comes. This sounds a little hedonistic on the face of it, but it need not necessarily be so. It depends upon our interpretation of how we are to enjoy ourselves. Remember, Solomon tried and dismissed many things which people think are enjoyable (money, wine, possessions, women). He ended up saying that men should find satisfaction in his toil, which almost sounds contradictory. However, throughout Ecclesiastes he repeats this wisdom many times, in a number of different ways. "A man can do nothing better than to eat and drink and find satisfaction in his work. This too, I see is from the hand of God, for without Him who can eat or find enjoyment?" (2:24, 25), It is only with God's help that we can find consistent enjoyment in what we do. Without that context we are back to seeing the futility and meaninglessness of everything.

I know that there is nothing better for men than to be happy and do good while they live. That everyone may eat and drink, and find satisfaction in all his toil – this is the gift of God. (Ecclesiastes 3:12-13)

Here Solomon adds a little more to what he has said before, and says men should do good while they live, and that finding satisfaction in their work is a gift from God. Doing good for others (unselfishness) leads to more satisfaction than anything else in this life. This is the ultimate God-given wisdom from Solomon.

Then I realised that it is good and proper for a man to eat and drink, and to find satisfaction in his toilsome labour under the sun during the few days of life God has given him – for this is his lot. Moreover, when God gives any man wealth and possessions, and enables him to enjoy them, to accept his lot and be happy in his work – this is a gift of God. He seldom reflects on the days of his life, because God keeps him occupied with gladness of heart. (Ecclesiastes 5:18-20)

Thus it is a gift from God to enjoy our work, our possessions, and to basically be happy with our lot in life. From the last sentence it seems that if we are kept fully and happily and usefully occupied, then we are unlikely to spend much of our time reflecting on how meaningless life is! When Solomon talked about his younger days, he said, "My heart took delight in all my work, and this was the reward for all my labour" (2:10). In those days he had not started thinking about the futility of life as he was so wrapped up in living it. The point is that there is nothing wrong in doing this as long as we are engaged in wholesome and moral activities. We need to spend our time usefully, helping others, doing good, and enjoying each moment as it comes. As far as enjoyment of life goes, if we can copy the example given us by little children, we won't go far wrong.

At the very end of Ecclesiastes, Solomon sums up everything he says in the final two verses.

Now all has been heard, here is the conclusion of the matter. Fear God and keep His commandments, for this is the whole duty of man. For God will bring every deed into judgment, including every hidden thing, whether it is good or evil. (Ecclesiastes 12:13-14)

Our whole duty is to obey the commands of God in this life, and it is only in this context that we can begin to understand the meaning of our lives while we are on this earth.

47. Luke 6 - Blessings and Woes

Sylvia Penny

The first part of the Sermon on the Mount in Matthew 5 has traditionally been referred to as "the beatitudes". In that passage there are nine sections of people described as "blessed". Here in Luke however, there are just four of these "blessing" sections, but in addition there are also four sections of "woe". A contrast is made between:

1. the poor and the rich
2. the hungry and the well fed
3. the sad and the happy, and
4. the rejected and the respected.

1. The poor and the rich (Luke 6:20,24)

> Blessed are you who are poor, for yours is the kingdom of God. (Luke 6:20)
>
> But woe to you who are rich, for you have already received your comfort. (Luke 6:24)

The poor

In Matthew 5:3 we read, "Blessed are the poor *in spirit*, for theirs is the kingdom of heaven." Luke omits the two words "in spirit", but from Matthew 5 it is immediately obvious that Jesus was not referring to people poor in material possessions (although this may also have been true), but rather those who were poor in spirit. *The New Bible Commentary* says that this "must be understood spiritually (as Matthew indicates) of those who feel dissatisfied with this present world and long for what God has to give to them." Those who are "poor in spirit" are those who are humble and contrite. Isaiah 66:2 says "This is the one I esteem: he who is humble and contrite in spirit, and trembles at my word." Thus, Jesus was not saying anything new and radical here. He was repeating what Isaiah had already stated 600 years earlier. Those who acknowledge their own spiritual poverty, and who come to God to seek real life, are those who God esteems and blesses. In this context to be blessed is to be happy, and those who are esteemed by God can be truly happy because of what is promised to them. Theirs is the kingdom of God, which means that they are a part of the family of God in this life, and will receive eternal life in the next.

The rich

Luke then contrasts the poor with the rich. Again, the rich here are not those rich in material possessions (although this may also have been true), but rather those who are rich in spirit. What does this mean? Set in contrast with those poor in spirit it means those who are self-exalted and rich in their own eyes. They feel they have no need of God, they are self-satisfied, and they take pleasure in only earthly things. Jesus says that people like this have already received their comfort, and the implication is that they will therefore have no part in the kingdom of God. Those who reject God and have no need of Him will not receive eternal life.

Although Jesus' words are spoken to His disciples and followers, it may well be true that some of His words referred particularly to the Pharisees. Later, in Luke 11:37-53 Jesus specifically addresses six "woes" to the Pharisees, and the equivalent passage in Matthew 23 has seven "woes" addressed to them. Thus, "woe to you who are rich" may well have been aimed at the Pharisees, who thought themselves rich in righteousness, as made clear by Jesus in Luke 18:9 which says "To some who were confident of their own righteousness and looked down on everybody else, Jesus told this parable …", and the parable which follows is about a Pharisee and a Tax Collector. Also, Luke 5:31,32 says "It is not the healthy who need a doctor, but the sick. I have not come to call the righteous, but sinners to repentance." Here Jesus was talking to the Pharisees, and ironically referred to them as "righteous", as that was their own assessment of themselves (see also Matthew 9:13, Luke 15:7). However, Romans 3:10 clearly states, "there is no-one righteous, not even one". Righteousness comes from God alone, and can only be ours through faith, as stated in Romans 3:22. "This righteousness from God comes through faith in Jesus

Christ to all who believe. There is no difference, for all have sinned and fall short of the glory of God".

Although Jesus refers to the rich figuratively in this passage to make a contrast with the poor, it is true that in many other parts of Scripture He warns against the love of literal riches. It is not the riches in themselves that are the problem, rather than the attitude towards them. It is implied many, many times that once a person is rich it is very difficult for them not to attach too great an importance to their wealth, and that they become over concerned in maintaining and increasing their wealth. The parable of the rich fool in Luke 12:13-21 concludes "But God said to him, 'You fool! This very night your life will be demanded from you. Then who will get what you have prepared for yourself?' This is how it will be with anyone who stores up things for himself but is not rich towards God." Although it does not say a person cannot be rich towards God *and* also have great riches, it implies that this is a rare person indeed. Luke 18:18-30 refers to a rich ruler, who although a good man, was unable to part with his wealth. When he realised how attached he was to his own money, he was very sad, *but still unable to part with it.*

So, in Luke 5:24 when Jesus says "woe to you who are rich", although predominantly figurative, it could well have a literal application, as wealth seems to become an effective barrier to accepting our need for God. This may well explain the decline in Christianity in the affluent west in recent years, as the majority of the population live in wealth and comfort beyond the wildest dreams of most people who have ever lived.

2. The hungry and the well fed (Luke 6:21,25)

> Blessed are you who hunger now, for you will be satisfied. (Luke 6:21)
>
> Woe to you who are well fed now, for you will go hungry. (Luke 6:25)

Again, if we compare this with Matthew 5:6, we will see that this should also be understood figuratively rather than literally. Matthew

5:6 says, "Blessed are those who hunger and thirst *for righteousness*, for they will be filled". The promise that they will be filled is in the future however. As we have seen, Romans 3:10 tells us that no-one is righteous in this life, but that we will be made righteous in the next, through Christ's death on the cross (Romans 5:19).

References to food and drink, and to hunger and thirst, are often figurative in the Scriptures. Isaiah 55:1,2 says, "Come, all you who are thirsty, come to the waters; and you who have no money, come, buy and eat! Come, buy wine and milk without money and without cost. Why spend money on what is not bread, and your labour on what does not satisfy? Listen, listen to me, and eat what is good, and your soul will delight in the richest of fare." Here the Lord is referring to His words, and telling the people if they listened to Him, they would have life.

When Christ talked to the woman at the well in Samaria, He also referred to this spiritual water. John 4:13,14 says, "Everyone who drinks this (literal) water will be thirsty again, but whoever drinks the water I give him will never thirst. Indeed, the water I give him will become in him a spring of water welling up to eternal life." A short time later, He spoke to a crowd, and told them "But here is the bread that comes down from heaven, which a man may eat and not die. I am the living bread that came down from heaven. If anyone eats of this bread, he will live for ever" (John 6:50,51). Christ was not saying anything new. Isaiah had said the same things many hundreds of years earlier.

On the contrary, those that think they have no need of God, and those that do not wish to listen to Him, will starve spiritually. They are under the illusion that they are filled with good things, primarily material things, but such things do not give lasting contentment or happiness. In the end they will go hungry. This is referred to, again, in Isaiah 65:11,13, "But as for you who forsake the Lord … who spread a table for Fortune … this is what the Sovereign Lord says: "My servants will eat, but you will go hungry; my servants will drink, but you will go thirsty."

3. The sad and the happy (Luke 6:21,25)

> Blessed are you who weep now, for you will laugh. (Luke 6:21)

> Woe to you who laugh now, for you will mourn and weep. (Luke 6:25)

The equivalent passage in Matthew 5:4 says, "Blessed are those who mourn, for they will be comforted." Here, although the mourning and laughing are not figurative, we still have to understand *why* there is weeping, and *why* there is laughter. The Lord does not spell this out. However, in the context of the two previous statements, about the rich and the poor and the hungry and the well fed, it makes sense to understand that the weeping and mourning results from sorrow over sinfulness, both personal sin, and also that of society around, while the laughter will be in the future, in eternal life, when their will be no more sin, and no more sorrow (Revelation 21:4).

James 4:8,9 says, "Come near to God and he will come near to you. Wash your hands, you sinners, and purify your hearts, you double-minded. Grieve, mourn and wail. Change your laughter to mourning and your joy to gloom." In this passage James tells believers that they should submit themselves to God. He tells them that anyone who chooses to be a friend of the world becomes an enemy of God. Those that purify their hearts, will recognise their own sinfulness, and so their laughter will turn to mourning, and their joy to gloom, just as we read in Luke 6:21.

In contrast, in the future, the mourning will turn to laughter, and those that mourn in this life will be comforted in the next. If we go back to Isaiah again, Isaiah 61:2,3 says, " … (He has sent me) to comfort all who mourn, and provide for those who grieve in Zion – to bestow on them a crown of beauty instead of ashes, the oil of gladness instead of mourning, and a garment of praise instead of a spirit of despair." Jeremiah 31:13 also refers to that time, " … I will turn their mourning into gladness; I will give them comfort and joy instead of sorrow." And Revelation 21:4, which we briefly mentioned above says, "He will wipe every tear from their eyes. There will be no more death or mourning or crying or pain, for the old order of things has passed away."

However, for those who laugh now, there will be mourning and weeping in the future. This refers to those who are happy with the standard of their own life, and the standard of society around them. They do not see the sinfulness surrounding them, or, if they do, they do not care. There are many verses in Matthew's gospel, and one in Luke, that refer to weeping and gnashing of teeth by such people in the future. Matthew 13:41,42 says, "The Son of Man will send out his angels, and they will weed out of his kingdom everything that causes sin and all who do evil. They will throw them into the fiery furnace, where there will be weeping and gnashing of teeth." Similar verses can be found in Matthew 8:12; 13:50; 22:13; 24:51; 25:30; 25:41; and Luke 13:28.

Although all of the verses quoted above refer specifically to Jewish believers and unbelievers, the verses in Luke 6 quoted at the beginning of this section may be applied just as much to believers and unbelievers today as they applied to those the Lord was speaking to in the Sermon below the Mount. We should feel as much sorrow today over our own sinfulness and shortcomings as they did then, and also over the standard of society around us, particularly in this day and age when moral standards seem to be deteriorating more and more swiftly.

4. The rejected and the respected (Luke 6:22,26)

> Blessed are you when men hate you, when they exclude you and insult you and reject your name as evil, because of the Son of Man. (Luke 6:22)
>
> Woe to you when all men speak well of you, for that is how their fathers treated the false prophets. (Luke 6:26)

Like those who weep and those who laugh in the previous section, this section is also literal. However, why should they be blessed (happy) when men hate them, yet woeful when men speak well of them? Again, this continues the same theme of the other blessings and woes. We have to understand the *reason why* they are hated, insulted and rejected. It is because of the Son of Man. In other words, the Lord is talking to believers here, and warning them they will suffer as a result of their faith in Him. 1 Peter 4:13-16 elaborates on this theme of suffering for being a Christian, and says, "But rejoice that you participate in the sufferings of Christ, so that you may be overjoyed when his glory is revealed. If you are insulted because of the name of Christ, you are blessed, for the Spirit of glory and of God rests on you. If you suffer, it should not be as a murderer or thief or any other kind of criminal, or even as a meddler. However, if you suffer as a Christian, do not be ashamed, but praise God that you bear that name."

Peter makes it clear that it is not suffering for *any* reason that is to be rejoiced in, but only suffering as a direct result of being a follower of Christ. In that case, we are not to be ashamed, but to praise God, and be happy. This has never been easy to put into practise, either 2000 years ago when this was written, or in this day and age, as no-one likes to be excluded, insulted or rejected.

However, Luke 6:23 gives some comfort to those who have to endure such treatment, as it says, "Rejoice in that day and leap for joy, because great is your reward in heaven. For that is how their fathers treated the prophets." Many passages in Scripture refer to there being a reward in heaven for those who endure suffering and rejection in this life as a result of their faith, and for those who put their faith into practise by helping others. It is not the suffering and rejection by itself that engenders a reward, nor is it doing good works by themselves that receives a reward, but rather it is the suffering and good works *motivated by faith in Christ* that results in a reward in heaven.

On the other hand, the Lord condemns those who all men speak well of, which seems strange until we understand *why*. He explains that the false prophets in the past were spoken well of by man. This was simply because the false prophets always told the people what they wanted to hear, rather than the truth, which has never been as popular. Jeremiah 23:32 refers to some of these false prophets, "They tell them and lead my people astray with their reckless lies, yet I did not send or appoint them." Just as in the previous 'woes', it is not the fact that men speak well of a person that is the problem, it is the *reason* that they are spoken well of. Generally speaking, it is those who try to live a holy and godly life that tend to be condemned and rejected by an unbelieving world, whereas those who go along with the ways of the world and endorse their actions become popular and well thought of. We can certainly see this principle in action all around us today, where the rich and famous are idolised despite their questionable activities and immoral lifestyles. On the other hand, principled and good living Christians are condemned as being intolerant when they refuse to condone the immoral behaviour they see around them.

Summary

So, these few verses concentrate on the contrast between two types of people. One sort is outwardly to be pitied by men, but are blessed by Jesus because they have a spiritual relationship with God through the recognition of their own sinfulness and their need of Christ. The other sort is self-satisfied, and are happy with material possessions and being respected by people around them. They are not concerned with receiving any blessings from Jesus, nor in having any sort of relationship with God.

The first two 'blessings' and 'woes' are figurative, whereas the last two are literal. However, all four can be applied to the contrast between believers and unbelievers in any day and age, whether in our modern twenty-first century western society, or in the Jewish society of 2,000 years ago.

48. Three Challenging Verses (1 Thessalonians 5:16-18)

Sylvia Penny

Be joyful always;
pray continually;
give thanks in all circumstances,
for this is God's will for you in Christ Jesus.
(1 Thessalonians 5:16-18)

It is not difficult to understand what these verses are saying – they are very straightforward. The difficulty is putting them into practice. The will of God is encapsulated here in just a few words. It is very clear, very concise, and very difficult!

Joy

Firstly, there is *joy*. Are any of us always joyful? Under the usual definition of this word – probably not. Webster's Dictionary defines *joy* as "a very glad feeling; happiness; great pleasure; delight." It is a temporary state depending on a recent event. So how can we be "joyful always"? Other Scriptures can help us understand this. Galatians 5:22,23 describes the fruit of the Spirit as "love, joy, peace, patience, kindness, goodness, faithfulness, gentleness and self-control". This is a list of spiritual qualities that a believer develops as a result of the indwelling Holy Spirit with Whom we are sealed from the day we believe (Ephesians 1:13).

These spiritual qualities are continual, and increase with our growing maturity as Christians. Romans 15:13 says "May the God of hope fill you with all joy and peace as you trust in him, so that you may overflow with hope by the power of the Holy Spirit." Here joy is linked with hope, and the power of the Holy Spirit. Similarly, Romans 12:12 says "Be joyful in hope". So, our joy as Christians is linked with our hope, and Hebrews 11:1 tells us "faith is being sure of what we hope for and certain of what we do not see." Through faith our hope is eternal life and righteousness, and Christian joy is linked with the certainty of this fact.

This spiritual joy does not therefore depend upon our circumstances. In a number of passages Paul talks about his own joy, *despite* his circumstances. In 2 Corinthians 7:4 he says "in all our troubles my joy knows no bounds". In the following verse he says "this body of ours had no rest, but we were harassed at every turn – conflicts on the outside, fears within." (For a comprehensive list of Paul's troubles, read 1 Corinthians 11:22-28.)

Many of us may not suffer conflicts on the outside, but maybe we can identify with the "fears within". Despite these, we can still experience the joy of knowing our future hope of eternal life is safe and secure. Paul goes on in verse 7 "He told us about your longing for me, your deep sorrow, your ardent concern for me, so that my joy was greater than ever." Paul was consoled by their concern for him. Despite his many troubles, the thought that others were concerned about him gave him strength and joy.

1 Thessalonians 1:6 says "You became imitators of us and of the Lord; in spite of severe suffering, you welcomed the message with the joy given by the Holy Spirit." Here again joy is described as being given by the Holy Spirit, and is experienced despite severe suffering.

James 1:2-4 adds another thought: "Consider it pure joy, my brothers, whenever you face trials of many kinds, because you know that the testing of your faith develops perseverance. Perseverance must finish its work so that you may be mature and complete, not lacking anything." Here, another reason for joy in the face of trials is given. It is because difficulties develop our character, and help to mature us in the faith. An easy life does not necessarily result in maturity, but quite often the reverse.

So then, what actually is joy in the Scriptural sense? *Strong* defines it as being "calmly happy and well off". Scriptural joy is therefore an appreciation of how well off we are (in Christ) in spite of any problems and sufferings we may have here on earth.

Finally, in Philemon 7 Paul says "Your love has given me great joy and encouragement". Again, it is other people, and their support and love that gave Paul great comfort and joy. He loved and supported them, and in return they loved and supported him. Thus, another way we can experience this spiritual joy is by helping and supporting one another, in the same way Paul and his fellow believers did.

Prayer

Secondly, there is prayer. 1 Thessalonians 5:17 simply says "pray continually". How can we do this? After all, most of us will have many duties and commitments to fulfil on a daily basis. We simply cannot kneel and pray continually. Therefore, many understand this to mean adopting a prayerful attitude. We should be aware of the Lord in everything we do and say throughout the day. If we remembered to do this all the time, it is likely our attitude, and hence our behaviour, would improve considerably. Often throughout the day, although we cannot spend a long time in thoughtful prayer, we are able to direct our thoughts towards God, and ask Him to watch over our next action, or our next conversation. If we are constantly aware of God's presence in our lives, it makes a difference. Many people are "on their best behaviour" if they feel someone is watching them – having a prayerful attitude is even more effective.

There are so many different things said about prayer throughout the Scriptures, that I have selected just a few helpful verses to look at. Paul himself said that we do not know what we should pray for (Romans 8:26), but that the Holy Spirit will help us in our weakness. We can take comfort from the fact that even Paul did not always find prayer easy.

Ephesians 6:18 says "pray in the Spirit on all occasions with all kinds of prayers and requests." This is very similar to 1 Thessalonians 5:17. It encourages us to pray on any and every occasion. Again, Colossians 4:2 says "Devote yourselves to prayer, being watchful and thankful." Here prayer is again linked to thankfulness. Philippians 4:6,7 says "Do not be anxious about anything, but in everything, by prayer and petition, with thanksgiving, present your requests to God. And the peace of God, which transcends all understanding, will guard your hearts and your minds in Christ Jesus." Here, if we pray with thanksgiving, we will have the peace of God. Once again, prayer is strongly linked with thanksgiving. It is a recurring theme!

In Philippians 1:3,4 Paul says "I thank my God every time I remember you. In all my prayers for all of you, I always pray with joy…" So, his prayers for them are linked with both thankfulness and joy. In fact, Paul's letter to the Philippians is full of joy, as the words "joy" and "rejoice" are used fourteen times.

Finally, 2 Thessalonians 1:11 says, "We constantly pray for you, that our God may count you worthy of his calling, and that by his power he may fulfil every good purpose of yours and every act prompted by your faith." Paul again refers to praying constantly. The Thessalonian believers had good intentions, and he prayed for them to follow these through, so that they actually carried them out.

Thankfulness

Thirdly, there is thankfulness. 1 Thessalonians 5:18 says we should give thanks in all circumstances. It doesn't tell us that this is easy. It just tells us that this is God's will. How can we do this?

Colossians 2:6,7 says, "So then just as you received Christ Jesus as Lord, continue to live in him, rooted and built up in him, strengthened in the faith as you were taught, and overflowing with thankfulness." Similar to joy, thankfulness here does not depend upon our outward circumstances. It depends on our relationship with the Lord, our acceptance of Him as our Saviour, and our dependence on Him for the security of our future hope of eternal life, and an appreciation of all the Spiritual blessings we have in Him (Ephesians 1:3). We can be thankful despite our circumstances, and not necessarily as a result of them. We may also possess many material things, but as many discover, once we have more than we need it is very easy to become discontented, focusing on those who have more than us. Unfortunately, materialism produces a society of malcontents rather than a society with gratitude at its heart.

Finally, the passage in Colossians 3:15-17 combines peace, thanks and gratitude. Paul says in these verses, "Let the peace of Christ rule in your hearts, since as members of one body you were called to peace. And be thankful. Let the word of Christ dwell in you richly as you teach and admonish one another with all wisdom, and as you sing psalms, hymns and spiritual songs with gratitude in your hearts to God. And whatever you do, whether in word or deed, do it all in the name of the Lord Jesus, giving thanks to God the Father through him."

Conclusion

These three verses combine many of the thoughts in this article. Christian joy, peace, prayerfulness, and thankfulness are often linked together in many different passages, and for good reason. They are very difficult to separate, and are difficult to practise and experience in isolation. They are all linked together, and depend upon one another. It is good to meditate on these verses, and bring them to mind frequently, in order to help us on our Christian pathway.

Spiritual Subjects

49. Is faith God's gift to man?

Sylvia Penny

It is quite clear from Scripture that salvation from sin to eternal life is a free gift from God, given to anyone who puts their faith in Him:

> For the wages of sin is death, but *the gift of God is eternal life in Christ Jesus our Lord.* (Romans 6:23)
>
> For God so loved the world that He gave His one and only Son, that *whoever believes in Him shall not perish but have eternal life.* (John 3:16)

However, is it true to say that faith itself is also a gift from God? If it is, then surely everyone would be saved, as God would not select some to receive the gift of faith, and exclude others. Yet everyone is not saved. Some people decide to put their faith in the Lord Jesus as their Saviour, whereas others do not.

The belief that all faith comes from God as a gift may be an attempt to show how absolutely nothing worthwhile can come from man, and how everything which is good must only come from God. Thus, the *motivation* for this view may be praiseworthy, but is it correct?

Ephesians 2:8, 9

One favourite Scripture on which this view is based is Ephesians 2:8-9:

> For it is by grace you have been saved, through faith – and this not from yourselves, it is the gift of God – not by works, so that no-one can boast

Here, some mistakenly suppose that the 'gift of God' refers to faith rather than to salvation. However, there are two good reasons to reject this view:

(1) *The New Bible Commentary*, on page 1111, says on this verse: "*This* is neuter in the Greek and cannot look back to *faith* (Gk. *Pistis*, a feminine noun) .... It is the whole process of salvation that forms the antecedent to the word 'this', as in 2 Corinthians 5:18." In other words, the Greek language makes it clear that *salvation* is the gift referred to, not faith, whereas the English language, being less precise, does not make it quite so clear.

(2) There are many other verses in Scripture which refer to salvation and eternal life being gifts from God, whereas there are *none* which refer to our faith in Christ as Saviour being a gift from God. If this is what this verse is saying it stands alone in Scripture.

Defining *faith*

It is helpful to know the definition of the word *faith* as used in the New Testament. The Greek word is *pistis*, and William Barclay in *The New Testament Volume II, The Letters and the Revelation*, page 300, states: "The main meaning of faith, the characteristically Pauline meaning, is total commitment to Jesus Christ (Galatians 2:16; 3:26; 3:34). It is accepting Jesus Christ at His word, both in His demands and in His promises."

This saving faith, this total commitment to Jesus Christ, is not therefore a gift from God, but rather *the channel by which* we receive the gift of salvation from God. By exercising this faith, by opening up this channel, we choose to let God give us this wonderful gift of salvation. He never forces Himself upon anyone.

It is this understanding of faith which helps us to avoid the extreme Calvinistic position, in which it is believed that a person will *only* be saved if *God chooses to give them the gift of faith*. If someone remains an unbeliever, then rather than being their own fault for lack of faith, it is God's fault for not giving them this gift.

So although at first sight it seems that by attributing all faith as a gift from God, His greatness and goodness is being magnified. In fact, it leads to the logical conclusion that God can be blamed for the lack of faith of all unbelievers, which is untenable.

Faith as a Gift

There is one verse in Scripture which does refer to faith as being a gift from God, but it is clear from the context that it is not '*saving*' *faith* which is referred to:

> To one there is given through the Spirit the message of wisdom, to another the message of knowledge by means of the same Spirit, *to another faith by the same Spirit,* to another gifts of healing by that one Spirit, to another miraculous powers, to another prophecy, to another distinguishing between spirits, to another speaking in different kinds of tongues, and to still another the interpretation of tongues. (1 Corinthians 12:8-10)

In *The Miracles of the Apostles*, (by Michael Penny) page 173, he says of this verse: "We read of the gift of faith in 1 Corinthians 12:9 and, possibly, in 13:2 and Romans 12:6. This cannot refer to the faith placed in Christ for salvation for that was, and is, possessed by all believers. This must be something extra, like the faith of those mentioned in Hebrews 11: the faith that overcomes, like David's faith when he faced Goliath, or Peter's and John's when they faced Caiaphas and company (Acts 4:8,13)."

During the Acts period many wonderful gifts were bestowed upon many different believers for different purposes. However, each believer did not receive *every* gift. The *gift of faith* was just one of these special gifts, given for a particular purpose. It was not the *saving faith* referred to in many other parts of Scripture. This gift was given by God to people who were *already believers*; those who already had a 'saving' faith.

Conclusion

Salvation is a wonderful gift we receive from God. How do we receive this gift? Simply by believing in the Lord Jesus Christ as our

Saviour and putting our faith in Him. Once we have heard the good news, the gospel, of our salvation all we have to do is accept it and believe it. As a result of *our* faith in the Lord, we receive righteousness and eternal life from Him. The faith comes from us; everything else that follows, and the many blessings we receive as a result, all come from the Lord.

50. Faith and healing

Sylvia Penny

In Scripture, was faith necessary for healing to take place? Many would answer "Yes!" There are a number of Scriptures which seem to say this, which may be why many Christians believe this to be true. However, if every reference to healing in the New Testament is looked at, it soon becomes apparent that this is not the case.

There are literally dozens of references to healing in the New Testament, and so it is beyond the scope of this article to cover them all. This is simply meant as an overview which will give a starting point for anyone who has ever wondered about the relationship between faith and healing in the New Testament.

John's Gospel

One of the clearest passages in the New Testament which gives the *reason* Jesus healed people is John 4:43-54. Here, Jesus healed an official's son. Verse 48 says: "'Unless you people see miraculous signs and wonders,' Jesus told him, 'you will never believe.'" Following on, in verse 53, *after* his son had been healed, it says, "Then the father realised that this was the exact time at which Jesus said to him, 'Your son will live.' So he and all his household believed." The official's son was not healed because of his faith. Instead, once the father saw that his son had been healed, it was then that he believed, and put his faith in Jesus. His faith was the *result* of healing, *not* the cause.

It was prophesied in the Old Testament that when the Messiah came He would make the blind see, the deaf hear, the lame leap, the mute speak and heal the sick (Isaiah 35:5,6). When John the Baptist had doubts as to whether Jesus was the Messiah, this was the very message Jesus sent to him (see Luke 7:21,22). Matthew 8:16,17 is similar where it says, "When evening came many who were demon-possessed were brought to Him, and He drove out the spirits with a word and healed *all the sick*. This was to fulfil what was spoken through the prophet Isaiah: 'He took up our infirmities and carried our diseases.'"

We can see that the reason for Jesus healing was to show that He was the promised Messiah, and such miracles were performed *so that* people would accept Him, and put their faith in Him. The concept of having to have faith *first*, before healing took place, is contrary to this.

Everyone was healed

As in the above two quotations, there are numerous other places in Scripture where it is recorded that *everyone* who came to Jesus was healed. He did not single out those who had faith from those who did not. In accordance with Old Testament prophecy He healed *all* those who came to Him (see Matthew 4:23, 24; 8:16; 9:35; 10:1, 8; 12:15; 14:36; 15:29, 30; 19:2; 21:14; Mark 1:34; 3:10; Luke 4:40; 5:15, 17; 6:18, 19; 7:21; 9:11; Acts 5:16). In addition, we are told in a number of passages that Jesus healed out of compassion for the people (see Matthew 9:35, 36; 14:14; 20:34; Mark 1:41; Luke 5:12; 7:13, 14). In *none* of these 25 or more references is there any mention of faith.

If it is our belief that faith is necessary for healing, then we would have to assume that all of these people, each and every one, was a believer. However, Scripture does not tell us this, and, as we have seen, expressly tells us that the official did *not* become a believer until *after* his son was healed. Therefore, it does seem more Scriptural to assume that many of these people put their faith in Jesus as a *result* of their healing.

No faith was required

In addition to the Scriptures cited above, there are others which refer to the healing of individuals, but again, no mention is made of faith being a requirement for healing in these passages (see Matthew 8:8, 13; Mark 7:31-37; 8:22-25; Luke 13:12; 14:4; 22:51; John 5:13; John 9:1-12; Acts 3:11; 9:34). It is therefore clear that the Scriptures refer to healing, independently of faith, many times. As this is so, why is it that many people believe that faith was necessary for healing?

Sozo means "to save"

As stated at the beginning, there are a number of Scriptures that seem to say this (Matthew 9:22, Mark 5:34 and Luke 8:48 about the woman bleeding; Mark 10:52 about blind Bartimaeus; and Luke 17:19 about one of ten lepers). On each of these occasions the NIV says: "Your faith has healed you." The Greek word used for 'heal' in these passages is *sozo*, which means 'to save'. However, this Greek word has several meanings depending on the context. It means salvation from danger, suffering, physical death, and sickness, but it also means the spiritual and eternal salvation granted to those who believe in the Lord Jesus Christ. In these passages, the translators translated *sozo* as 'healed' rather than 'saved'. However, a quick glance at an Englishman's Greek Concordance of the New Testament shows that the Greek word *sozo* is used 106 times in the New Testament, and on 91 occasions it is translated 'saved'!

One of these 91 occurrences is in Luke 7:50: "Jesus said to the woman, *'Your faith has saved you;* go in peace.'" Here, the word *sozo* is correctly translated 'saved', as on this occasion the woman was not healed of any sickness, and it is therefore obvious that it must mean spiritual salvation. However, in Luke 8:48 the identical Greek word is used, in an identical phrase, but this time it is translated 'healed': "Then He said to her, 'Daughter, your faith has healed you. Go in peace.'" Because the woman had indeed been healed of a sickness the translators decided to use the word 'healed' instead of 'saved'. By doing so they make it appear that it was her faith which healed her, rather than that it was faith which *saved* her. However, if they had translated this consistently, it would have been translated in the same way as Luke 7:50. It is probable that her healing led to her putting her faith in Jesus, which resulted in her salvation, just as it did in the passage in John 4:43-54 where the official became a believer as a result of his son being healed.

In Luke 18:42 the KJV translates *sozo* as 'saved': "And Jesus said unto him, 'Receive thy sight: thy faith hath saved thee.'" However, the NIV has altered this to 'healed'. On this occasion a blind man received his sight. Which translation is closer to the original meaning in this instance? Surely again, the answer is 'saved' rather than ‘healed’. In order to be consistent, each of the passages cited above would have been better translated, “Your faith has saved you” rather than “Your faith has healed you”.

The ten lepers

The passage in Luke 17:11-19, which describes the healing of the ten lepers, uses three different Greek words for ‘healing’. Each of these Greek words has a different shade of meaning and the NIV attempts to capture the differences by using different English words:

- verse 14: And as they went they *were cleansed* (*katharizo*)
- verse 15: One of them, when he saw he *was healed* (*iaomai*)
- verse 19: Rise and go; your faith *made you well* (*sozo*)

Katharizo is mostly used for cleansing from leprosy in the New Testament. It is *never* used in conjunction with faith. *Iaomai* is mostly used of healing in a physical sense. Again, this word is *never* used in conjunction with faith. In fact, in all the passages of Scripture quoted earlier in this article the Greek words used for ‘heal’ (*katharizo*, *iaomai*, or *therapeuo*), are never used in conjunction with ‘faith.’

However, sozo, as we have seen, is mostly translated ‘saved’, but on occasions has been translated ‘heal’. It is translated ‘heal’ when used in conjunction with faith, but as we have seen, it would be far more consistent to translate it ‘save’, as on this occasion of the ten lepers. It is clear that although Jesus physically healed all ten lepers, only one was grateful enough to return and give thanks and praise to Jesus. It was his faith which led him to return and give thanks, and so Jesus told him, “Your faith has saved you.” He did not say this to the other nine. They were physically healed (*iaomai*), but not saved (*sozo*). Again, this is in accordance with John 4:43-54 where it was shown that healing led to faith, and *not* that faith resulted in healing. If faith were required for healing, then the other nine lepers would not have been cleansed of their leprosy.

Conclusion

There are further passages which also deal with the relationship between faith and healing which have not been included in this article. For instance, those who already had faith and were saved were, of course, not excluded from being healed, and there are examples in Scripture of such people being healed. However, perhaps the passages quoted above are enough to give a Scriptural overview of this subject, and to show that rather than faith being necessary for healing, instead the reverse was true. *Healing resulted in faith.*

51. Is prayer scientific?

Sylvia Penny

Some time ago I read an article entitled *The Science of Prayer*. It described a variety of scientific experiments that had been conducted in the USA in order to test whether prayer really works. My first reaction to this was to be sceptical. Then I wondered what good such experiments might do. Then I wondered what God would think of such experiments.

The first verse quoted was Mark 11:24 where Jesus says, "Therefore I tell you, whatever you ask for in prayer, believe that you have received it, and it will be yours." However, Jesus was speaking to His chosen twelve disciples, and at a time before His death and resurrection. It was a special time, a special group of people, and a special place, and His words may well not be applicable to all people living at all times in history. Such verses taken out of context, can lead to disappointment and confusion when prayers are not answered in the way expected or desired. At worst, they can lead to disillusionment with Christianity, in the mistaken belief that God has in some way let us down, or that we do not have "enough" faith. So, I continued reading the article, wondering what conclusions would be reached.

Scientific Studies

A number of studies were cited, which I have summarised below:

- A 30-year long California study of 2,600 people showed that prayer improved the immune system and lessened depression/anxiety
- Psychologists from Sheffield Hallam University and Ulster University studied the church attendance, prayer and faith of 474 UK students. Those who attended church and prayed daily or often, were found to be less depressed and anxious and felt better psychologically than those who rarely prayed.

- In 1988, a ten-month, double blind study by San Francisco cardiologist Randolph Byrd involved 383 coronary patients. Half were prayed for by Christians, half weren't. The patients not prayed for needed five times more antibiotics, and developed three times as many complications.
- In 1998, a twelve-month study of 1,000 coronary patients at Mid-American Heart Institute in Kansas City was conducted, and the findings supported the earlier study.
- Dr Elisabeth Targ conducted a double-blind study on 20 Aids sufferers in the mid-1990s, and a further study in 1998 on 40 Aids patients. Unknown to the patients, 40 people were praying for them from a distance. The patients receiving prayer spent less time in hospital and developed fewer Aids-defining diseases than the patients without prayer support.
- Columbia University College of Physicians and Surgeons conducted a distant praying study involving 219 women undergoing IVF treatment at Cha Hospital in Seoul, Korea, with people praying for them in the USA, Canada and Australia. Half the prayed-for group became pregnant, while a quarter of the not-prayed-for group conceived.
- In 1997, in Arnold, Nottinghamshire, 15 local churches and the police combined prayer and practical action. Juvenile crime, anti-social noise, verbal abuse, petty damage and car break-ins there dropped by 15%.
- When Manchester police combined prayer and social action, crime on the Swinton Valley Estate in Salford dropped by 45%.

Encouragement to pray

As I said, my first reaction was to be sceptical. However, the article was written by a Christian, it was published in a Christian magazine, and its aim was to encourage people to pray. There was no good reason to believe that the information supplied was unreliable. Therefore, if I accept this at face value, it appears that God is *more likely* to act in a situation if people have prayed about it, than if they haven't. This in itself is a good reason to pray.

However, it was clear that prayer did not *always* result in what was asked for, so the article concluded that although God *always* answers prayers, they are not necessarily answered in the *way* we would wish. In other words, He does not always heal people, and does not always give them what they ask for, no matter how worthy the motive, and how faithful the person doing the praying. The difficult part is for us to accept this, and to understand that God did answer our prayer, even if it doesn't seem like He has.

I am not sure about this explanation. To me it seems that God does *not* always answer our prayers. What is difficult to understand is *why*. It is also difficult to understand why prayer should make a *statistical difference* to the outcome, as shown in the studies above, rather than a complete, one hundred percent difference.

God likes us to ask for things!

The key may be in the *asking*. There are a number of verses in which God expresses a wish for us to ask for things. Mark 11:24, quoted above, is one of those, "...whatever you ask for in prayer ... will be yours". A number of others are below:

Matthew 7:7	Ask and it will be given to you
Matthew 7:11	... how much more will your Father I heaven give good gifts to those who as him!
Matthew 18:19	... if two of you on earth agree about anything you ask for, it will be done for you by my Father in heaven
Matthew 21:22	If you believe, you will receive whatever you ask for in prayer
John 14:14	You may ask me for anything in my name, and I will do it
John 16:24	Until now you have not asked for anything in my name. Ask and you will receive, and your joy will be complete
James 1:5,6	If any of you lacks wisdom, he should ask God ... and it will be given to him. But when he asks, he must believe and not doubt ...

James 4:2,3	You do not have, because you do not ask God. When you ask, you do not receive, because you ask with wrong motives, that you may spend what you get on your pleasures
1 John 3:21,22	… we have confidence before God and receive from him anything we ask, because we obey his commands and do what pleases him

A number of points are made clear in these verses:

- People needed to ask God for what they wanted. Although He already knew what they wanted, He still wished them to ask for it, before He gave it to them. (Matthew 6:8; "… for your Father knows what you need before you ask him.")
- During the Acts period, if a person asked, they received their request, unless they lacked faith, or asked with wrong motives.
- If they obeyed His commands and did what pleased Him, they received anything they asked.

However, we have to consider whether these verses are relevant to us in this day and age. All these verses were written before Acts 28, and were relevant to the Jews to whom they were addressed. But if we look at a few verses addressed to Gentiles after Acts 28, we will see a different emphasis:

Eph. 3:20	Now to him who is able to do immeasurably more than all we ask or imagine …
Eph. 6:18	And pray in the Spirit on all occasions with all kinds of prayers and requests
Phil. 4:6	Do not be anxious about anything, but in everything, by prayer and petition, with thanksgiving, present your requests to God
Col. 4:2	Devote yourselves to prayer, being watchful and thankful

1 Tim. 2:1 I urge, then, first of all, that requests, prayers, intercession and thanksgiving be made for everyone

The main point that is repeated in these verses addressed to Gentiles is that we should continue to ask God for whatever we wish. However, there is no promise that all our prayers will *definitely* be answered if we pray with faith and the right motives. What is important is that we continue to pray, and continue to ask.

Going back to the scientific studies conducted, the results bear this out. When people and situations are prayed about, God *sometimes* chooses to act, and answer those prayers. He does not *promise* to act in any and every situation in this day and age, but he does want to be asked. If we do not ask, it seems that God may well restrict Himself, and not act. Certainly, the experiments mentioned earlier do seem to show that prayer prompts God into action.

I am not sure that we will ever understand *why* He chooses to answer on some occasions, and not on others. We just have to trust that He knows what is best for us. It may be that, as for the Jews, occasionally we ask for things with the wrong motivation, or with doubtful hearts that God could ever do such a thing, and maybe this results in God's choosing not to act.

What good do these studies do?

What good do such scientific experiments do? I think they confirm Scripture for us, they encourage us to continue in prayer, and they are interesting enough to use in conversations with non-Christian friends. However, they also raise other questions, which we should think through, such as why God would only answer a selection of such prayers, rather than all of them.

This brings me to my last point, which was, what would God think of these experiments? He obviously knew such studies were taking place, so He had a choice to:

- Answer all of the prayers

- Answer a selection of them
- Answer none of them

He chose the second option, which is what He has always done. The results bore out the fact that *without* prayer fewer people recovered, situations improved less, and people did not get what they wanted as often. *With* prayer, God helped many more people, significantly more so than without prayer. However, there will never be a one hundred percent answer rate, as undoubtedly if there were, with our fallen human nature, it is likely that our prayers would become progressively more frivolous and trivial.

Finally, I will close with one of my favourite verses:

Be joyful always;
pray continually;
give thanks in all circumstances,
for this is God's will for you in Christ Jesus.
(1 Thessalonians 5:16-18)

52. Problems with prayer

Sylvia Penny

One problem we sometimes have with prayer is trying to understanding why the Lord doesn't always answer positively. We feel that our hearts are right with the Lord, we feel that what we have asked for is reasonable and should be within the Lord's will, and yet for some reason it doesn't happen. Quite often this involves prayer for the healing of a person.

However, the simple answer to the problem is that if the Lord did answer all such prayers positively, it is likely that most Christians would never die! We all wish our loved ones to recover whenever they are ill, no matter how old or how sick they may be. None of us look forward to the final parting. And so we pray for the people we love, trusting that the Lord will answer our prayers.

However, if we look at just three examples of prayers in the Old Testament, we will see that we can never predict how the Lord will act in any given situation. We have to learn, like Job did, that we do not understand God in His entirety, and that we never will. The Lord speaks to Job in Job 38:2 and says to him, "Who is this that darkens my counsel with words without knowledge?" and Job finally says to the Lord in Job 42:2, "I know that you can do all things; no plan of yours can be thwarted." The problem is not with the Lord's ability, the problem lies with man not having the knowledge to understand God and His ways. Sometimes we try to apply human logic to the way we feel God "should" work, and when He doesn't act according to our expectations we get disappointed, or for some, it leads to a crisis of faith.

I have selected three examples of characters from the OT who all wanted the Lord to save them (or a loved one) from illness or death. They greatly contrast with one another, but the factor they have in common is their complete trust and faith in the Lord, no matter what the outcome.

Hezekiah (Isaiah 38:1-8)

This passage tells us about Hezekiah's illness, and how Isaiah was sent to him by the Lord to tell him "This is what the Lord says: Put your house in order, because you are going to die; you will not recover" (Isaiah 38:1). However, rather than accepting this as an absolute certainty, Hezekiah prays to the Lord, weeps bitterly, points out how faithfully he has walked with the Lord, and how devoted he has been to Him. Of course, the Lord must have known all this already, but as a result of Hezekiah's pleas, He changes His mind and sends Isaiah to him with another message. "I have heard your prayer and seen your tears; I will add fifteen years to your life" (Isaiah 38:5).

Sometimes people argue that, as the Lord already knows what we want there is no point praying about things. However, this example challenges that view. Here it is Hezekiah's response to being told he is going to die, his prayers and his tears, that result in the Lord changing His mind. Amazing as it seems, the Lord is concerned with individual feelings! However, it also seems it is important that we ask Him. In this case, if Hezekiah had accepted what Isaiah told him, and had put his house in order ready to die just as the Lord told him, one presumes his life would not have been extended. It was his asking that made the difference. On the other hand, neither can we conclude that this is a "prayer formula". God is not bound to do for one person what He may, in His grace and mercy, do for another, and we have to accept this. This leads on to the second example.

David (2 Samuel 12:1-23)

I kings 15:5 tells us that David had always done what was right in the eyes of the Lord, except in the case of Uriah the Hittite. This of course refers to David committing adultery with Uriah's wife Bathsheba, and subsequently ensuring the Uriah was killed in the front line of the fighting so that David's adultery would not be discovered. However, the Lord revealed this to Nathan, and sent him to David to rebuke him, and to tell him how the Lord was going to punish him. One of the punishments was that David's son, through Bathsheba, was going to die. When the child was struck ill, David pleaded with the Lord for the child, and fasted and wept. However, the Lord kept to His word and the child died, despite the pleading of David. David hoped the Lord would change His mind. However, when He did not, David accepted what had happened, got up, washed and changed, went to worship the Lord, and then went home to eat. His servants were bemused by this extraordinary behaviour. But David explained that while the child lived there was hope that the Lord would be gracious and grant his wish, but once he had died, he had to accept what the Lord had determined would happen.

Although in this case we can understand, to a certain extent, the justice in the Lord's decision to carry out His word, it is David's reaction which is important as an example to us. He did not question the Lord. He did not give up his faith. Instead, he accepted what had happened, and continued to worship the Lord as usual. The application for us is that we should try to have the same attitude as David, even when our prayers are not answered in the way we would like them to be.

Shadrach, Meshach and Abednego (Daniel 3)

The third example is Shadrach, Meshach and Abednego. Daniel 3 tells how King Nebuchadnezzar of Babylon made a huge image of gold and decreed that everyone should fall down and worship it. Those who did not were to be thrown into a blazing furnace. However, Shadrach, Meshach and Abednego refused to bow down to it. Nebuchadnezzar gave them a second chance to do so, asking them what god would be able to rescue them from his hand. They replied to the king, "O Nebuchadnezzar, we do not need to defend ourselves before you in this matter. If we are thrown into the blazing furnace, the God we serve is able to save us from it, and he will rescue us from your hand, O king. *But even if he does not*, we want you to know, O king, that we will not serve your gods or worship the image of gold you have set up." (Daniel 3:16-18)

Shadrach, Meshach and Abednego were convinced that God could save them from the fire if He wanted to. They were also absolutely determined not to compromise their faith by bowing down to the image. And thirdly, although they had absolute faith that God could save them if He wished, if He chose not to, it would not change their faith, or change their determination to obey God's laws, even if it ended in their death. In other words, their faith did not depend upon God conforming to a preconceived idea of how they wanted Him to act in a given situation. The application for us again is very clear. We can pray for anything we like; ("Do not be anxious about anything, but in everything, by prayer and petition, with thanksgiving, present your requests to God", Philippians 4:6). However, that does not mean we should expect Him to do everything we ask!

Getting everything we ask for?

There are a number of passages in the New Testament that say things like "whatever you ask for in prayer it will be yours". For example, Mark 11:24 says, "Therefore I tell you, whatever you ask for in prayer, believe that you have received it, and it will be yours." However, if we turn back only one chapter to Mark 10 we find James and John ask Jesus to do for them whatever they ask (verse 35), and the Lord's reply in verse 40 is "… to sit at my right or left is not for me to grant." In other words, what they had asked for was not possible. Blanket statements like "whatever you ask for will be yours" are always given in a context, to certain people for a certain time. Seldom can they be taken out of context and applied to everyone, no matter when or where they live.

However, what is clear is that the Lord likes us to pray! He likes us to come to Him in prayer and thank Him, praise Him, present our concerns to Him, and yes, also ask Him for things. As mentioned above, Philippians 4:6 tells us not to be anxious about anything, but to pray with thanksgiving to God, and as a result, verse 7 says "the peace of God, which transcends all understanding, will guard your hearts and your minds in Christ Jesus." Here the promise is not that we will get what we requested, but that we will receive the peace of God: that perfect peace that transcends all understanding.

53. Serendipity and prayer

Sylvia Penny

Webster's definition of *serendipity* is "a seeming gift for finding something good accidentally". Serendipity is the art of experiencing "happy accidents". By its very definition, someone experiences good things happening around them more often than would be statistically expected. In other words, they attract more than their fair share of good coincidences.

Archbishop William Temple said "more coincidences happen the more you pray." This, of course, is a contradiction in itself. A coincidence is only one if there is no cause. In this case, prayer may be the cause, but of course because there is no proof, we cannot be certain that the good event, whatever it is, wouldn't have happened anyway, even if we hadn't prayed!

There may be a number of explanations of "happy accidents" occurring after we have prayed:

1) we *notice* the good things that happen more when we pray for them
2) we affect the outcome by what we say/do after we have prayed for something
3) more good things do actually happen – God listens and acts

A coincidence, or an answer to prayer?

I read an article in a magazine a while ago about a Christian girl who had decided to spend a year in a Canadian University. However, later she got cold feet, and didn't really want to go. She wanted God to intervene so she didn't have to go! However, the summer before she was due to go, she went to a church summer camp, and met a girl from Canada there, and you can guess the rest! Yes, the Canadian girl attended the very university she was due to go to. Yes, they became good friends at the summer camp, and yes, the girl's family in Canada welcomed her into their home, and eased her passage into the Canadian University.

It is very easy to be sceptical about such articles. It is easy to say that the course of events would have happened anyway. She didn't even pray for help in going to Canada – she asked for help with a way out! Certainly, God does not *promise* any answers to such prayers in Scripture. But, and this is a big but, Ephesians 3:20 *does* say, "(He) is able to do immeasurably more than all we ask for or imagine, according to his power that is at work within us". In this case, she asked for a way out, but received a (much better) way through. We, and she, will never know whether this would have happened anyway. However, after an event like this, looking back, we can always give thanks and praise to God.

Trivialities unimportant to God

We may reason that such trivialities must be unimportant to God in the grand scheme of things. We may tell ourselves that He has much better things to be attending to. However, we do know that the Lord said "Are not five sparrows sold for two pennies? Yet not one of them is forgotten by God. Indeed, the very hairs of your head are all numbered. Don't be afraid; you are worth more than many sparrows." (Luke 12:6,7). If the Lord is interested in such tiny details of sparrows and hairs, then perhaps He is also interested in some of the trivialities of our lives, especially when they are important to us. However, it does seem that He likes to be asked. If we do not pray, it may indicate to Him that we do not care enough.

I prayed that our daughter would get the grades she needed to go to her chosen university, despite the fact that her predicted grades were lower than she needed. Fortunately, she got the exact grades she required – no more and no less. I can look at this in several ways. It could have been luck. It may have been hard work. It may have been an answer to prayer. The Lord may have helped her to concentrate at the crucial moments, or helped her to remember important facts at the right time. It may have been the result of sending her for some extra tuition. We will never know. I just thank the Lord for the outcome.

However, I also know that life is not as simple as that. It is never made up of one event in isolation. Her chosen university may not work out to be as wonderful as expected. If the course does not live up to expectations, then do I amend my original thoughts and thanks, and doubt whether God had a hand in it? After all, if things do not work out well, do we reason that God can have had nothing to do with it? Or alternatively, do we blame God for the outcome? There are no easy answers to many of these questions. What *is* easy to say is that we should still pray about anything we wish to. Ephesians 6:18 says, "And pray in the Spirit on all occasions with all kinds of prayers and requests." It is very clear that God likes us to pray, and likes us to ask Him for things. Whether He will *always* give us what we ask for is unlikely, but it is much more unlikely He will give us anything if we *do not ask*.

Pray about everything

Philippians 4:6 says, "Do not be anxious about anything, but in everything, by prayer and petition, with thanksgiving, present your requests to God." Here we are told to pray about everything, and to pray with thanksgiving. Often prayer and thanks go together. God likes to be asked, and He likes to be thanked. In fact, that does not sound very different from me as a parent. I like my children to be able to ask me for things, but I also like to be appreciated. 1 Thessalonians 5:16-18 says "Be joyful always; pray continually; give thanks in all circumstances, for this is God's will for you in Christ Jesus." Again, we see prayer and thanksgiving going hand in hand. We also see that it is God's will for us to do so. In other words, He likes us to pray for things.

Returning to Archbishop William Temple's comment "more coincidences happen the more you pray", we can see why this is the case. People who ask for more, are more likely to receive more answers, than those who ask for nothing. So, when we sometimes receive an answer to what may seem a fairly trivial prayer request, maybe we should attribute the answer to the Lord, and be thankful, rather than assume it is just a "happy accident".

54. The Good Wolf and the Bad Wolf

Sylvia Penny

There is a native American tale that goes like this. A Cherokee was teaching his grandson about life. "A struggle is going on inside me," he said to the youngster. "It is a tough one and it is between two wolves. One is evil – he is envy, greed, guilt, resentment, self-pity, lies, and false pride. The other is goodness – he is joy, serenity, humility, benevolence, truth and compassion. "The same fight is going on inside you and inside every other person, too." "But tell me, which wolf will win?" the grandson asked. "The one you feed," came the reply.

This story sounds good, until you compare it with that the Bible says. It's then that you realise that although it sounds very similar, something very important is missing. If you read what Paul says in Romans 7, which he wrote more than 20 years of being a Christian, he still had a struggle with doing what was right.

> I do not understand what I do. For what I want to do I do not do, but what I hate I do. And if I do what I do not want to do, I agree that the law is good. As it is, it is no longer I myself who do it, but it is sin living in me. I know that nothing good lives in me, that is in my sinful nature. For I have the desire to do what is good, but I cannot carry it out. For what I do is not the good I want to do; no, the evil I do not want to do – this I keep on doing. Now if I do what I do not want to do, it is no longer I who do it, but it is sin living in me that does it. So I find this law at work: When I want to do good, evil is right there with me. For in my inner being I delight in God's law; but I see another law at work in the members of my body, waging war against the law of my mind and making me a prisoner of the law of sin at work within my members. What a wretched man I am! Who will rescue me from this body of death? Thanks be to God – through Jesus Christ our Lord! So then, I myself in my mind am a slave to God's law,

but in the sinful nature a slave to the law of sin. (Romans 7:15-25)

The native American story implies that as long as a person concentrates on feeding the "good wolf" this one will win. In other words, if we try hard enough good will triumph over evil. However, when we read Paul's words in Romans, written many years after he became a Christian, this was not his experience. He just recognised all the more acutely the great struggle going on inside himself.

Martin Luther's struggle

The great reformer, Martin Luther, experienced the same problem acutely. He was so troubled by personal guilt that this led directly to him becoming convinced of the truth of "justification by faith alone", recognising that in and through his own efforts he would *never* be good enough to reach God's standard. He understood the truth of Ephesians 2:8-10, which says "For it is by grace you have been saved, through faith – and this not from yourselves, it is the gift of God – not by works, so that no-one can boast. For we are God's workmanship, created in Christ Jesus to do good works, which God prepared in advance for us to do."

The new nature and the old nature

What is missing from the native American story is the effect that the Holy Spirit can have on our lives once we have believed in Jesus Christ as our Saviour. Like Paul, we have the struggle between the good wolf and the bad wolf – that is, the struggle between the good nature and the sinful nature, or as it is sometimes referred to, the new nature and the old nature.

The first ten verses of Romans 8 contrast the new nature with the old nature, the spiritual nature with the sinful nature. Verse 5 sums this up by saying "Those who live according to the sinful nature have their minds set on what that nature desires; but those who live in accordance with the Spirit (new nature) have their minds set on what the Spirit (Holy Spirit) desires." Here, the sinful mindset is set in contrast with the spiritual mindset. Both are present in the believer, but it is the indwelling Holy Spirit Who can help us with the struggle we have between the two.

The indwelling of the Holy Spirit

When we become Christians, we acquire a "new nature" (Romans 8:5), and we receive the permanent indwelling of the Holy Spirit as a deposit guaranteeing our inheritance (Ephesians 1:13,14). There is therefore a big difference between a believer and an unbeliever. A believer has a new nature and the indwelling of the Holy Spirit. An unbeliever does not.

The story says we can feed our "good wolf" all by ourselves, and this is what an unbeliever may try to do in their own strength. But the Scriptures say we can never be good enough in our own strength. It's the Holy Spirit living in us that can enable our "new nature" to do this, if we let Him. However, our "bad wolf", (i.e. our sinful nature) never dies through lack of feeding. Believer or unbeliever, it is always there, ready to rear its ugly head if we let it.

Galatians 5 and the fruit of the Spirit

Galatians 5:16-26 is very similar to Romans 8:1-17 and describes the spiritual life as contrasted with the sinful life - again contrasting the new nature and the old nature. Galatians 5:17 says "For the sinful nature desires what is contrary to the Spirit, and the Spirit what is contrary to the sinful nature. They are in conflict with each other, so that you do not do what you want." It is made clear that there is a never-ending struggle going on inside a believer between their new nature and their old nature. The acts of the sinful nature are listed, and then contrasted with the fruit of the Spirit which is described in another of my favourite verses. Galatians 5:22 says, "But the fruit of the Spirit is love, joy, peace, patience, kindness, goodness, faithfulness, gentleness and self-control."

Conclusion

There is a lot of truth in the old Cherokee story, but the most important element is missing. That missing element is salvation by grace through faith in the Lord Jesus Christ and the consequent indwelling of the Holy Spirit. He is the one Who can help us with the struggle between our new nature and our old nature – our "good wolf" and our "bad wolf". But, with Paul, we have to recognise that this will be a life-long struggle. Unfortunately, it will not be until we have eternal life that we will be free of our "bad wolf".

55. The Christian Hallmark

Sylvia Penny

What is the difference between a believer and an unbeliever? There are many answers that could be given to this question, but one important one is that believers are sealed with the Holy Spirit, whereas unbelievers are not. The indwelling of the Holy Spirit is the hallmark of a Christian.

There are many Scriptures that refer to the indwelling of the Holy Spirit, and the fact that He is a permanent possession of believers. What difference does this make? There are a number of answers to this:

1. He gives unity among believers (Ephesians 4:3)
2. He confirms our identity as God's children (Romans 8:16)
3. He helps us understand Spiritual truths (1 Corinthians 2:12,13)
4. He develops His fruit in our lives (Galatians 5:22-25)
5. He helps us in our prayer life (Romans 8:26)

We will look at these later, but first we will look at some of the Scriptures that refer to the indwelling of the Holy Spirit in believers.

The Holy Spirit lives in believers

> Don't you know that you yourselves are God's temple and that God's Spirit lives in you? (1 Corinthians 3:16)
>
> He anointed us, set his seal of ownership on us, and put his Spirit in our hearts as a deposit, guaranteeing what is to come. (2 Corinthians 1:22)
>
> Now it is God who has made us for this very purpose and has given us the Spirit as a deposit, guaranteeing what is to come. (2 Corinthians 5:5)

> And this is how we know that he lives in us: We know it by the Spirit he gave us. (1 John 3:24)

> Having believed, you were marked in him with a seal, the promised Holy Spirit, who is a deposit guaranteeing our inheritance until the redemption of those who are God's possession – to the praise of his glory. (Ephesians 1:13,14)

> I pray that out of his glorious riches he may strengthen you with power through his Spirit in your inner being" (Ephesians 3:16)

The seal of the Holy Spirit is described as a deposit that *guarantees* what is to come –righteousness and eternal life for those that believe. This guarantee is eternal, not like manufacturer's guarantees that last for a year or two at best. It lasts for ever, and is sure and certain. This confirms what Romans 8:38,39 tells us, that *nothing* can separate us from the love of God that is in Christ Jesus our Lord.

Unbelievers do not have the Holy Spirit

The same truth is also expressed negatively in a number of Scriptures.

> You, however, are controlled not by the sinful nature but by the Spirit, if the Spirit of God lives in you. And if anyone does not have the Spirit of Christ, he does not belong to Christ. (Romans 8:9)

> The man without the Spirit does not accept the things that come from the Spirit of God, for they are foolishness to him and he cannot understand them, because they are spiritually discerned. (1 Corinthians 2:14)

> These are the men who divide you, who follow mere natural instincts and do not have the Spirit. (Jude 19)

Unbelievers follow natural instincts, many of them good, but they do not accept truths that are spiritually discerned, as "they are foolishness to him". Have you ever thought of trying to explain some of your beliefs to an unbeliever, and realised that they are most unlikely to understand, let alone accept them. A person has first to hear and accept the gospel message before they stand any chance of understanding many of the deeper spiritual truths in Scripture, for example identification, substitution, righteousness, atonement, redemption, forgiveness, *agape* love, and the return of Christ, to name but a few.

The Holy Spirit *became* a permanent possession of believers after Jesus' death

Was this always the case, or was there a time in the past when believers did not experience the permanent indwelling of the Holy Spirit? The Lord Jesus answers this question very clearly in a number of places in John's gospel:

> "Whoever believes in me, as the Scripture has said, streams of living water will flow from within him." By this he meant the Spirit, whom those who believed in him were later to receive. Up to that time the Spirit had not been given, since Jesus had not yet been glorified. (John 7:38,39)
>
> I will ask the Father, and he will give you another Counsellor to be with you for ever – the Spirit of truth. The world cannot accept him, because it neither sees him nor knows him. But you know him, for he lives with you and will be in you. (John 14:16)
>
> But I tell you the truth: It is for your good that I am going away. Unless I go away, the Counsellor will not come to you; but if I go, I will send him to you. (John 16:7)

From what Jesus said it is clear that it was not possible for the Holy Spirit to become a permanent possession of all believers until Christ was glorified, after His death and resurrection. It is not explained why, but this is stated as a fact.

However, it *is* explained why unbelievers do not accept the concept of the Holy Spirit – it is because they neither see Him nor know Him.

"Seeing is believing" is a popular expression, but Jesus says to Thomas, after His resurrection "Because you have seen me, you have believed; blessed are those who have not seen and yet have believed," (John 20:29) and that of course includes us.

The result of the indwelling of the Holy Spirit

So, what are the results of the Holy Spirit living within us? We briefly listed a few at the beginning of this article.

1. Unity among believers

> Make every effort of keep the unity of the Spirit through the bond of peace. (Ephesians 4:3)

The Holy Spirit has made a unity between all believers. All are sealed with the same deposit and all are guaranteed an eternal inheritance. We are all in the same boat. However, we have to make every effort to guard this unity through the bond of peace. Verse 2, just before this, directs us how to do this, when it says "Be completely humble and gentle; be patient, bearing with one another in love."

2. Confirms our identity as children of God

> The Spirit himself testifies with our spirit that we are God's children. (Romans 8:16)

This appears near the end of a whole passage about life through the Spirit in Romans 8:1-17 which culminates in saying that those who are led by the Spirit of God are sons of God. The whole of this passage is well worth reading through to put this into context.

3. Understanding spiritual truths

> We have not received the spirit of the world but the Spirit who is from God, that we may understand what God has freely given us. This is what we speak, not in words taught us by human wisdom but in words taught by the Spirit,

> expressing spiritual truths in spiritual words. (1 Corinthians 2:12,13)

The Holy Spirit helps us understand what God has given us, and helps us understand spiritual truths. By implication this means that He helps us when we read Scripture, as today this is our main source of spiritual understanding, whereas in Paul's day they had the spoken word of the apostles as well.

4. Fruit of the Spirit

> But the fruit of the Spirit is love, joy, peace, patience, kindness, goodness, faithfulness, gentleness and self-control. Against such things there is no law. (Galatians 5:22,23)

As a result of the indwelling of the Holy Spirit, His fruit should be self-evident in our lives, and He will help us to develop this fruit if we let Him. As in all things with God, this is a two-way relationship. God never forces us to do things against our will. In fact, 1 Thessalonians 5:19 says "Do not put out the Spirit's fire". We have to let Him work in our lives, and showing such fruit is no exception.

5. Prayer life

> In the same way, the spirit helps us in our weakness. We do not know what we ought to pray, but the Spirit himself intercedes for us with groans that words cannot express. And he who searches our hearts knows the mind of the Spirit, because the Spirit intercedes for the saints in accordance with God's will. (Romans 8:26,27)

So, the Holy Spirit also helps us with our prayer life. Often, we feel helpless in knowing what to pray for, but through the Spirit, God knows what is in our hearts, and understands what we really want to pray for if only we had the right words. This is very comforting to know in times of trouble, but also uplifting to know in times of rejoicing. We have a heavenly Father who understands us fully through the Holy Spirit who dwells in us. We do not have to find the right words – He understands our thoughts before they are expressed.

Conclusion

The work of the Holy Spirit in our lives as believers is wonderful. He can help us in so many ways if we allow Him to. The first stepping stone is understanding that we are sealed with the Holy Spirit from the very moment we believe, and that once sealed, He can never be taken away from us. However, fully understanding what the implications of this are, and allowing Him to develop us as Christians and go on to maturity will take a lifetime.

56. Water miracles and the miracle of water

Sylvia Penny

It is amazing how often water figures in miracles. How many occasions can you think of?

In the Old Testament we soon reach the flood in Noah's time. We have the parting of rivers and seas at least four times – Moses parted the Red Sea, (Exodus 14:21,22), Joshua parted the Jordan (Joshua 3:15-17), to let the people of Israel into the promised land, Elijah struck the Jordan with his cloak, and it parted to let him and Elisha cross over (2 Kings 2:7,8), and Elisha did the same coming back after Elijah had been taken to heaven (2 Kings 2:14). We have Moses striking a rock and producing water in the desert (Exodus 17:6) and we have an iron axe-head floating on water for Elisha (2 Kings 6:6). Also, Naaman was cleansed from leprosy by bathing in the Jordan seven times (2 Kings 5:14).

In the New Testament we have the turning of water into wine, the calming of the storm including the waves of the sea, and Jesus walking on the water. This is by no means an exhaustive list, but it gives an indication of the wide variety of water miracles that took place in Biblical times.

Mary's attitude of belief

So many miracles involve water, and as Christians who believe in the inspiration of Scripture, we tend not to question *whether* such events took place. Instead, we are maybe more interested as to *how* they took place and *why* they took place. When Mary was told she was going to have a child, she asked "*How* will this be, since I am a virgin." (Luke 1:34). In his reply, the angel Gabriel concluded by saying "For nothing is impossible with God." (verse 37). We are like Mary in our attitude. Through faith she accepted what she was told without question. However, she still wondered "*how*"? Later, when Jesus was about to begin his ministry she knew *without doubt* that He could turn water into wine. Another water miracle!

Each of the water miracles mentioned above are, humanly speaking, impossible. However, if we wonder *how* such miracles took place, this does not indicate unbelief, but rather, like Mary, that we are interested in what God has done, and is able to do, both now and in the future.

Zechariah's attitude of unbelief

This can be contrasted with Zechariah's attitude when he was told that his wife Elizabeth was going to have a child, even though she was well past the age of child-bearing. He did not believe what he was told, (Luke 1:20) and as a result he was struck dumb, until the child was born. The Lord honoured Mary who questioned with an attitude of belief, whereas He condemned Zechariah who questioned with an attitude of unbelief.

Explanations of miracles

Returning to the water miracles, I have read many explanations for Noah's flood, a few for the parting of the Red Sea, but little or none for the floating axe head, the turning of water into wine, and the walking on the water. That is, until I read a small piece in the Guardian newspaper recently – a most unlikely journal to include a piece headed up "Bible Study"! The sub-heading was "Jesus 'walked on thin ice.'" The report stated that a team of American and Israeli scientists had published a study in the Journal of Paleolimnology (the study of prehistoric lakes) and stated that unique freezing processes would have occasionally allowed a crust of ice to form on the surface. This scientific fact, it went on to say, "may have provided an origin to the story that Christ walked on water."

The Lord is in control of creation

Although we do not need such explanations, it is always interesting to read about continuing scientific thoughts and discoveries. The more that is discovered, whether archeologically, geologically, biologically, and so on, the more it seems the content of the Bible is confirmed and upheld. To me, it makes no difference whether the Lord Jesus miraculously walked on thin ice, or whether he even hovered on the surface of the water! Either way, it shows His divinity, by being in control of His creation, rather than being in subjection to it. Since the Lord Jesus is God incarnate, for Him to be able to do such things is to be expected rather than denied.

As limited human beings, we learn by experience and observation. If people hovered over water every day, or if water became wine instantaneously all the time, we would think nothing of it. We would eventually discover how the phenomenon happened by observation, testing and scientific analysis. However, if it only happens once, we are unable to do this. This makes it a miracle. Women who have given birth to a child will often describe it as "miraculous" even though it happens all the time!

Water is unique

Scientists know that water has unique and unexpected properties, totally different to any other known substance. Unlike most materials, as liquid water cools down it reaches its maximum density at four degrees centigrade, at which point its density decreases as it becomes ice. Thus, colder water and any ice floats on the warmer liquid water below. If it did not possess this unusual property, life on earth would be very limited, maybe impossible. We accept this as a fact because we observe it all the time. However, we still do not know *why* this is so. Except as Christians we presume that God created water in just this way so that life could exist. So maybe it is not surprising that many of the miracles in the Bible involved water. Water is a miraculous and life-giving substance in itself. To use and control this substance in other ways than those normally observed in nature is to show a greater power and authority. It indicates the Creator Himself at work in His Creation.

Belief or incredulity?

So, whether we accept these miracles at face value simply because of our faith in the Lord Jesus, and our acceptance of the Scriptures as the inspired word of God, or whether we question *how* they happened and why, I believe the Lord honours and accepts such attitudes, as He did with Mary. What He does not accept is the questioning prompted by an attitude of disbelief and incredulity, as in the example given by Zechariah.

57. Made in the image of God

Sylvia Penny

> Then God said, "Let us make man in our image, in our likeness, and let them rule over the fish of the sea and the birds of the air, over the livestock, over all the earth, and over all the creatures that move along the ground." (Genesis 1:26)

The very first thing the Bible tells us about man is that he is made in the image of God. This is the very first reference to man in the Scriptures, and thus undoubtedly the first thing that God wished to convey to man about Himself. What does it mean to be "made in the image of God"? In what way is man His image? Does this make us different from the rest of His creation, and how are we different? There are many questions we can ask about this statement made in the very first chapter of the first book in the Bible. In this article we shall look at some of the answers.

Man is not divine, but he is unique

An image exists only by *derivation*. It is not the original. Without the original it is nothing. Being an image stresses man's dependence on God, Who is the Original. An image is not an exact replica. It is created, and therefore cannot be exactly the same as the original. Man is creature, not Creator, and as such is infinitely lower than his Creator. Thus, from the first page of Genesis, the Bible excludes the pagan idea of man being divine.

However, we are told *only* humans were created in the image of God. None of the animals were. Neither does Scripture say the angels were, even though 2 Peter 2:11 says "they are stronger and more powerful" than humans. So, on the one hand man's dependence upon God is made very clear, while on the other hand it is clear that, out of all creation, man is special to God.

What does the word "image" refer to?

The New Bible Commentary Revised has this to say about the image and the likeness:

> The words used, image (*selem)* and likeness (*demuth*), have an undoubted reference to outward form (e.g. 1 Sam. 6:5; 2 Ki. 16:10), and we must not resist the implication that while God is Spirit (Is. 31:3) and outward appearance does not belong to His essence, yet there is an outward appearance which is suitable to the invisible glory of God (e.g. Nu. 12:8) and in this likeness man was created. This affords a basis for the dignity which Scripture ever accords to the human body.

The image is therefore the outward form, and man is this image, a copy made according to the Original (God). If the "image" refers to man, rather than to God, then it may be clearer if Genesis 1:26 said "Let us make man *as* our image" rather than "*in* our image." 1 Corinthians 11:7 supports this reading, as in this verse Paul, referring to man, says he *is* the image and glory of God. Thus man is the visible image of the invisible divine glory. What an amazing thought! And this is the first thing that God chose to reveal to man about Himself. Perhaps this is why He so strongly prohibited the making of images of Himself, *because He had already created His own image*, and He needs no others.

Pagan writings

Early pagan writings often suggested that *only* kings could be described as being images of God. The Bible stands apart in attributing this to *all* mankind. If Moses was the author of Genesis 1, perhaps he was inspired to write this as a reaction against the ideology of only the pharaoh being the "image of God".

What does the word "likeness" refer to?

The word "likeness" specifies the nature of the image – it is one which *resembles* but that is *not* identical to it. 2 Corinthians 3:18 says

"And we, who with unveiled faces all reflect the Lord's glory, are being transformed into his *likeness* with ever-increasing glory, which comes from the Lord, who is the Spirit."

Perhaps it is because of this resemblance between God and His image, that Christ linked two commandments together when He was asked which the greatest commandment was. He replied in Matthew 22:37-40: "'Love the Lord your God with all your heart and with all your soul and with all your mind'. This is the first and greatest commandment. And the second is like it: 'Love your neighbour as yourself.'" Loving our fellow men, in Christ's mind, is how our love for God is manifested. Maybe this is why John wrote: "If anyone says 'I love God', yet hates his brother, he is a liar'" (1 John 4:20). Also, there is a similar train of thought in James 3:9: "With the tongue we praise our Lord and Father, and with it we curse men, who have been made in God's likeness." The implication is that in so doing we are being self-contradictory.

How does mankind resemble God?

Three attributes of God that come across in Genesis 1 are:

(1) His Spirit
(2) His use of speech
(3) His transcendence over creation

The second chapter of Genesis concentrates on man in close-up and describes the composition of his nature, and shows how man also has these attributes.

(1) Genesis 2:7 says God "breathed into his nostrils the breath (*ruach* = spirit) of life, and the man became a living being." This spirit, this 'inner life' of men, this 'spirituality', is part of what sets man apart from the animals, and part of what makes him the image of God.

(2) The use of speech also sets man apart from the rest of creation. God brought all the animals to Adam for him to name them (Genesis 2:19). This confirmed his delegated

authority over the animals, and also shows his use of speech, and his mastery of language.

(3) Although mankind also resembles God in the authority he is given by God over the rest of creation, this is not so much a part of being the image of God, rather than a consequence of it. Although God said, "fill the earth and subdue it. Rule over the fish of the sea and the birds of the air and over every living creature that moves on the ground" (Genesis 1:28) this did not imply Sovereignty, but rather a position of deputy to the Sovereign. Man was subject to God from the very beginning, and has to account to Him.

Is man still the image of God after the fall?

Some have argued that the image was lost by man at the fall. However, it is not righteousness that makes man the image of God, as we have seen. Despite his sinfulness, man is still referred to as the image of God (Genesis 9:6; 1 Corinthians 11:7; James 3:9). Genesis 9:6 says "Whoever sheds the blood of man, by man shall his blood be shed; for in the image of God has God made man." It is wrong for man to kill man, *because* he is the image of God.

Others have argued that it is *only* saved and redeemed human beings who are now the image of God. This they base on Colossians 3:9,10 which says "Do not lie to each other, since you have taken off your old self with its practices and have put on the new self which *is being renewed in knowledge* in the image of its Creator." They say this implies that it is *only* the redeemed who are now in the image of the Creator. However, this is not what this verse is saying. Rather, it says that when we believe in Christ our new nature is renewed in knowledge (enabling us to be more like Him in character), not that the image is renewed.

The perfect image of God

There is no doubt that God's original intention was to create mankind as the perfect image of Himself. Before Adam fell, he was sinless, and would have been the "exact representation" of God. Genesis 5:1 says, "When God created man, he made him in the likeness of God."

Genesis 5:3 says, "Adam … had a son in his own likeness, in his own image." Thus, God created Adam as His earthly son, just as Adam in turn was enabled to have a son in *his* likeness. Although Genesis does not refer to Adam as being the son of God, Luke 3:38 actually does so. In the same way, when we are in Christ Jesus, we are not only images of God, but we also become sons of God, just as Adam was.

Christ Himself is referred to as the image of God, but in contrast to the rest of mankind, He is the perfect and righteous image, as shown in the verses below:

Colossians 1:15	He is the image of the invisible God.
John 14:9	Jesus said: "Anyone who has seen me has seen the Father."
2 Corinthians 4:4	Christ, who is the image of God.
Hebrews 1:3	The Son is the radiance of God's glory and the exact representation (express image, KJV) of his being.

Thus, Christ as the perfect man is the perfect image of God. In eternal life, when we receive our resurrection bodies, we too, once again, will also be perfect images of God as He always intended us to be.

58. The Judgment seat of Christ and the Great White Throne

Sylvia Penny

What is the difference between the judgment seat of Christ, and the great white throne in Scripture? First, we will look at the judgment seat of Christ. There are two passages in Scripture that refer to the judgment seat of Christ, the divine tribunal, before which all believers will stand on the day of resurrection in order to give an account of their lives and service.

> You, then, why do you judge your brother? Or why do you look down on your brother? For we will all stand before God's judgment seat. It is written: "'As surely as I live,' says the Lord, 'Every knee will bow before me; every tongue will confess to God.'" So then, each of us will give an account of himself to God. (Romans 14:10-12)

> For we must all appear before the judgment seat of Christ, that each one may receive what is due to him for the things done while in the body, whether good or bad. (2 Corinthians 5:10)

Bema – the believers' assessment at the "Judgment Seat"

The Greek word translated "judgment seat" is *bema*. Vine's Expository Dictionary says it was used "to denote a raised place or platform, reached by steps, where was a place of assembly; from the platform orations were made. The word became used for a tribune (i.e. magistrate), two of which were provided in the law-courts of Greece, one for the accuser and one for the defendant". Thus, it was used of a tribunal. In the NIV *bema* is translated "court" in Acts 18:12,16,17 (Paul brought before Gallio, the proconsul of Achaia), and in Acts 25:6,10,17 (Paul's trial before Festus at Caesarea). It is also translated "judge's seat" in Matthew 27:19 (Pilate was sitting on the judge's seat) and John 19:13 (Jesus brought before Pilate, who sat on the judge's seat).

As we can see from the two quotes above where *bema* refers to the judgment seat of Christ, this is a place where believers will bow the knee and worship the Lord, where each person will give an account of themselves to God, and where he will then receive what is due to him for what he did during this life on earth, *whether good or bad.* It is clear from these two occurrences in Scripture, that the *bema* is only for believers, and that this is a place of assessment, rather than condemnation. John 3:18 says "Whoever believes in him is not condemned, but whoever does not believe stands condemned already because he has not believed in the name of God's one and only Son" and Romans 8:1 tells us that "there is now no condemnation for those who are in Christ Jesus".

1 Corinthians 3:10-15 explains in more detail how this assessment works:

> By the grace God has given me, I laid a foundation as an expert builder, and someone else is building on it. But each one should be careful how he builds. For no-one can lay any foundation other than the one already laid, which is Jesus Christ. If any man builds on this foundation using gold, silver, costly stones, wood, hay or straw, his work will be shown for what it is, because the Day will bring it to light. It will be revealed with fire, and the fire will test the quality of each man's work. If what he has built survives, he will receive his reward. If it is burned up, he will suffer loss; he himself will be saved, but only as one escaping through the flames.

On that Day (of resurrection), a believer's work for the Lord will be assessed. A reward will be given for the gold, silver and costly stones, whereas the worthless wood, hay and straw will be destroyed permanently. All that will be left for eternity will be the good. Each believer will receive a reward for whatever good he has done for the Lord during his life on earth.

Krino – the unbelievers' judgment at the "Great White Throne"

This is quite different from the "Great White Throne" judgment of Revelation 20:11 where unbelievers are judged "according to what they had done" (Revelation 20:12).

> Then I saw a great white throne and him who was seated on it. Earth and sky fled from his presence, and there was no place for them. And I saw the dead, great and small, standing before the throne, and books were opened, which is the book of life. The dead were judged (*krino*) according to what they had done as recorded in the books. (Revelation 20:11,12)

Here the Greek word *krino* is used for judgment. Vine says this means (among other things) "to assume the office of a judge …, to give sentence…, to condemn…, and to execute judgment upon." It is often translated "condemn", and is used in many passages referring to the judgment of sin. One of the most famous passages using *krino* for this type of judgment is John 3:16-18, part of which we quoted above.

> For God so loved the world that he gave his one and only Son, that whoever believes in him shall not perish but have eternal life. For God did not send his Son into the world to condemn (*krino*) the world, but to save the world through him. Whoever believes in him is not condemned (*krino*), but whoever does not believe stands condemned (*krino*) already because he has not believed in the name of God's one and only Son.

This word *krino* is never used of believers. God's purpose in sending Jesus Christ into the world was not to judge or condemn, but to save the world from sin and death through His substitutionary death on the cross.

Christ the righteous judge and Christ the lamb of God

It is significant that the two passages that refer to the believer's assessment before God use a totally different Greek word, *bema*, as we have seen above. The judgment seat of Christ is likened to a Greek court where there would have been two tribunes, one as accuser and one as defender. However, in this divine tribunal, Christ is both accuser and defender! Christ is the righteous judge, but He is also the Lamb of God, who paid the penalty for sin on the cross, so for all those that have accepted Him as their Saviour, there is no case to be heard. The price has been paid, and the sins have been cancelled.

In 2 Timothy 4:7,8 Paul refers to Christ as the righteous judge:

> I have fought the good fight, I have finished the race, I have kept the faith. Now there is in store for me the crown of righteousness, which the Lord, the righteous Judge, will award to me on that day – and not only to me, but also to all who have longed for his appearing.

John 1:29 refers to Christ as the Lamb of God:

> The next day John saw Jesus coming towards him and said, "Look, the Lamb of God, who takes away the sin of the world!

On that day of assessment, each believer will stand before Christ, and for each one He will declare there is no case against them. Their sin is covered by the blood of the Lamb. All that remains to be seen is which of our deeds done while we were still on earth merit a reward, and which require burning up.

59. Augustine and the problem of evil

Sylvia Penny

The fact that there is evil in the world gives rise to one of the most difficult of philosophical problems, particularly for Christians. Why is there evil in the world, and what is the source of evil? If God is good, and all-powerful, then where did evil come from, and why didn't God eliminate it when it appeared?

Augustine came to faith through rational argument

As a teenager Augustine rejected Christianity, despite being brought up by a devout Christian mother, partly because he had problems with this very question of evil in the world. He felt the Bible did not explain how a good God could allow evil. He grappled with this problem, intellectually, for many years, until he finally came to faith at 31 years old. Although it is often said that no-one has ever been argued into faith, it seems that Augustine, to a large extent, was. It was through the strength of rational arguments that he finally became a Christian, and came to an appreciation of the God of love Who he had turned his back on for so many years. It was important to Augustine when he converted to Christianity that it was intellectually credible, as well as a decision of the heart. Both his will *and* his mind had to be involved.

Manichaeism

In his first attempt to solve the problem of evil in the world he became a follower of the Manichaean sect. This was because they asserted there was not a single good and all-powerful God, but two divine powers that ruled the universe. The principle of light was the good force in the world, and this was the realm of the soul, while the principle of darkness was the origin of evil, and this is what dominated the body. There was therefore a dualism, which helped Augustine understand his own internal moral struggle between doing good and evil. Manichaeism solved the problem of evil by denying there was one all-powerful, good divine being. Instead, there were two divine beings, and the good one, the principle of light, was not powerful enough to overcome the principle of darkness. However, after some years he became intellectually dissatisfied with this explanation of the way things were, and so he abandoned this religion.

Neo-Platonism

Later he became interested in Neo-Platonism, mainly because it dealt with the problem of evil in an entirely different way. It denied the separate existence of evil. It stated that evil was not something in and of itself, but rather an absence or deficiency of goodness. Thus, evil could not exist by itself. Good can exist without evil, but the reverse could never be true. Evil can only exist where there is goodness to corrupt.

Evil is "disordered love"

When he became a Christian, his writings about evil still reflected the influence of Neo-Platonism. He described evil as "defective goodness" and as "disordered love". At the beginning of Genesis, we have a creation which is described as being "very good". If evil is not created by God, and is not a part of the original state of the universe, where does it come from? Augustine says it arises from the rejection of the highest level of goodness, which is God. God is the only fully perfect being, followed by a hierarchy of spiritual beings, then humans, then animals, then plants and then the earth and all inanimate objects.

Evil arises when lower levels of created things are loved more than the highest level – i.e. God, who possesses perfect goodness. Evil is therefore not the love of bad things (as God did not create any bad things). Evil results when good things are valued more highly than the best, i.e. God. If we love the lower things more than we love God Himself, it results in leaving us unhappy and incomplete. We were created to love God. If love of God does not take priority over all other loves, we will consequently be incapable of loving anything else properly, since we will expect from these lesser things what they are unable to deliver. If we invest our life in the lower things, we will ultimately damage ourselves.

Does evil come from Satan?

There is a lot of truth in what Augustine thought and wrote. Many Christians today, if they are asked the question "where does evil come from" may answer that it comes from Satan. However, this does not solve the problem of evil, because they then have to explain why God created an evil being, or they have to say that Satan was not created by God, which is contrary to Scripture. Augustine's thoughts on the problem of evil go some way towards solving this dilemma. Satan had a choice. He could choose to love and obey God, or he could choose to love himself and go his own way, and persuade others to go with him. We know which way he chose. It was Satan's free will which led him away from God.

Adam's free will

It is the same for the human race. Adam was given a choice. He could choose to obey God and not eat the fruit of the tree of the knowledge of good and evil (Genesis 2:17), or he could choose to go his own way and bear the consequences. Again, we know which way he chose. Despite fully knowing what the result would be, Adam chose to join Eve in disobeying God. Was it because he had a greater love for Eve than he did for God that led him to do this? Scripture does not say. However, this would tie up with Augustine's view of evil being "disordered love" – following a love of the lesser good (Eve) at the expense of the greater good (God).

Eve was deceived

Satan's role in this is interesting. He approached Eve, not Adam. It was Eve who he successfully deceived, not Adam. 1 Timothy 2:14 tells us clearly, "Adam was not the one deceived; it was the woman who was deceived and became a sinner." Why did Satan pick Eve rather than Adam? I don't believe this is because women are more easily deceived than men. Rather, it may have been because God hadn't spoken directly to Eve. Maybe because God's words were related to her by Adam, Satan thought they would carry less weight in her mind, so she was the one most likely to be swayed by his words. As it turned out, he was right. Scripture tells us that Eve was deceived by Satan whereas Adam wasn't.

Satan's deception was subtle. He mixed a lie with the truth. He implied God was lying, and told Eve that she would not "surely die" (Genesis 3:4) if she ate the fruit, (which was a lie) but that instead she would become like God, knowing good and evil, (which was the truth – Genesis 3:22). He implies that God was deceiving her, because He didn't want her and Adam to become like Him. Eve was tempted by the fruit itself because it looked good, and she was tempted by the thought of gaining wisdom. Both were good things in themselves, but again, her fault was in loving and desiring other things more than God Himself. She disobeyed God because her love for something else other than Him was greater.

God's foreknowledge thwarts Satan

What was Satan's downfall? He wanted something other than God - he wanted God's place for himself (Isaiah 14:14). As a result he was driven in disgrace from "the mount of God" (Ezekiel 28:16). When he observed the creation of man, it seems he wanted to show God that this new bodily creation would also disobey Him, if they were given the chance. He therefore presented Eve with the same temptation that had tempted him. He had wanted to be like God, so he put this possibility before Eve, and she fell. She was completely taken in by Satan and believed what he said, whereas Adam knowingly disobeyed God. What Satan did not know was that God had foreseen all that would happen, and had planned in advance for this "before the creation of the world" (Ephesians 1:4). Satan had no idea that God planned to come, as a Man, in the Person of Christ to save mankind. So, although Satan was subtle and crafty, he could not outwit God, as God has the advantage of foreknowledge (Romans 8:29), and Satan does not.

Why do we naturally consider evil a problem?

Returning to Augustine, and the problem of evil in the world – another interesting question to ask is why most people *naturally* view evil as a problem. Before Adam and Eve ate the fruit it seems they were unaware of evil. The potential was there, but until they exercised their free will to disobey God, it did not exist. They did not have a problem with evil as we do. Everything God created was "very good" (Genesis 1:31). This included Adam and Eve themselves. God created mankind to be good, and to love what is good. We are created in the "image of God" (Genesis1:26), and therefore, even in our sinful and fallen state, we recognise that there is something wrong with the world when we see evil in it. It is clear to the vast majority of people that something is not right. That is why no-one ever asks why *good things* happen, because this is how the world was created, this is the default setting, and this is how the world would have remained as long as man had chosen to love and follow God above everything else. On the other hand, people often ask why *bad things* happen.

Are humans intrinsically evil?

Some Christians will describe humans as intrinsically evil. However, that view of humankind poses problems with the idea that God is our Creator. Why would God create us with an evil nature if He is good and loving? He would not. Why would God wish to save us if we are innately evil? He would not. He created us in His image to be good, and to love Him and others. The reason that this did not work out is that human choice *resulted* in evil by their loving lesser things more than the greatest - i.e. God.

Conclusion

Augustine's views on the problem of evil are a good place to start thinking about this subject. He had such a problem with this himself, that he spent years thinking about it before coming to faith, and then later committing his thoughts to writing. I think he is right about the essential goodness of creation, and that our natural inclination is to love the creation and everything in it. What spoils this is our own sinful nature, and our continuing to make the wrong choices throughout our lives. However, once we have made the most important decision in our lives – to accept the Lord as our Saviour – we can rest assured that one day we will be able to live the perfect life in the heavenly realms and then, at last, evil will no longer be a problem.

60. Prophecy at Easter

Sylvia Penny

Prophecy is one of the aspects of the Bible that makes it absolutely unique among books. It is the only book in which dozens of prophecies have been recorded and subsequently seen to come true and confirmed by history. Some of the most amazing prophecies (but not the only ones) relate to the birth and the death of the Lord Jesus Christ. At Easter it seems a good time to look again at the prophecies that were made concerning the Lord's death, and realise just how amazing and how accurate they were.

There are at least fourteen specific prophecies that all came true, literally, within a 24-hour period, and that are very difficult to explain, other than there being an eternal, all-knowing God, Who can reveal the future in advance, when it is in accordance with His purpose to do so.

They are listed below, in the order in which they were fulfilled:

1. Prophecy	**The Lord's disciples were to forsake him**
Zechariah 13:7	"Awake, O Sword, against my shepherd, against the man who is close to me!" declares the Lord Almighty. "Strike the shepherd, and the sheep will be scattered
Fulfilment	
Mark 14:27	"You will all fall away," Jesus told them, "for it is written: "'I will strike the shepherd, and the sheep will be scattered.'"
2. Prophecy	**He was to be dumb before his accusers**
Isaiah 53:7	He was oppressed and afflicted, and yet he did not open his mouth; he was led like a lamb to the slaughter, and as a sheep before

	her shearers is silent, so he did not open his mouth.
Fulfilment	
Matthew 27:12-14	When he was accused by the chief priests and the elders, he gave no answer. Then Pilate asked him, "Don't you hear how many things they are accusing you of?" But Jesus made no reply, not even to a single charge – to the great amazement of the governor.
3. Prophecy	**He was to be wounded and bruised**
Isaiah 53:5	But he was pierced for our transgressions, he was crushed for our iniquities; the punishment that brought us peace was upon him, and by his wounds we are healed.
Fulfilment	
Matthew 27:26,30	But he (Pilate) had him flogged, and handed him over to be crucified. … They spat on him, and took the staff and struck him on the head again and again.
4. Prophecy	**His hands and feet were to be pierced**
Psalm 22:16	… a band of evil men has encircled me, they have pierced my hands and my feet.
Fulfilment	
Luke 23:33	When they came to the place called The Skull, there they crucified him
5. Prophecy	**Yet none of his bones would be broken**
Exodus 12:46	It (the Passover lamb) must be eaten inside one house … Do not break any of the bones.

Fulfilment

John 19:31-36	The Jews … asked Pilate to have the legs broken … The soldiers therefore came and broke the legs of the first man who had been crucified with Jesus, and then those of the other. But when they came to Jesus and found that he was already dead, they did not break his legs … These things happened so that the Scripture would be fulfilled: "Not one of his bones will be broken."
6. Prophecy	**He was to be crucified with thieves**
Isaiah 53:12	He was numbered with the transgressors
Fulfilment	
Mark 15:27-28	They crucified two robbers with him … and the Scripture was fulfilled which says, "He was counted with the lawless ones."
7. Prophecy	**He was to pray for his persecutors**
Isaiah 53:12	For he bore the sin of many, and made intercession for the transgressors.
Fulfilment	
Luke 23:34	Jesus said, "Father, forgive them, for they do not know what they are doing"
8. Prophecy	**The people were to ridicule him**
Psalm 22:7-8	All who see me mock me; they hurl insults, shaking their heads. "He trusts in the Lord; let the Lord rescue him. Let him deliver him, since he delights in him."

Fulfilment

Matthew 27:41-43 In the same way the chief priests, the teacher of the law and the elders mocked him. "He saved others," they said, "but he can't save himself! He's the king of Israel! Let him come down now from the cross, and we will believe in him. He trusts in God. Let God rescue him now if he wants him."

9. Prophecy His garments were to be parted and lots cast for his vesture

Psalm 22:18 They divide my garments among them and cast lots for my clothing.

Fulfilment

John 19:23-24 When the soldiers crucified Jesus, they took his clothes, dividing them into four shares, one for each of them, with the undergarment remaining … "Let's not tear it," they said to one another. "Let's decide by lot who will get it." This happened that the Scripture might be fulfilled which said, "They divided my garments among them and cast lots for my clothing."

10. Prophecy The cry from the cross

Psalm 22:1 "My God, my God, why have you forsaken me?"

Fulfilment

Matthew 27:46 About the ninth hour Jesus cried out in a loud voice, "*Eloi, Eloi, lama sabachthani*?" – which means, "My God, my God, why have you forsaken me?"

11. Prophecy	**They were to give him gall and vinegar to drink**
Psalm 69:21	They put gall in my food and gave me vinegar for my thirst.
Fulfilment	
Matthew 27:34	There they offered him wine to drink, mixed with gall; but after tasting it, he refused to drink it.
12. Prophecy	**His body was to be pierced**
Zechariah 12:10	They (Israel) will look on me (the Lord, verse 8), the one they have pierced, and mourn for him …
Fulfilment	
John 19:34-37	One of the soldiers pierced Jesus' side with a spear, bringing a sudden flow of blood and water. The man who saw it has given testimony, and his testimony is true. He knows that he tells the truth, and he testifies so that you also may believe. These things happened so that the Scripture would be fulfilled: "Not one of his bones will be broken," and, as another Scripture says, "They will look on the one they have pierced."
13. Prophecy	**His heart was to be broken**
Psalm 22:14	I am poured out like water, and all my bones are out of joint. My heart has turned to wax; it has melted away within me.
Fulfilment	
John 19:34	One of the soldiers pierced Jesus' side … bringing a sudden flow of blood and water.

14. Prophecy	**He was to be buried in a rich man's grave**
Isaiah 53:9	He was assigned a grave with the wicked (plural), and with the rich (singular) in his death.
Fulfilment	
Matthew 27:57-60	As evening approached, there came a rich man from Arimathea, named Joseph … Going to Pilate, he asked for Jesus' body, wrapped it in clean linen cloth, and placed it in his own new tomb that he had cut out of the rock.

These prophecies speak for themselves

These prophecies speak for themselves, and need very little comment. They were all prophesied between 500 and 1500 years before the Lord's death, and they all happened precisely as described. Ten of these fourteen prophecies come from just two passages of Scripture – Psalm 22 and Isaiah 53 – and reading these two passages alone makes it very difficult for the reader to ignore the amazing accuracy of the descriptions included in them.

Sceptical of Prophecy

Some who are sceptical of prophecy in Scripture have argued that Jesus, knowing the prophecies in the Old Testament, set out to fulfil them. Although they could possibly argue this way in the case of prophecy no. 2 (dumb before his accusers), no. 7 (pray for his accusers) and no. 10 (the cry from the cross), it is difficult to argue this for the remaining eleven.

He is not likely to have purposely encouraged these:

- Make his disciples forsake Him.
- Make the soldiers wound and bruise Him.
- Got the people to ridicule Him.

Nor would it have been possible for Him to have planned these:

- His hands and feet to be pierced (crucifixion),
- His legs not broken,
- His crucifixion with the thieves,
- His garments being parted, and lots cast for his clothes,
- Being offered gall and vinegar to drink,
- His side being pierced with a sword after he died,
- His heart being broken,
- Where he was buried,

Revealed by an omnipotent and eternal God

The more we look at these prophecies, and the more we read them over and think about them, the more we realise that there is no other good explanation for them than that they were inspired by an omnipotent and eternal God who knows everything from everlasting to everlasting, and Who, occasionally, let people know what will happen in the future.

61. A Valentine Letter from God

Laura Kestly

Dear Beloved Child,

How great is the love I lavishly have for you. You are a child of mine (1 John 3:1; Ephesians. 1:5-6).

I not only express love. I am love (1 John 4:16). I have revealed what is true about myself to you through the Bible, the written words that express my plans and instructions for you (2 Timothy 3:16).

I also have revealed what is true about myself through my creation, (Romans 1:19-20) and through Jesus Christ, the Eternal Word who became flesh and dwelt among you thousands of years ago (John 1:14).

I love you so much that before the foundation of the world you now live in I made a way for you to be near me (Ephesians 1:4). This is how I expressed my love for you, not because you loved me, but because I loved you and sent my Son to be the atoning sacrifice for your sins (1 John 4:10).

I am rich in mercy and, because of my great love for you, I have made you alive with Christ my Son, even when you were dead in your sins – it is by grace you have been saved (Ephesians 2:4-5).

There is nothing that you can do to earn my love. I have freely given it to you. You must just believe me when I tell you about my Son and the sacrifice that he made on the cross so I could be with you.

Please accept this gift that I offer freely to you. When you do this you will never be separated (Romans 8:35-39; Ephesians 1:13).

Since my Son was raised from the dead and made alive, through Him you will also be raised (1 Corinthians 15:20-22).

I am the Almighty Eternal One Who Is, and Who Was, and Who Is to come (Revelation 1:8). My love is limitless because I am infinite. My love is pure because I am holy. I love you with an almighty and pure love that is beyond anything that you've experienced. I so desire you to be able to grasp and feel this love. I want you to understand … how wide and long … and how high and deep is the love I have for you in Christ. I want you to know that this love, a love that surpasses knowledge, will fill you to measure of the fullness of Me (Ephesians 3:18-19).

I desire the best for you. *Do not be deceived by the false lover*. He isn't a lover at all. All his sweet and flattering words are lies to enslave and entrap you and to distract you from the plan and the full life that I called you to live through my Son. This false lover is smooth and his lies are subtle but *he comes as a thief to steal, kill and destroy*; I sent my Son to come that you may have life, and have it to the full (John 10:10). Cast all your cares to Him because He cares for you. (1 Peter 5:7).

The false one is a liar and has been from the beginning when he deceived Adam and Eve. They missed out on the abundant life that I had planned for them because they chose to believe him (Genesis 3; John 8:44). This enemy of mine prowls around like a roaring lion looking for someone to devour (1 Peter 5:8). He will just use you for his own selfish desires and then leave you, but I will ***never*** leave you nor forsake you (Hebrews 13:5).

When you understand the deep and unconditional love that I have for you, you will want to tell others about me and love them the way I have loved you (1 John 4:11). No one has ever seen me; but if you love one another, as I have loved you, they will be able to see me through you.

I have created within you a free will. It allows you the choice whether to accept me or not. My love is not forced and conditional. I have given you the hope of eternal life. I do not lie. I have made this promise before the beginning of time (Titus 1:2).

Dearly beloved child, won't you choose me the way that I've chosen you? Won't you be Mine? Please if you haven't yet accepted the gift that I am so longing that you'll receive – consider it now. It is the one wrapped in crimson red. Believe in Me. I am patient, not wanting anyone to perish but everyone to come to repentance (2 Peter 3:9). I am anxiously waiting to lavish you with so many good things. Every spiritual blessing is waiting for you in the heavenlies (Ephesians 1:3), and in the coming ages I want to show you the incomparable riches of My grace (Ephesians 2:7).

I love you dear child.

Love, your Heavenly Father

62. Christmas and the Promised Seed

Laura Kestly

The celebration of the Christmas season is quickly approaching. As Christians, we have much to celebrate as we commemorate, "For unto you is born this day in the City of David a Saviour (Deliverer) which is Christ the Lord" (Luke 2:11). Seldom do we reflect on the effort that took place for the birth of Christ to have even happened.

The Two Seeds

The Bible records an epic saga by first revealing a spiritual foe of great power and a conflict that will involve two seeds. This story's starting point is Genesis 3. There we find our first parents, children of God, being deceived by the serpent. Because of their one act of disobedience, a conflict of major proportion commenced. In Genesis 3:15 God reveals, with pronouncement, the plot and prophecy as He speaks directly to the serpent:

> "And I will put enmity (a state of opposition) between you and the woman, and between your seed and her seed. It shall bruise your head and you shall bruise His heel."

When one realises this is the major theme and the common thread that runs throughout the Bible, it can become a fascinating journey for the reader when the Bible is studied in this light. Here is a preview of some of the events that lead to the birth of the seed of the woman.

In Genesis 4, the arch enemy of God attacks through his instrument Cain, who John states was "of that wicked one" (1 John 3:12). Cain commits the first murder. However, after Abel's death God, through His infinite wisdom and foresight, appointed (through the principle of substitution) another "seed" (Seth) to carry on the line leading to Christ (Luke 3:23-38).

The reader should be warned that the enemy of this grand drama is an enemy of cunning subtlety. For example, note the line of Cain (given in Genesis 4:16-24). It contains names identical (in some cases), and similar (in others), to names that are found in the true line through Seth.

Deception and misdirection are constant methods used by Satan throughout this complex story, to sway and divert the participants and readers away from the true seed, to the false.

Additional events

Some additional events need to be highlighted. In Genesis chapters 6 and 7 God commands Noah to build an ark, with the express purpose of keeping the seed of the woman alive upon the face of the earth (Genesis 7:3), while destroying the corrupt seed of the enemy (Genesis 6). With the true seed preserved the covenant of Genesis 9:9 was made.

After the flood, it is indicated that through the line of Noah's son, Shem, the seed will come (Genesis 9:26-27, 11:10, Luke 3:36).

The next reference to a seed is that of Genesis 12:7 (see also Galatians 3:16), where the promise made by God to Abraham is expressed in one sentence: "Unto thy seed will I give this land."

Ishmael is passed by and Isaac is chosen (Genesis 21:12). Esau is set aside and Jacob chosen (Genesis 28:13-15). Of the sons of Jacob, Judah is chosen (Genesis 49:10), and of Judah, comes the family of David. And so on, up to the birth of Christ in Bethlehem (Matthew 1:1).

Satan's agents

The reality of this battle between good and evil, darkness and light, God and Satan, is intensely real. God has allowed Satan to use various agents/vessels (Romans 9:22) throughout the ages, as recorded in the pages of Scripture. Satan's aim has been to try and prevent the seed from coming forth.

In each case Satan's willing human 'puppets' have had their own interests to serve, while Satan ultimately keeps his own great object in view. Exodus 1:22 shows a prime example of the type of vessel Satan uses. It is the Pharaoh, in this case, who tries to have every Hebrew son that is born thrown into the river.

2 Chronicles, chapters 21-22, reveals another attempt of Satan to break up the Royal line by which the seed of the woman is to come, reducing it to just one life.

In the book of Esther there is yet another plot on the part of the arch enemy, to destroy the whole nation. Here he used Haman's pride.

New Testament attacks

In Matthew 2:4-7, it is King Herod who is used. When, after finding out the time and place that Christ is to be born, he sends out a decree to have all the males under the age of 2 years old in Bethlehem slain (v. 16). In this case as well as in all the others, God faithfully intervenes to prevent the seed from ultimate destruction (vs. 13-15). After Christ is born the attacks intensify.

In Matthew 4:6, it is Satan himself who tries to tempt Christ to cast himself down, but to no avail.

When Christ dies on the cross Satan thinks he's finally achieved victory but, as God has done in every other situation, He intervenes (see Job 5:12; Proverbs 19:21, 21:30; Psalm 33:10-11) and so *His* purposes prevail.

God demonstrated incomparably powerful strength when He raised Christ from the dead, defeating the power which Satan used to wield through sin – the last enemy, death (1 Corinthians 15:24-28)

.

So the seed came and remains alive forever, but Satan's enmity against the purposes of God, in Christ, has not ceased. Satan's present human instruments appear and work as "ministers of righteousness" (2 Corinthians 11:13-15).

What they preach must appear to be right and true, or they would not be able to deceive. They preach not the righteousness of God that is by grace through faith in Christ. Rather they speak of a righteousness by works. They teach a righteous living for mankind, one which occupies believers with what they can do for God, not with what God has already done for them. The emphasis is upon works, not upon the promises we can receive through faith in Christ.

This Christmas we can celebrate Christ's birth and the faithfulness of God and His promises (Hebrews 10:23). And let us be occupied with the Giver and His grace (not with our gifts), as we await with joy and peace the coming glory of Him in Whom all the promises find their centre and their end.

63. Christmas – A True Story

Laura Kestly

Once upon a time (in the beginning) the first man and woman (who were allowed the freedom to choose) chose to believe a lie from a stranger rather than to believe what their Creator, God had told them. God called this 'sin'

A great promise and prophecy was pronounced by the almighty Creator, spoken to the stranger (who was God's enemy):

> "I will put enmity (opposition) between you and the woman and between your seed and her Seed; It will bruise your head and you will bruise His heel." (Genesis 3:15)

The man and woman were driven out of their home and a curse of death was placed upon them and the world that they would now live in. They would no longer have direct access to their Creator (Genesis 3:16-24), and all born after them would inherit this sin nature, along with the curse of death (Romans 5:19; 1 Corinthians 15:22).

The stranger (the enemy of God) was allowed to occupy their world and continue to deceive the people who lived there with all his lies (2 Corinthians 4:3-4; Ephesians 2:2; John 12:31, 14:30, 16:11).

Over time, under enemy occupation, the world had grown very dark. Their Creator, God, had a plan that would use all of this for His purposes, but in His time (Proverbs 16:4; Ephesians 3:11).

Throughout the pages of the Creator's special Book the accounts of the attacks of the enemy on God's people were recorded. Through God's faithfulness and loving plan, the Seed of the woman, through all of this, was protected.

The hour had come when the seed of the woman entered into the world (John 1:13; Romans 1:3; 2 Timothy 2:8; Galatians 3:16; 1 Peter 1:23; Philippians 2:5-7; Hebrews 2:14). The prophecy was becoming fulfilled. The Creator, Himself, was stepping into the framework of the already existent natural world that He has previously created (Genesis 1-2; John 1:1-3; Ephesians 3:9; Colossians 1:16).

The light entered the dark, enemy-occupied world to save and redeem it (John 8:12).

> "For unto you is born this day in the city of David a *Saviour* which is Christ the Lord." (Luke 2:11)

The story continues after Christmas until all God has prophesied and promised is fulfilled (1 Corinthians 15:27-28; Revelation 22:3).

> For God Who commanded the light to shine out of darkness; has shined in our hearts to give the light of the knowledge of the glory of God in the face of Jesus Christ. (2 Corinthians 4:6)

64. Grace Reigns

Vicky Wilkinson

Reading: Romans 6:15-23

Before we came to know the Lord as our Saviour, our only standing before God was in condemnation. The law of sin that reigned in our lives pointed us to death with no hope. However, the rich mercy of God and the great love with which He loved us has reversed this situation (Ephesians 2:4-10). Verse 8 says, "For by grace you have been saved through faith…" The faith of the Lord Jesus Christ and the faith we demonstrated when we believed were brought together and the result was the salvation of our souls (lives) and also a change in our standing before God. We now stand before God forgiven and justified in His sight – there is no condemnation to those who are in Christ Jesus (Romans 8:1).

God has dealt with our sins through the shed blood of Christ and we are now under grace. However, in the reading above, the Apostle Paul reasons that because grace now reigns this is not to be at the expense of righteousness. The presence of the flesh, the old man, who is still with us, is no excuse for walking in it. Positionally, in the reckoning of God, it was crucified with Christ and we were made alive as a new creation. Therefore, we are no longer the slaves of sin but rather slaves of righteousness and are exhorted to make this good in our daily experience by putting off the deeds of the old man (or nature) and putting on the new man (Colossians 3:8-14).

In other words, because we are under grace, we should never spurn it by continuing to walk in sin. How shall we who died to sin live any longer in it? This is not the way to make grace abound (Romans 6:1). In the way that we would not purposefully hurt those such as our parents, our partners, our children or those who are particularly close to us, because of their unconditional love toward us, even more so we do not want to treat with contempt the riches of grace and the great love God has bestowed on us through our Lord Jesus Christ. Acceptance by faith into God's grace gives us peace and enables us to rejoice in the hope of the glory of God. Furthermore, closely associated with grace is the glory that awaits us, when God will continue to show the exceeding riches of His grace to us in the ages to come.

65. Let the weak say "I am Strong"

Vicky Wilkinson

Reading: 2 Corinthians 12:1-10.

> Therefore I take pleasure in infirmities, in reproaches, in needs, in persecutions, in distresses, for Christ's sake. For when I am weak, then I am strong (v. 10)

The above words of the Apostle Paul seem quite absurd, even contradictory. How can one take pleasure in adverse conditions? How can one who is weak be strong? First we need to look at the context of the preceding verses to understand why Paul made such a statement.

Paul had received great revelations and visions from the Lord, and in order that he would not feel lifted above his station, he spoke of receiving a 'thorn in the flesh' lest he be exalted above measure. What this thorn in the flesh was, we are not told, but it was obviously very distressing to Paul because it caused him to plead with the Lord to remove it. This he did three times. However, the Lord did not remove it but instead said to Paul, "My grace is sufficient for you, for my strength is made perfect in weakness" (v. 9).

When we undergo problematic and distressing periods it drains us of all our physical energies and depletes us emotionally. If we have an active faith, then it is at times like this that instead of relying on our own strength, which may have disappeared, we have no choice but to turn to Christ to carry us through. Our wholehearted submission to Christ allows Him to work fully in our lives, so in this way we can echo Paul's words and say, "When I am weak, then I am strong." That is why we can look back on tough times and understand how we managed to survive such traumatic episodes of our lives.
Hebrews 11 speaks of great men of faith who out of weakness were made strong because of their trust in God (v. 34). Isaiah the prophet said: "He gives power to the weak, and to those who have no might

He increases strength" (Isaiah 40:29). With this in view we can join the Old Testament prophet and say: "Let the weak say, I am strong" (Joel 3:10).

66. Never too late to repent

Vicky Wilkinson

Reading: Luke 23:39-43

> Repent therefore and be converted, that your sins may be blotted out. (Acts 3:19)

At Easter our thoughts are particularly directed to the death of Christ. The sacrifice of His life that Christ made at Calvary was the price of redemption. By it He redeemed us from sin and death and gave us a hope for the future. When the Apostle Paul speaks of our redemption through His shed blood, he immediately links it with 'forgiveness of sins' (Ephesians 1:7). When Christ died and was buried, He took our sins with Him and left them there in the grave – never to be seen again. He wiped the slate clean for us in order that we can be righteous before God.

Before we can benefit from the death of Christ, we must first turn to Christ in faith and acknowledge that great sacrifice He made for our sins. This means that repentance will have taken place in our hearts. The Apostle Paul declared to the Gentiles that they should repent and turn to God (Acts 26:20).

Repentance means a change of heart which causes us to turn about – to turn away from the world and turn to God. On the Cross of Calvary Christ had two criminals also being crucified on either side of Him. Whilst one of them blasphemed and mocked Jesus, the other seemed to have a last-minute change of heart – He repented and turned in faith to Jesus saying, "Lord, remember me when you come into your kingdom." Because of this, Christ promised him a place with Him in paradise.

There is a lesson we can learn from this and this is highlighted in 'the workers of the vineyard parable which Jesus related to the people (Matthew 20:1-16). Those who worked only from the eleventh hour were paid the same wages as those who had worked from early morning. Whilst some people repent and come to faith early in their lifetime, others, like this criminal, have a death-bed conversion. This tells us that it's never too late to repent and turn to Christ Jesus in faith.

Index of Quoted Scriptures References

Genesis
1:26 238
2:9 175
2:16-17 175
3:2-6 175
3:15 263,267
3:16 9
3:22,24 175
12:1-3 33
Exodus
12:46 254
34:6 100
Numbers
14:18 100
Deuteronomy
30:15 97
33:26 149
1 Samuel
25:30-31 46
2 Samuel
22:23 151
1Kings
8:27 147
Job
42:1-2 151
Psalms
22:1 256
22:7-8 255
22:14 257
22:16 252
22:18 256
44:21 154
46:10 107
62:11 151
69:21 257
94:11 154
103:8 100
103:14 154
139:7-10 147
139:15-16 154
139:17-18 107
145:8 101
146:5 83
Proverbs
3:18 176
11:30 176
13:12 176
15:4 176
16:20 83
28:14 84
Ecclesiastes
1:2,18 182
2:22,23 183
3:1 70
3:12-13 185
3:14 184
5:12 68
5:18-20 185
12:13-14 186
Isaiah
9:6 136,152
40:31 110
53:5 254
53:7 253
53:9 258
53:12 255
57:15 149
66:1-2 147
Lamentations
3:22-24 96
Ezekiel
47:6-7 178
47:12 178
Daniel
2:21-22 154
Micah
5:2 150
Habakkuk
1:12 149
Zechariah
12:10 257
13:7 253
Matthew
7:7,11 213
18:19 213
18:20 147
19:4-5 171
21:22 213
25:21 75
27:12-14 254
27:26,30 254
27:34 257
27:41-43 256
27:46 256
17:57-6 258
28:19-20 148
Mark
14:27 253
15:27-28 253
Luke
2:11 268
6:20 187
6:21 189,191
6:22 192
6:24 187
6:25 187,191
9:43 152
11:50-51 172
17:26-27 172
17:28 173
21:27 152
23:33 254
23:34 255

John
1:1-2 150
1:14 150
1:29 246
3:16 202
7:38,39 230
8:44 172
8:56 173
10:27-30 134
10:30-33 134
14:9-10 136
14:14 213
14:16 230
15:12 102
16:7 230
16:24 213
19:23-24 256
19:31-36 255
19:34-37 257
Acts
3:19 273
7:49 147
16:12-15 53
16:40 54
Romans
1:18-20 158
1:20 151
1:21-22 159
1:28-31 159
4:10-12 243
6:23 202
7:15-25 225
8:9 229
8:16 231
8:26-27 232
11:33 146
12:17-21 78
16:26 149
1 Corinthians
2:12-13 232
2:14 229
3:10-15 244
3:16 228
12:8-10 204
13:1-8 86
13:4-8 100
13:12 138
13:13 86
15:22-23 140
2 Corinthians
1:22 228
4:6 268
4:6 268
5:5 228
5:10 243
12:10 271
Galatians
5:22-23 232
Ephesians
1:3-6 160
1:13-14 229
2:8-9 202
3:16 229
3:17 148
3:20 214
4:1-3 101
4:3 231
4:9-10 148
4:15-16 102
5:2 60
5:10 68
6:18 214
Philippians
1:3-5 56
4:6 214
4:8-9 92
4:11-13 105
4:15-16 56
4:17-18 57
Colossians
1:10-11 101
1:17 150
3:12-14 102
3:18 60
4:2 214
1Thessalonians
5:16-18 195,216
5:18 103
1 Timothy
2:1 215
2 Timothy
3:16 167
3:16-17 164
4:7-8 246
Hebrews
1:3 152
1:8 136
1:10-12 150
James
1:5-6 213
4:2-3 214
1 John
3:18 85
3:24 229
4:20-21 85
Jude
1:19 229
Revelation
2:7 176
2:10 177
2:11-12 245
2:17 177
2:26-28 177
3:5,12 177
3:21 178
22:2 176
22:14 176
22:19 176

Index of Books Quoted and Referred to

Barclay, William, *The New Testament Volume II: The Letters and the Revelation* ... 203
Chapman, Steven Curtis, *Declarations of Dependence* ... 107
Davies, Paul, *The Goldilocks Enigma: Why is the Universe Just Right for Life?* ... 153
Keener, Craig S, *Paul, Women and Wives* ... 61
McDowell, Josh, *The Resurrection Factor* ...130
New Bible Commentary ... 203,239
Oxford Dictionary ... 154
Penny, Michael, *The Miracles of the Apostles* ... 204
Sowell, Thomas, *A Personal Odyssey* ... 104
Vine, W E, *Expository Dictionary of New Testament Words* ... 132
Wilkinson, Bruce, *The Prayer of Jabez* ... 85

About the Author

Sylvia Penny was born in Bexleyheath, Kent, in 1956. She was educated at Basingstoke High School and Queen Mary's College, before studying accountancy at Oxford Polytechnic. She qualified as a Chartered Accountant and practised in the profession for a number of years, until she went to live in the USA with her husband and was a pastor's wife, taking an active role in the church. On returning to Britain she went back to the accountancy profession and has recently retired.

As well as compiling the first volume of *Woman to Woman* she has written three other books: *Satan through the Bible, Salvation: Safe and Secure,* and a novel, *Eve and the Angel of Light*, based on Genesis chapters 1-3. She has also written *Introducing God's Plan* (with Michael Penny), and *Abraham and his Seed* (with W M Henry and Michael Penny)

She is a regular contributor to *Search* magazine and has written a number of booklets including *Arminianism or Calvinism?, Christ and Redemption, The Seven Deadly Sins, Loving Your Enemies, Lying, Forgiveness, Theories of Creation, Noah's Flood, Song of Songs: An Alternative Vie, Universalism! True or False? And Resurrection! When?.*

These publications are available as paperbacks from Amazon and as e-books from Amazon and Apple.

Details of these and other publications can be seen on the website

www.obt.org.uk

Also by Sylvia Penny

Woman to Woman

Compiled and edited by Sylvia Penny

The first volume, containing sixty articles by women and for women, covering such subjects as:

- Old Testament Women
- New Testament Women
- Roman and Greek Women
- Jesus and Women
- Paul and Women
- Husbands & Wives
- Raising Children.
- Christian Living
- Modern Day Issues

A great book for women's ministry.

****

Satan through the Bible

Sylvia Penny

An excellent book dealing with every reference to Satan in the Bible.

Salvation: Safe and Secure

Sylvia Penny

This important book is a thorough treatment of the subject of salvation, asking such questions as …

- What is it, exactly, that saves us?
- Is salvation secure?
- Can it be lost?
- What is 'conditional security'?

It deals with a wide range of issues such as …

Salvation and works	The doctrine of rewards
Lordship salvation	Free grace theology
Assurance of salvation	Why people lose their faith

****

Eve and the Angel of Light

Sylvia Penny

A thought provoking novel based on Genesis chapters 1-3, giving some unique insights as to what may have happened in the Garden of Eden.

Manufactured by Amazon.ca
Bolton, ON

37424617R00155